DATE DUE

DEC 1 1 2015			
	DEC 0 8 2015		
GAYLORD			PRINTED IN U.S.A.

OEMCO

*Shakespeare's Development
and the Problem Comedies*

(She moved in circles, and those circles moved)
THEODORE ROETHKE

Shakespeare's Development and the Problem Comedies

Turn and Counter-Turn

◆══════►

RICHARD P. WHEELER

UNIVERSITY OF CALIFORNIA PRESS

BERKELEY · LOS ANGELES · LONDON

University of California Press
Berkeley and Los Angeles, California

University of California Press, Ltd.
London, England

© 1981 by
The Regents of the University of California

ISBN: 0–520–03902–5
Library of Congress Catalog Card Number: 79–63550

Printed in the United States of America

1 2 3 4 5 6 7 8 9

For Joanne

Preface

My subtitle, like the epigraph, is from Theodore Roethke's poem "I Knew a Woman." The line from which it is taken, "She taught me Turn, and Counter-turn, and Stand," wonderfully assimilates the movements of a woman's body to those of a Grecian ode. I find Roethke's line also conveys for me the mutually balancing movements I try to follow in this book. In the actions of single plays, but also in transitions from one play to another, from one genre to another, and from one phase of Shakespeare's development to another, movements of extraordinary complexity radiate from simple, rhythmically recurring oppositions: attraction and repulsion, union and separation, trust and autonomy, love and authority. The troubled comic resolutions of *All's Well That Ends Well* and *Measure for Measure* dramatize polarized extremes grounded in such oppositions. In detailed readings, I situate problematic turns in the actions of these plays within some large patterns of Shakespeare's development. In the last chapter I effect a counter-turn of my own, foregoing close readings of individual plays in order to sketch various turns and counter-turns that shape the main lines of Shakespeare's development. It is part of my purpose to suggest how the interpretation of any one play by Shakespeare depends upon an interpretive context constructed from the others—as readers of Shakespeare, we move in circles and those circles move.

The tortuous route toward the completion of this book has been
shaped by questions I could not answer, and often could not pose,
in a doctoral dissertation on *All's Well That Ends Well* written a
decade ago at the State University of New York at Buffalo. Parts
of this route are recorded in print. The first and fourth sections of
chapter 2 still resemble essays published in *Bucknell Review*, 21
(Spring 1973), and in *Comparative Drama*, 8 (Winter 1974–75).
My comments on the *Sonnets* in chapter 2 and chapter 4 draw upon
an essay on *Sonnets* 88–96 published in *Literature and Psychology*,
22, No. 3 (1972). An essay adapted mainly from the fifth section
of chapter 4 of this book is included in *Representing Shakespeare:
New Psychoanalytic Essays* (Baltimore: Johns Hopkins University
Press, 1980); the editors of that volume, Murray M. Schwartz and
Coppélia Kahn, have patiently overseen this essay through major
revisions. Papers based on my work in progress have found helpfully
critical audiences at meetings of the Shakespeare Association of
America and the Modern Language Association of America, at lectures given at the University of California, Berkeley and Santa Cruz,
and at gatherings of the English Renaissance group of the University
of Illinois, Urbana-Champaign.

So many friends and colleagues have offered telling commentary
on various drafts of part or all of this book that I have at times found
myself as much editor and arbitrator as author; prominent among
them are Richard O. Allen, Peter Garrett, Jan Hinely, Cary Nelson,
Murray M. Schwartz, Michael Shapiro, and Leon Waldoff—whose
supportive criticism has been important from the beginning. The
readers of the submitted manuscript—expertly typed by Marlyn
Ehlers—far exceeded their duty to the University of California Press
in their responses to it: my long-standing debt to Norman N. Holland's pioneering work in psychoanalytic criticism has been compounded by his incisive comments; Janet Adelman's invaluable
page-by-page commentary, which regularly identified both vulnerabilities and potential strengths I had been unable to see myself, led
to substantial revisions in every chapter. At the press, Doris Kretsch-
mer gracefully oversaw the progress from manuscript to published
book, and Christine Taylor's scrupulous editing tactfully sent me
back for a last struggle with many sentences I had given up on.

Carol Thomas Neely, who has gone over one draft after another
with painstaking care, has kept before me standards of clarity and

responsibility that I have taken as my most challenging and trust-worthy guides; my debt to her penetrating understanding of Shake-speare extends to every page. C. L. Barber, my friend and teacher, has given my work the ground from which it grows, and has over-seen that growth with a generosity that only those who knew him will fully appreciate; the importance to me of his work, his conver-sation, and his encouragement is only inadequately conveyed by the references to him scattered through the following pages.

No indebtedness do I acknowledge with more gratitude and pride than my oldest and deepest, that to Clifford and Irene Wheeler, my father and mother. Natalie, Gregory, and Ellen Wheeler have tol-erated and, I hope, forgiven the unreasonable demands made on me, for as long as they can remember, by their verbal sibling. But in see-ing this book through to completion, no one has given as much, in as many ways, or at more cost to herself, than Joanne Elizabeth Wheeler.

R. P. W.
Champaign, Illinois
August, 1979

Note on Texts

All quotations from Shakespeare are from the Pelican edition of the *Complete Works*, gen. ed. Alfred Harbage (Baltimore: Penguin Books, 1969); *All's Well That Ends Well* is edited by Jonas A. Barish, *Measure for Measure* by R. C. Bald. I have also consulted extensively the Arden editions of *All's Well*, ed. G. K. Hunter (London: Methuen, 1959), and *Measure for Measure*, ed. J. W. Lever (London: Methuen, 1965).

Contents

Contents

I

"When our deep plots do pall":
The Problem Comedies
and Shakespeare

SHAKESPEARE's comedy undergoes continuous change. New possibilities are explored and old strategies altered, amplified, or discarded in a succession of plays from *The Comedy of Errors* to *The Tempest*. Two groups of comedies, however, reflect a relative stabilization in plot, characterization, conventions, and theme. First in the festive comedies, and again in the very different mode of the late romances, Shakespeare writes within a stable but richly flexible set of assumptions regarding what can be dramatized in a comic action. *All's Well That Ends Well* and *Measure for Measure*, however, pose unique problems. These plays, written between the festive comedies and the late romances, share attributes with both groups without quite belonging to either. Their dramatic worlds seem alternately more realistic and more fantastic than those of earlier comedies. Characters who on some occasions are secondary functions of the action are on other occasions centers of powerfully individualized feeling pressing the action in unexpected directions. Conventions they share with other comedies may be used straightforwardly or may be subjected throughout to corrosive ironies. In both plays, love relations completed in comic movements toward marriage seem to put unusual stresses on those marriages. These problematic areas and others have persistently troubled critics of *All's Well* and *Measure for Measure*, and perhaps provide the main reason for the endurance,

1

to no one's complete satisfaction, of the expression *problem plays* or *problem comedies* to describe them.[1]

1. The label *problem comedies* belongs to and reflects the troubled critical heritage of these plays. The habit of setting off *All's Well* and *Measure for Measure* as problem plays was begun in 1896 with the publication of F. S. Boas's *Shakspere and his Predecessors* (New York: Charles Scribner's Sons). Linking these plays by "general temper and atmosphere" (p. 345) with *Troilus and Cressida* and *Hamlet*, Boas overemphasized their resemblance to modern problem plays of Ibsen and Shaw. The group of plays since designated by the term *problem plays* (or one of its variants, *problem comedies*, *dark comedies*, *bitter comedies*) has varied as different critics have taken the term to mean different things. W. W. Lawrence, in *Shakespeare's Problem Comedies* (New York: Macmillan, 1931), scratched *Hamlet* from Boas's group in order to emphasize genre as well as atmospheric considerations. For widely different reasons, E. M. W. Tillyard (*Shakespeare's Problem Plays* [Toronto: University of Toronto Press, 1949]) and William B. Toole (*Shakespeare's Problem Plays* [The Hague: Mouton, 1966]) restored *Hamlet*. Peter Ure kept *Hamlet* and added a fifth play, *Timon of Athens*, in his pamphlet *Shakespeare: The Problem Plays*, rev. ed. (London: Longmans, Green, 1964). Since Lawrence, however, the only critic to make the term indicate a clearly defined type of drama has been Ernest Schanzer, but he included only one of the plays ordinarily designated as problem plays. Schanzer found in *Julius Caesar*, *Measure for Measure*, and *Antony and Cleopatra* problematic presentations of a "moral problem" (*The Problem Plays of Shakespeare* [New York: Shocken Books, 1963], p. 6).

Most critics, however, seem most often to think of the three plays specified by Lawrence as the problem plays or problem comedies: *All's Well*, *Measure for Measure*, and *Troilus and Cressida*. Whatever its genre, *Troilus and Cressida* clearly is, as Boas noted, linked by "general temper and atmosphere" to plays roughly contemporaneous with it. Its action, however, does not have close formal affinities to the comic actions of *All's Well* or *Measure for Measure*, nor does it share the close relations of those plays to the earlier comedies or the late romances, all of which move through comic actions that culminate in marriage and some form of social reconciliation, however fragile or problematic the endings in some cases may seem. I will use the term *problem comedies* to refer only to *All's Well* and *Measure for Measure*, two plays that together occupy a transitional place in Shakespeare's development of comic form.

Some critics have, sensibly enough, questioned the appropriateness of keeping a term that has been used in so many different ways. Leo Salinger, for instance, recently observed of the label *problem play* in connection with *All's Well* and *Measure for Measure*: "One is sometimes left under the impression that the problem lies in the critics' difficulty of deciding what kind of plays they really are" (*Shakespeare and the Traditions of Comedy* [Cambridge: Cambridge University Press, 1974], p. 321). G. K. Hunter writes in his introduction to the Arden edition of *All's Well* that "there is a strong case for avoiding the traditional separation of 'problem-plays' from 'romances' and considering as a group the 'later comedies'—*All's Well*, *Measure for Measure*, *Pericles*, *Cymbeline*, and the rest" ([London: Methuen, 1959], p. lv). I find

In the festive comedies, social and internal obstacles to love impede the movement toward marriage; the action culminates when obstructed love relations are consummated in marriages arranged or completed in the closing scene.[2] Marriage rituals clarify the relations of individual longings to both the natural and social orders.[3] The actions of the festive comedies move toward dramatic reconciliations of conflicts that develop in the interrelations of sexuality (a source of both desire and fear), mutuality (a goal that expresses a need but also poses a threat), and society (an external structure of authority and order perpetuated by characters who impulsively seek release from internalized authoritarian constraints). *All's Well* and *Measure for Measure* become problematic, become problem comedies, when strategies that succeed wonderfully in the festive comedies prove no longer adequate to conflicts that have become increasingly intense. If, as I think F. S. Boas rightly suggested long ago, "the issues raised preclude a completely satisfactory outcome, even when, as in *All's Well* and *Measure for Measure,* the complications are outwardly adjusted in the fifth acts,"[4] it is because the familiar "issues" of comedy have undergone transformations more radical than Shakespeare's transformations of his comic art. That art remains, amid many instances of daring and inventive adaptation, closely linked to the designs of the festive comedies. Individual fulfillment, marital intimacy, and communal renewal are celebrated together in the festive endings of earlier comedies; the marriages that conclude *All's Well* and *Measure for Measure* seem only superficially to resolve antagonisms that have developed between degraded sexual desire and the moralized social orders of these two plays.

All's Well and *Measure for Measure* sufficiently removed from the romances, however, both by chronology and by dramatic strategy, to justify setting them off with a term specific to them. The expression *problem comedies* serves this purpose conveniently, if imperfectly.

For an excellent review of modern critical interest in these plays, see Michael Jameison, "The Problem Plays, 1920–1970," *Shakespeare Survey,* 25 (1972): 1–10.

2. See Northrop Frye's widely influential discussion of comic form in "The Argument of Comedy," in *English Institute Essays 1948,* ed. D. A. Robertson, Jr. (New York: Columbia University Press, 1949).

3. Here and throughout this book I am greatly indebted to C. L. Barber's understanding of these comedies as expressed in *Shakespeare's Festive Comedy* (Princeton: Princeton University Press, 1959).

4. *Shakspere and His Predecessors,* p. 345.

The special difficulties presented in *All's Well* and *Measure for Measure* can only be fully identified by examining carefully the action of each. But these difficulties can be illuminated by setting the problem comedies in the context of patterns running through Shakespeare's works. Because Shakespeare writes in a number of genres, changing and extending each through a lengthy appropriation of it, it is possible to recognize, both in shifts within a single genre and in movements from one genre to another, large developmental patterns. The chronological position and the genre status of the problem comedies link them closely to nearly all the major developments in Shakespeare's mature work. *All's Well* and *Measure for Measure* share many formal characteristics with earlier comedies, anticipate the comic mode of the late romances, and reflect concerns central to tragedies written at about the same time. But in these plays, possibilities for comic expression that were alive in the festive comedies seem to have been at least partially closed off; new ways of making comic sense of experience that go with the late romances have not yet been fully discovered; and the qualities in *All's Well* and *Measure for Measure* that have consistently posed the most difficulties for critics are the qualities that seem to link them most closely to the tragic worlds of *Hamlet, Troilus and Cressida, Othello,* and *King Lear.*

This book is an exploration both of problematic qualities specific to *All's Well* and *Measure for Measure* and of some large patterns in Shakespeare's development. In chapter 2 I will look closely at the tension between comic design and deep psychological conflict in *All's Well* and relate that play to earlier comedies, to the *Sonnets,* and to the late romances. Chapter 3 is a reading of *Measure for Measure* that emphasizes the relation of that play to conflicts Shakespeare masters more fully in the tragedies. In chapter 4 I will present a large schema of Shakespeare's development, of which the movement from *All's Well* to *Measure for Measure* forms a part. In this introductory chapter I will first single out *Measure for Measure* to indicate briefly what I find problematic about the designs of the problem comedies and then suggest how this problematic dimension can be illuminated by placing *All's Well* and *Measure for Measure* in the context of Shakespeare's development; in its last section I will explore how my reading of Shakespeare's plays relates to my understanding of Shakespeare the author of those plays.

The Problem with the Problem Comedies:
Measure for Measure

Any one play can be measured both by the inclusiveness of its action (the mastery it exercises over the specific circumstances dramatized in it) and by the exclusiveness of its action (the absence or subordination of powerful conflicts present in Shakespeare's works but never all fully present in any one play). As *You Like It* masters a set of dramatic circumstances fully presented and carefully limited; love receives triumphant clarification in a forest of Arden invaded by various illusory ways of loving but sheltered from the violence tragically released in connection with similar illusions in *Othello*. *King Lear* is inclusive in a similar way, but it includes more; it masters in a tragic action circumstances that drastically expand the range of conflict engaged in the festive comedies. *Measure for Measure*, like *King Lear*, engages a larger range of experience than As *You Like It*. But the action of *Measure for Measure* does not culminate in the kind of inclusive symbolic mastery achieved in either As *You Like It* or *King Lear*. The range of feeling dramatized in *Measure for Measure* is diminished rather than sustained and controlled as the play moves toward completion. Shakespeare seems not to finish quite so large and powerful a play as the one he starts, but to change the rules—excluding powerful trends of feeling already admitted into the action—so that the play can be finished at all.

The mastery of psychological conflict achieved in dramatic action corresponds in many ways to that achieved in the activity of childhood play. Erik Erikson uses the expression *play it out* to suggest the kind of completion that typifies such play; the *it* refers to the whole arrangement of potentially anxiety-provoking personal and social circumstances engaged by the child within a play space and time that can be trusted to remain the zone of play and subjected there to symbolic mastery by the child's integrative, adaptive ego.[5]

5. *Childhood and Society*, 2nd ed. (New York: Norton, 1963), p. 222. Subsequent page references in the text refer to this edition. In a later essay, Erikson compares a boy's presentation of himself through play construction to "the dramatist's job," which he regards as "the closest analogy to our play constructions in adult life":

> If, in this small boy's life, the classroom and the home setting are an early equivalent of the sphere of adult actuality with its interplay of persons and

Successful play coordinates inner impulse with outer reality: the "microcosmic" activity of play creatively synthesizes the "autocosmic" demands of the inner self with the "macrocosmic" world "shared with others" (pp. 220–21). Play fails when the urgency of inner demands or the intractability of an alien world subvert the ego's effort at symbolic mastery.

Erikson uses the term *play satiation* to indicate the psychological achievement of successful play (p. 229). Perhaps a corresponding term for literature is Kenneth Burke's use of *artistic felicity* to describe "an exaltation at the correctness of the procedure, so that we enjoy the steady march of doom in a Racinian tragedy with exactly the same equipment as that which produces our delight with Benedick's 'Peace, I'll stop your mouth (*Kisses her*)' which terminates the imbroglio of *Much Ado About Nothing*."[6] I find that, for myself, the "same equipment" that exalts at the inclusive "correctness" of *Much Ado* or *As You Like It* or *King Lear* or *The Winter's Tale* is first fully engaged by *Measure for Measure*, but responds ultimately with a sense of distrust—an uneasy sense both of a letdown and of something left over—that undermines my satisfaction when I try to take in its whole action. *As You Like It*, by contrast, "plays out" the tension it establishes between inner impulse and external reality; the celebration of love completed in marriage culminates what C. L. Barber summarizes as a dramatic movement "through release to clarification" (*Festive Comedy*, p. 6). The festive poignancy of the celebration is amplified by an understanding that identifies qualities within the experience of love that are anything but objects of celebration and that places love within larger patterns of life that romantic love as an exercise in self-deception subordinates to itself. In the whole movement, as Barber observes, the power of inner impulse is sustained while its initially obscured relation to the outer world is made clear; at the end, "love has been made independent of illusions without becoming any less intense" (p. 236).

---

institutions, then his solitary construction is the infantile model of the playwright's work: he, too, condenses into scenes of unitary place and time, marked by a "set" and populated by a cast, the tragic (and comic) dilemma of representative individuals caught in the role conflicts of their time.

("Play and Actuality," in *Play and Development*, ed. Maria W. Piers [New York: Norton, 1972], p. 133)

6. "Psychology and Form," in *Counter-Statement*, 2nd ed. (Los Altos, California: Hermes Publications, 1953), p. 37.

The festive measures danced at the close of As You Like It can be as rich as they are because they have won their place at the center of a comic awareness that acknowledges Touchstone's exploitation of marriage for sexual pleasure, the perverse Petrarchanism enacted by Silvius and Phebe, the sweeping subordination of love to life articulated by Rosalind, the artificiality in such comic devices as the instantaneous love of Celia and Oliver, and even melancholy Jaques's exclusion of himself from the comic community formed at the end of the play. The play clarifies its relation both to a world of extravagant possibility offered by the conventions of comedy and to a human world that in fact perpetuates itself at that point, always under stress and always essential, where social custom intersects with the large rhythms of nature. Each marriage at the end of As You Like It culminates a relationship subtly clarified in its own right, but ultimately subordinated with all the others to the celebration of marriage itself, of Hymen, who is "god of every town" because he presides at that intersection of social order and instinctual release shared by the action of comedy and the perpetuation of society.

The action of Measure for Measure culminates not only in four marriages but in several important acts of forgiveness as well. Both marriage as a social ordering of sexuality and forgiveness as an essential adjustment to transgression are clearly appropriate gestures to end a play that dramatizes deep transgressions within the relations of sexuality and the social order. But the complications that terminate the plot—"rather intricate than artful"[7] in Dr. Johnson's neat distinction—cannot integrate into the precarious comic conclusion of this play complex developments that lead into it. Gestures of mercy are essential if the ending is to be comic at all. But the mercy granted to Barnardine, Claudio, and Angelo does little to clarify the issues these characters have raised in the play, and the mercy granted to Lucio seems to be a form of punishment—"Slandering a prince deserves it" (V.iii.519). Similarly, the marriages of Angelo to Mariana, Claudio to Juliet, and especially of Vincentio to Isabella do not dramatize a freeing of these characters from conflicted attitudes toward sexuality and marriage developed with great intensity earlier. The marriage of Lucio to Kate Keepdown—a degraded relationship forced to take the stamp of official respectability—comes perilously

7. Johnson on Shakespeare, ed. Arthur Sherbo, in The Works of Samuel Johnson, vol. 7 (New Haven: Yale University Press, 1968), p. 216.

close to providing an emblem for the entire play. The conflicted inner worlds of the characters are not clarified either by bringing them to resolution or by dramatizing their continued irresolution; they are simply sacrificed to the effort to create the theatrical appearance of an outer social order. After dramatizing instances of greatly intensified conflict within an expanded comic action, *Measure for Measure* retreats from the force of such conflict into a kind of theatrical simulation of mastery.

A discrepancy between a superficial dramatic resolution in *Measure for Measure* and the intensity of conflict that precedes it has been often perceived and stated in many ways.[8] Anne Barton, for example, finds that Shakespeare "suddenly imposes upon a play which hitherto has probed uncomfortably deep into the dark places of society and the human mind, which has been essentially realistic, an ending which is that of fairy-tale: conventional, suspect in its very tidiness, full of psychological gaps and illogicalities."[9] Barton's position is particularly interesting because she sees in this discrepancy not only "the problems of a Shakespeare now seemingly disillusioned with that art of comedy which, in the past, had served him so well" (p. 549), but also an artful comment on that art. The "confusion of values in *Measure for Measure*," if "desperate," is "surely deliberate" (p. 548). "Shakespeare seems perversely to stress the hollowness, in a sense the falsehood, of the happy ending of this comedy" (p. 547). *Measure for Measure*, Barton suggests, is a com-

8. Mrs. Charlotte Lennox found (*Shakespear Illustrated*, vol. 1 [London, 1753]) that "Shakespear made a wrong Choice of his Subject, since he was resolved to torture it into a Comedy." For Mrs. Lennox, Shakespeare resorted to "low Contrivance, absurd Intrigue and improbable Incidents . . . in order to bring about three or four Weddings, instead of one good Beheading, which was the Consequence naturally expected." Mrs. Lennox's remarks are quoted by Rosalind Miles (*The Problem of "Measure for Measure"* [New York: Barnes and Noble, 1976], p. 16), who reviews exhaustively and often rather condescendingly "the bad old days" of critical discontent with *Measure for Measure*. But Miles's confidence that she can demonstrate the play's coherence by historical investigation gives out by the time her project is completed: "It is not a fully satisfying emotional experience because it deprives us of the sense of harmony and completeness, even the harmony and completeness of a consistent ironic vision, which is the accompanying sensation of a great work. Full creative assimilation of the various elements in the play has not taken place . . ." (pp. 287–88).

9. Introduction to *Measure for Measure*, in *The Riverside Shakespeare*, ed. G. Blakemore Evans (Boston: Houghton Mifflin, 1974), pp. 547–48.

edy that clarifies its relation to the conventions of comedy by demonstrating their inadequacy. But whether or not Shakespeare self-consciously dramatizes the "hollowness" of the ending (I think otherwise, as will be clear in my discussion of *Measure for Measure* in chapter 3), it is important to recognize the limitations of such a view with regard to the whole design of the play. The kind of clarification Barton suggests for the play can in itself do nothing to clarify the extraordinary crises that have been forcefully developed earlier, and it is in this regard that the last scene is strikingly inadequate to the action it brings to an end.

The fate of Isabella typifies the impoverishment of dramatic potential in the ending of *Measure for Measure*. The prior characterization of Isabella is realized through her speech and action in a series of closely interrelated dramatic situations: her flight from a secular society that perpetuates itself through marriage and the family to a religious sisterhood that excludes sexuality; her effort to argue before Angelo that her brother Claudio's life be spared, despite her abhorrence of his "vice"; her horror when confronted by Angelo's sexual advances; her outrage when Claudio, in an effort to save his own life, begs her to submit to Angelo; and her daughterly dependence on Vincentio, disguised as a holy father, to save her from Angelo's lust. As these situations succeed and complicate each other, Isabella's experience helps to focus the major concerns of the play. Her characterization is part of an intricate dramatic network of interrelated conflicts—authority/sexuality; order/liberty; justice/mercy; virtue/vice; self-awareness/self-deception—that intersect in her experience. But what she says and does in the last scene and what is said and done to her are meaningful only within a much more narrowly circumscribed range of meanings than that suggested by her prior experience. The extraordinary complexity of Isabella's situation is kept alive into the final scene, but finds there no dramatic clarification responsive to the whole experience she has undergone.

The richest parts of this scene are rich precisely because they keep open possibilities already developed. When Isabella accuses Angelo of sexual coercion, for instance, her outrage finds its place within one deception she is party to (that Angelo has violated her virginity) and within another deception she regards as true (that Claudio has been executed). The situation presents an Isabella whose predicament is still being complicated and whose final position in the play clearly belongs to a future fast approaching. And when she later, at Mariana's request, begs for Angelo's pardon, the play seems to move toward a way of understanding what Isabella has become through her experience of intense conflict in relation to both Angelo and her brother.

> Most bounteous sir,
> Look, if it please you, on this man condemned
> As if my brother lived. I partly think
> A due sincerity governed his deeds
> Till he did look on me. Since it is so,
> Let him not die; my brother had but justice,
> In that he did the thing for which he died.
> For Angelo,
> His act did not o'ertake his bad intent,
> And must be buried but as an intent
> That perished by the way. Thoughts are no subjects,
> Intents but merely thoughts.   (v.i.439–50)

Because these are the last words she speaks, critics have often taken this speech as a final revelation of Isabella's character, an authoritative presentation of what she has become, or failed to become, in the course of being tested by the play's action. But I think the potential importance of the speech lies chiefly in its suggestiveness, in its power not to resolve questions of Isabella's character, but to keep them open. This suggestiveness is abundantly reflected in the criticism. Does Isabella speak from a Christian charity she has learned in the play, as G. Wilson Knight thought?[10] Does she participate in a moral outrage by forgiving Angelo, as Coleridge implied?[11] Does her forgiveness of Angelo betray an astonishing vanity ("Till he did look on me") as Empson found, following Dr. Johnson?[12] Can she forgive Angelo so easily because she is in some sense

10. *"Measure for Measure and the Gospels,"* in *The Wheel of Fire,* 5th ed. (New York: Meridian Books, 1957), p. 93.

11. *Shakespearean Criticism,* ed. Thomas Middleton Raysor, 2nd ed., vol. 1 (London: J. M. Dent and Sons, 1960), p. 102.

12. William Empson, *The Structure of Complex Words* (London: Chatto and Windus, 1951), p. 279. Dr. Johnson: "I am afraid our varlet poet intended to inculcate, that women think ill of nothing that raises the credit of their beauty, and are ready, however virtuous, to pardon any act which they think incited by their own charms" (*Johnson on Shakespeare,* p. 213).

relieved that Claudio is dead (" 'Tis best that thou diest quickly," she has told him in III.i)? Is she right in thinking that her "brother had but justice"—that justice has in some way been served by a law that punishes fornication by death? How does her sharp distinction between Angelo's thoughts and deeds relate to the complex interconnections between thoughts and deeds established repeatedly in the earlier action?

The problem is not that such questions provoked by Isabella's speech are not answered, but that the issues they address are not allowed, by the whole context of the final scene, to interact with and illuminate each other. Throughout the play Shakespeare has presented an Isabella whose experience is sufficiently complex to make such questions meaningful, all the more so because they cannot be easily answered and cannot be separated from one another. But just as such questions seem to come into final focus, they are skirted, not made unanswerable so much as unaskable; the world presented as the action closes is simply too fragile to sustain them as meaningful interrogation. After Vincentio makes Isabella's relation to Angelo even more complex by noting that the deputy has speeded up Claudio's execution, has essentially murdered her brother before the legally scheduled execution could take place, he drops that matter in order to pardon Barnardine. Then, in nine lines, Vincentio produces a living Claudio, proposes marriage to Isabella, and pardons Angelo. At this moment, all of the relationships that have defined Isabella's experience in the play—to her chosen vocation, to her own sexuality, to Angelo, to her brother, to a Vincentio she has known as a celibate, fatherly priest—are given a final turn that puts them all under special stress. And Isabella is given nothing to say at all. Vincentio himself simply goes on to the matter of Lucio, parenthetically tucking issues central to the entire play between the absurd pardon of Barnadine and the problematic mercy shown to Lucio.

Or rather, since Vincentio's actions also pose problems regarding his place in the play that the comic design provides no coherent way of addressing, I should say Shakespeare nervously goes on to other matters. The ending of Measure for Measure does not "play out" earlier developments, it plays them down; it looks back to the previous action with an averted, mystifying gaze that has its emblem in Vincentio's anxiety-denying movement from one character and one issue to another in the final scene. The failure of these characters (and these issues) to respond to him—as in Isabella's silence and the silence of Claudio and Angelo—mirrors Shakespeare's inability to find an ending that responds fully to the whole action. The kind of integration of inner impulse with external reality that is established in successful play, and which provides a paradigm for the comic action of *As You Like It,* is not achieved in *Measure for Measure.* Characters who have been centers of deep conflict earlier are denied the dramatic reality they have acquired; psychological tensions their crises have expressed are neither resolved nor sustained but simply deprived of a location in the play world. Instead of clarifying, either positively or negatively, the relations between individual longings and the social order, or between comic art and experience, Shakespeare seeks unearned reassurance in a comic ending that cannot fully acknowledge previous developments in *Measure for Measure.*

Placing the Problem Comedies: Shakespeare's Development

By looking at the failure of *Measure for Measure* to provide a fully persuasive comic ending, I have sketched part of a pattern that, in a very general sense, is also applicable to *All's Well.* Sexual conflict tends to separate individual desire from the demands of the social order in each play; the *bed trick* both dramatizes this estrangement and points toward a possible resolution of it; as with *Measure for Measure,* many have found strained or inadequate the rather abrupt comic turnabout that proposes to close this gap at the end of *All's Well.* But beneath such similarities are important differences that must be recognized in order to clarify the relation that binds these two plays closely together.

Although the problem comedies have in common the use of the bed trick as a plot device for insuring a comic ending, this sexual duplicity is not arranged, and does not function, in quite the same way in the two plays. In *All's Well,* Helena substitutes her own body for that of Diana. Although Bertram's unacceptable effort to seduce Diana is thereby diverted, the bed trick's chief purpose is to consummate a sexual union that binds the woman who arranges it to the man who has fled from her. The bed trick, part of Helena's general function as manipulator of the plot, enlarges upon the roles played by earlier heroines who have taken charge of love relations in the festive comedies. But Helena's counterpart in *Measure for Measure* is not the comic heroine, Isabella—who is powerless to deal with her situation except by a flight of her own—but a man, Duke Vincentio. The bed trick is the key element in the Duke's master plan.[13] Although it leads eventually to the marriage of Angelo and Mariana, the bed trick in *Measure for Measure* is designed primarily to prevent the unacceptable sexual union of Angelo and Isabella and to preserve the already consummated union of Claudio and Julietta. Whereas the bed trick further concentrates the action of *All's Well* on the central movement toward the marriage of Helena and Bertram, in *Measure for Measure* it further disperses a dramatic movement that will eventually culminate in four marriages, none of which completes a relationship that has held a place at the center of the action throughout the play.

Vincentio's role has no clear precedent among men in the comedies that immediately precede *Measure for Measure*. His control over an action he never participates in directly until he proposes to Isabella also contrasts sharply with Helena's deep involvement in the action she manipulates in *All's Well*. From this vantage point, the movement from *All's Well* to *Measure for Measure* indicates a profound reorientation of Shakespearean comedy, an essential shift in the movement from the festive comedies to plays in which Vincentio's fabrication of spiritual fatherhood will give way to such actual fathers as Pericles, Cymbeline, Leontes, Polixenes, and Prospero. But despite this shift in focus, the deep affinities of *All's Well* to *Measure for Measure* are reconfirmed when these two plays are placed within the context of Shakespeare's development. Although they present very different comic responses to them, both plays open onto psychological conditions central to tragedies contemporaneous with them. These links to the tragedies, marked particularly by a deep preoccupation with the place of sexuality in the social order, lead to

13. Both the substitution of Mariana for Isabella in particular and the function of the Duke as plot manipulator in general represent striking departures from Shakespeare's sources for *Measure for Measure*. See *Narrative and Dramatic Sources of Shakespeare*, ed. Geoffrey Bullough, vol. 2 (London: Routledge and Kegan Paul; New York: Columbia University Press, 1958), pp. 409–10.

the intuitive grouping of *All's Well* and *Measure for Measure* as problem comedies, and they determine the nature of the transitional place these plays occupy between the festive comedies and the late romances. The following comments, which are indebted to C. L. Barber's study of the transformation of comic form in *Pericles* and *The Winter's Tale*,[14] sketch a way of seeing the problem comedies in relation to the festive comedies, the tragedies, and the late romances.

In the festive comedies, the main action moves away from ties of family and friendship to new relationships completed in marriage. The late romances emphasize the recovery of family and friendship bonds that have been disrupted in ways often reminiscent of the violent rendings of the tragedies. The central experience in these later plays is that of an older generation finding its bearings in reconstructed social and familial orders it has earlier helped to disrupt. Often central to the pattern of love and desire dramatized in the festive comedies is the controlling presence of a strong, wise, loving young woman, particularly Portia in *The Merchant of Venice* and Rosalind in *As You Like It*.[15] In the late romances, women have different relations to the main plots, serving as both victims and saviors in a reciprocal working out of a loss and recovery pattern linking them to husband or father. The central conflict in *Pericles*, *The Winter's Tale*, and *The Tempest* resides in the experience of a noble, basically good, fatherly man who in some way brings great suffering on himself and those most closely related to him, but who is restored to dignity and power. Perhaps *Cymbeline* is an exception that helps clarify the rule. The extraordinary diffuseness of its action seems to reflect the absence of a strongly asserted masculine presence at the center of conflict, loss, and recovery in the design of this play, an absence that makes necessary the spectacular intervention of Jupiter in the last act.

All's Well is curiously linked to the designs of both the festive

14. " 'Thou that beget'st him that did thee beget': Transformation in *Pericles* and *The Winter's Tale*," *Shakespeare Survey*, 22 (1969): 59–67. I return to this seminal essay in chapter 2.

15. Other heroines like Beatrice and Viola often dominate their plays dramatically, but compared with Portia and Rosalind they are relatively powerless in directing the course of the action. In chapter 4 I consider development within the festive comedies, and discuss the roles played by these heroines as they differ from one another.

comedies and the late romances. Helena extends the controlling role of Portia and Rosalind, but in a world that calls her into very different and often more complexly troubled relations with the other characters, particularly the object of her love. Helena's main task is to overcome a difficulty that originates in Bertram's revulsion from her. Essential to Helena's success are her cure of the king and her own apparent death, both of which point forward to the roles played by daughters in the late romances. But after *All's Well* Shakespeare will never again write comedy brought to resolution primarily by the active presence of a woman in love. Crucial as they are to their respective plays, Marina, Perdita, and Miranda can do little to control actions in which each of them will give new life to a father and find a mate for herself. Imogen, the closest counterpart of the comic heroines in the late romances, is the most forceful dramatic presence in *Cymbeline,* but her ingenuity is not given the power to resolve an action that requires divine, patriarchal intervention.

In *Measure for Measure* the recentering of the control over comic action in a man, Duke Vincentio, suggests a reaction against the power that comes to be invested in Helena in *All's Well.* But the Duke's control is accompanied by telling limitations on his characterization. Vincentio, to bring *Measure for Measure* to its comic conclusion, must be kept at a distance from the powerful experience of conflict in this play. Many critics have noted that Vincentio seems in many ways to anticipate Prospero. But unlike the all-too-human fathers of the late romances, Vincentio is a "ghostly father." He also seems to be a rather ghostly lover when, in Shakespeare's attempt to bring *Measure for Measure* into line with the usual comic design, the Duke abruptly proposes to Isabella in the last scene.

The actions of the festive comedies are grounded in and protected by trust that the experience of love and the conventions of comedy are compatible with each other, that they make sense of each other. I do not have in mind here trust as a theme self-consciously explored in these plays, in the sense that the trusting of others becomes important in the plot of *Much Ado About Nothing* when Claudio cannot sustain his belief in Hero's virtue. Severe crises of trust brought on by real or apparent betrayal will become more central within the actions of Shakespeare's later plays: one need only think of Hamlet's excruciating struggle to compose a self capable of taking decisive action, of Antony's experience of a self as elusive and intangible as the shifting shapes of clouds, or of Prospero's embittered brooding over his misplaced trust in his brother. In the tragedies, failures of trust lead to violent mistrust, madness, desperate repudiations of self and others; trust in the comedies is stabilized by characters who, like Rosalind, balance their faith in human impulse with a shrewd mistrust of human folly and self-deception. The trust that will undergo such terrible pressures in the tragedies and romances is less important as a theme in the festive comedies, or as an experience of individual characters in them, than as a condition of their very existence.

Throughout the festive comedies, loving motives that will create tragic vulnerabilities in later plays are strengthened and refined through confrontations with stubborn but finally surmountable obstacles—in the lovers themselves, and in antagonistic elements in their society. Trust in the resourcefulness of human action underlies the affirmation of love and community in the festive comedies. The complications of these plays do not force conflict toward an irreconcilability that can undermine such trust. Orlando, though stripped of his rightful place in his family and in the dukedom, energetically celebrates the recentering of his life through his love for Rosalind in *As You Like It*; Claudio, after a moment of angry disorientation, seems scarcely affected in *Much Ado* by Hero's apparent betrayal of his love.

Trust in the self's inner resources and their compatibility with an external world, which sustains the festive comedies, becomes problematic in the problem comedies. Bertram, once his nerves are shattered by his forced marriage to Helena in *All's Well*, can only recover for himself the prospect of manly identity through a warrior's commitment to Mars and a quest for illicit sexual conquest. Angelo, after his desire has been provoked by Isabella in *Measure for Measure*, can only cling desperately to an empty semblance of respectability while he is driven to pursue the object of his lust. In the festive comedies, such trustworthy heroines as Portia and Rosalind provide assurance that the calamities of comedy can be, and will be, brought to a renewed order. But for Bertram's revulsion from Helena, neither Helena nor Shakespeare has a fully adequate solution. And for Angelo, who is shaken into violent and debasing confrontation with apparently alien forces within himself, there is only the problematic mercy of Vincentio. Comic action does not release longings for mutual intimacy in Bertram and Angelo, but fear of marital sexuality in one, desperate self-alienation in the other, and degraded, compulsive sexual longings in both. Both plays dramatize the men's fundamental mistrust of the inner impulses released in encounters with women.

Women's powers, which protect the comic actions of *As You Like It* and *The Merchant of Venice*, become threatening in the tragedies. In these plays, written in years that include the composition of *All's Well* and *Measure for Measure*, fierce struggles follow from erosions of masculine power or wisdom that result, at least partially, from relations to women. The failure of trust, often in a man's relation to a woman, is central to much Shakespearean tragedy. From Hamlet's estrangement from Gertrude and Ophelia and Troilus's naive faith in Cressida to the dramatization of Coriolanus, whose life has been shaped almost entirely by his deference to Volumnia, the tragedies present men either inhibited or excessive in their capacity for trust in women, and for whom such trust is inseparable from their capacity for trust in themselves. *The Winter's Tale* and *The Tempest*, like the tragedies, turn on the issue of trust, but these late plays move beyond catastrophe to a restored order that includes the main characters. The recognition scenes of the late romances dramatize the recovery from a calamitous crisis of trust that has taken a key figure beyond hope, away from the matrix that has given his life meaning. The problem comedies, however, are written during that phase in which Shakespeare's imagination is deeply preoccupied with catastrophic developments engendered by the failure of trust—in the most intimate relations with others and in the deepest inner resources of the self.

Failures of trust in the tragedies almost invariably lead to expressions of rage and disgust regarding sexuality, often presented in close connection with family tensions. In *Antony and Cleopatra*, an explicitly sexual relation is directly implicated in a crisis of trust, but often, as in *King Lear*, the sexual dimension is absent from the surface structure of key bonds. *Timon of Athens* provides a spectacular instance of violent rant about sexuality apparently unprovoked at the surface level of the action. Timon has invested his trust entirely in relations to men who eat his food and accept his lavish gifts. But when that trust is exposed as groundless, Timon turns immediately to often fiercely misogynous tirades that center on debased sexuality and family relationships:

> Matrons, turn incontinent!
> Obedience fail in children!
>
> . . . .
>
> To general filths
> Convert o' th' instant, green virginity!
> Do't in your parents eyes!　(IV.i.3–4, 6–8)

When Shakespeare brings Alcibiades to Timon's cave, Timon urges the wayward general to heed not the "yells of mothers, maids, nor babes" in destroying Athens (IV.iii.125). The "counterfeit matron," Timon counsels, is a "bawd," virgins are sources of treachery whose breasts menacingly "bore at men's eyes," the babe is a "bastard" whose destiny is to cut throats (IV.iii.113, 115, 117, 121). Timon urges the two "sluts" who accompany Alcibiades toward a more insidious form of destruction:

> Be whores still;
> And he whose pious breath seeks to convert you—
> Be strong in whore, allure him, burn him up,
> Let your close fire predominate his smoke,
> And be no turncoats.　(IV.iii.140–44)

The misogyny in Timon's rage is partly comprehensible as a reaction against his earlier quasi-maternal giving. Feeding Athenian men, Timon has himself fed on their responses to his bounty. When his "mouth-friends" (III.vi.86) abandon him, he turns savagely on the maternal identity he has earlier incorporated. The repressed sexual component neutralized by Timon's giving is released and projected in images of corrupt and dangerous female sexuality. Timon's ill-fated identification of himself with the recipients of his own generosity can in turn be related to the efforts of other tragic figures who seek nurture by merging their identities with the women they love. Violent denunciations of female sexuality follow when Desdemona seeks to be fully a wife rather than the reservoir of absolute content Othello has sought, for instance, or when Cordelia, instead of collaborating in Lear's perverse desire that she love her father all, asserts her rightful need to grow beyond the bonds of family.

Such developments in the tragedies, which explosively link sexuality, trust, and actual or symbolic family bonds, can also elucidate special pressures generated when consummated sexual unions are introduced into Shakespearean comedy in *All's Well* and *Measure for Measure*. The actions of these plays extend a comic design in which release leads to marital union. But these actions are subjected to the stresses of an imagination that presents its most compelling dramatization of sexuality's power in and over individuals in Hamlet's brooding over his mother's incest, Othello's hideous evocations of sexual disgust, Lear's raging against the "sulphurous pit" in the "centaur" half of the female anatomy.

Anxious mistrust for the sexual dimension of living, not fully acknowledged within the dramatic orderings of relations among the characters, pervades *All's Well* and *Measure for Measure*. Pressures that undermine trust in liberated human desire engender much of the formal experimentation with comic design in the problem comedies, especially the increased emphasis on an older generation's authority and on conflicted family bonds in *All's Well* and, conversely, the introduction of a disguised male figure of authority—a symbolic father with no actual family ties—who manipulates the plot of *Measure for Measure*. But Shakespeare is unable to dramatize in these plays an action that moves beyond failed trust to sexual bonds both persuasively completed in themselves and fully integrated into a reaffirmed social order. This achievement must wait for the late romances. Shakespeare must discover, must find himself able to discover, a comic ordering principle equivalent in power and scope to the destructive logic of tragedy. Such art must wait for Shakespeare's comic imagination to develop a route beyond the tragedies to a pattern of restored trust and a new ordering of human impulse in *The Winter's Tale* and *The Tempest*.

But what is the nature of an interpretive remark, like those above, that resorts to "Shakespeare" to account for something that occurs in Shakespearean drama? The question raises the vexed critical problem of relating literary works to the concept of an author used as an interpretive paradigm. In the following section I address this problem, not in order to make a thorough exploration of this elusive theoretical issue, but to make explicit some assumptions that underlie the interpretive framework I bring to this book.

Shakespeare and the Problem Comedies: What Is Shakespeare?

My way of reading *All's Well* and *Measure for Measure* in some respects recalls, and is indebted to, a critical tradition that indulged freely in speculation about Shakespeare's life to account for changes in the drama; it also raises the same difficult issue of determining the constraints that shape interpretive remarks about these plays. *All's Well* and *Measure for Measure* came to be regarded as "problem" or "dark" or "bitter" comedies because they seemed to represent an interruption of Shakespeare's characteristic comedy by concerns alien to it. A broad historical dimension for this intrusion was found in the "depths of Jacobean negation" inhabited alike by Shakespeare and the dramatists who were his contemporaries.[16] But the primary cause was sought in speculation about the personal depths of Shakespeare's experience at the beginning of the seventeenth century.

Before the term *problem comedy* had been introduced, Edward Dowden associated *All's Well* and *Measure for Measure* with the "out of the depths" period of the major tragedies. For Dowden, observations about particular plays were inseparable from "an inquiry after the personality of the writer." If the plays revealed "the mind of the creator," their chronology showed "the growth of his intellect and character from youth to full maturity."[17] Within that growth, Dowden argued, it was necessary to trace "in chronological order the three separate lines of Comedy, History, and Tragedy" (p. x). As Shakespeare wrote *All's Well* and *Measure for Measure*, "the genial spirit of comedy was deserting him." After *Twelfth Night*, "the change comes; *All's Well That Ends Well* is grave and earnest; *Measure for Measure* is dark and bitter" (p. vi).

Dowden's view influenced and was extended by many critics, among them E. K. Chambers and J. Dover Wilson. Of *All's Well* Chambers concluded, "Behind comedy so unsmiling as this some perturbation of the once sunny spirit must needs lie."[18] *Measure*

16. Una Ellis-Fermor, *The Jacobean Drama*, 4th ed. (1957; reprint ed., New York: Vintage Books, 1964), p. 260. The first edition of *Jacobean Drama* was published in 1935.

17. *Shakspere: A Critical Study of His Mind and Art*, 3rd ed. (New York: Harper and Brothers, 1881), p. xiii.

18. *Shakespeare: A Survey* (London: Macmillan, 1925), p. 207.

for Measure he found to be a "painful" play that sprang "out of a vexed, not out of limpid mood" (pp. 211, 216–17). Grouping these plays with *Troilus and Cressida*, Chambers declared that they were "the utterances of a puzzled and disturbed spirit, full of questionings, sceptical of its own ideals, looking with new misgivings into the ambiguous shadows of a world over which a cloud has passed and made a goblin of the sun" (p. 210). Wilson proceeded to make even more confident reconstructions of Shakespeare's spiritual crises. Wilson jumped, for instance, from the modestly stated claim "that Shakespeare's tragedies reflect personal feeling and inner spiritual experience" to the "irresistible" conclusion that "Shakespeare was subject at this time [1601–1608] to a dominant mood of gloom and dejection, which on one occasion at least brought him to the verge of madness."[19] Wilson sought corroboration both in historical circumstances—"the crash of Essex, and the squalid peace of James"—and in an autobiographical reading of the souring of " 'Sweet Desire' " in the *Sonnets* (p. 118).

Such speculations, not surprisingly, have been vigorously repudiated by critics who have objected both to the correctness of the particular attributes assigned to Shakespeare and to the general assumption that biographical inferences can be made on the basis of the drama. Although these two objections are very different—to rely on either one of them logically nullifies reliance on the other—they have often tended to blur in this critical debate. C. J. Sisson, for instance, in a barrage of eloquent indignation, sought to rescue Shakespeare from "mythical sorrows" fabricated by critics who assumed "that the actual evolution of Shakespeare's personal life must be read into his poetic and dramatic work" and that "dramatists write tragedies when their mood is tragic, and comedies when they are feeling pleased with life."[20] But Sisson, rather than dispensing

19. *The Essential Shakespeare: A Biographical Adventure* (Cambridge: Cambridge University Press, 1932), pp. 114–15. This conclusion is "irresistible" only if Shakespeare is identified totally with the darkest utterances of the protagonists of the tragedies and not with the mastery of deeply conflicted feeling achieved in tragic form—an identification Wilson endorses without reservation: "Collect these passages together, face them as they should be faced, and the conclusion is inescapable that the defiled imagination of which Shakespeare writes so often, and depicts in metaphors so nakedly material, must be his own" (p. 119).

20. "The Mythical Sorrows of Shakespeare," in *Studies in Shakespeare: British Academy Lectures*, selected and introduced by Peter Alexander (Lon-

with Shakespeare's life as an explanatory paradigm, merely replaced a Shakespeare subject to disillusionment and despondency with a perennially buoyant Shakespeare who "maintained throughout his robust and transcendent faith in God and in his creature Man" (p. 32). Sisson and others, outraged by efforts to understand the problem comedies in relation to dark turns in Shakespeare's life, have often tended, as A. P. Rossiter notes, to substitute not an approach freed from biographical speculation but "what amounts to spiritual biography—of an 'optimist' and Christian cast." [21]

More recent critics have attempted more rigorously than Sisson to dispense with an author in any way revealed in the drama. Northrop Frye, for instance, in his important book on the comedies and the romances, distinguishes critics who would write Shakespeare's "fictional biography," "a kind of allegory" suggested by the chronology of his writings, from those wiser critics who are concerned to demonstrate a "broader view of Shakespearean artistry." [22] Frye, relieved that the "foolish procedure" of fictional biography "is now happily discredited," argues that it should be replaced by the critical principle "that there is no passage in Shakespeare's plays, certainly written by Shakespeare, which cannot be explained in terms of its dramatic function and context" (p. 36). [23] "Shakespeare's plays,"

---

don: Oxford University Press, 1964), p. 11. Sisson's lecture was delivered in 1934.

21. *Angel with Horns* (New York: Theatre Arts Books, 1961), p. 113.

22. A *Natural Perspective: The Development of Shakespearean Comedy and Romance* (New York: Columbia University Press, 1965), pp. 35, 37.

23. For Frye, the "problems of the problem comedies" are circumscribed by a literary universe; characters caught up in the conflicts of these plays do not reflect the inner world of a Shakespeare responding to personal experience, but "have to be looked at first of all as conventional descendants of myths" (p. 64). In *All's Well*, Helena does not engage the "social problem of how a woman gets her man," but a "mythical problem" which she dispatches, "like her ancestress Psyche," by solving "three impossible tasks." If we "still find it a problem that she should want to do all this just to get Bertram" (p. 64), this is because we bring to the play inappropriate expectations. Frye's discussion of *All's Well* and *Measure for Measure* as completions of mythic paradigms perhaps provides the most sophisticated version of a widespread tendency in the criticism of these plays. Many modern commentators, faced with the rich and unsettling range of conflict that eludes full dramatic mastery in the problem comedies, abstract from the complexity of attitudes released by their actions a coherent and identifiable pattern—based on a motif from myth or folklore, a scriptural analogue, or a dramatic convention—and regard the completion of that pattern as the play itself. W. W

Frye argues, "reflect the anxieties of his time; they do not show that he shared those anxieties. He may have done so as a man—there is no evidence one way or the other . . ." (pp. 41–42). When Frye

---

Lawrence seemed to be convinced that many of the difficulties *All's Well* poses for modern audiences would be minimized with a recognition that the motifs of the "Healing of the King" and the "Fulfilment of the Tasks" are enacted by a "wholly noble" version of the "Clever Wench" (*Shakespeare's Problem Comedies*, ch. 2). Eric LaGuardia sees *All's Well* as a "symbolic drama in which a regenerate condition of natural order is reached as a result of both the purification of the whole society of the play, and the initiation of the central characters into a life of mature virtue" ("Chastity, Regeneration, and World Order in *All's Well That Ends Well*," in *Myth and Symbol,* ed. Bernice Slote [Lincoln: University of Nebraska Press, 1963], p. 128). For LaGuardia, "the special equilibrium between the natural and the divine which the play ultimately asserts" (p. 121) emerges efficiently from the interaction of chastity, virtue, purity, sensuality, and a few other abstractions the characters "embody."

Frye finds that Isabella's chastity, "always a magical force in romance" (*Perspective,* p. 64), solves the main "problem" of *Measure for Measure,* but modern critics have more typically looked to Vincentio as the central figure and to the Bible instead of mythic and folk motifs for the pattern of that play. For G. Wilson Knight, Vincentio is "a symbol of the same kind as the Father in the Parable of the Prodigal Son (Luke xv) or the Lord in that of the Unmerciful Servant (Matthew xviii). The simplest way to focus correctly the quality and unity of *Measure for Measure* is to read it on the analogy of Jesus' parables" (*The Wheel of Fire,* p. 83). Roy Battenhouse ("*Measure for Measure* and the Christian Doctrine of Atonement," *PMLA,* 61 [1946]: 1029–59) and Neville Coghill ("Comic Form in *Measure for Measure,*" *Shakespeare Survey,* 8 [1955]: 14–27) see the action of *Measure for Measure* as an allegory of Christian atonement presided over by the "omnipresent Friar-Duke" (Coghill, p. 25).

Even Robert G. Hunter's instructive study of *Shakespeare and the Comedy of Forgiveness* (New York: Columbia University Press, 1965) seems to me flawed by a tendency to regard the completion of a moral/thematic pattern as the completion of a whole dramatic movement in his readings of *All's Well* and *Measure for Measure.* Hunter, like many other critics who look to historical or mythic or Biblical parallels for keys to these plays, is convinced that modern audiences simply do not respond correctly to patterns Shakespeare's contemporaries would have found completely plausible. "The final scene of *All's Well* draws upon and refers to a belief in the reality of the descent of grace upon a sinning human," Hunter argues, a reality Elizabethans regarded as "an everyday psychological possibility." "A Renaissance audience would not, I think, have considered even Bertram incapable of that alteration" (p. 131). Even if one assumes that *All's Well* does suggest such a transformation, however, the problem for modern audiences is not that they cannot imaginatively conceive of Bertram's possible alteration, but that the play does so little to dramatize it—or to dramatize responses in other characters that demonstrate the capacity for forgiveness of sins in a Christian community.

asks us to "conceive of an imagination so concrete that for it the structure is prior to the attitude, and prescribes the attitude" (pp. 43–44), the separation between Shakespeare the man and Shakespeare the artist is apparently complete and absolute.

To conceive of Shakespeare in this way, however, is to construct a kind of fictional biography, one that takes its place beside the Shakespeare of spiritual turmoil and the Shakespeare of imperturbable Christian faith. In his effort to divorce "biographical" from critical considerations, Frye must invent a remote and invisible and godlike Shakespeare whose essence is a superhuman detachment from historical and psychological forces that shape human experience. This notion of a Shakespeare who could separate absolutely tensions in his life from the structuring power of his literary imagination is biographical speculation that seems to me to put Shakespeare outside the reach of human possibility. Frye, indeed, constructs a new version of the "impersonal," "Olympian" Shakespeare Dover Wilson enthusiastically set out to dismantle in his "biographical adventure" of 1932.

The different ways I have mentioned of imagining Shakespeare do not serve the same purposes, nor assume the same importance, for the critics who employ them. For Dowden, "to come into close and living relation with the individuality of a poet must be the chief end of our study"; the project is completed when we "pass through the creation of the artist to the mind of the creator" (*Shakspere*, p. 2). Wilson wished to put Shakespeare's "spiritual development, which is evident in the poems and plays, . . . in relation to the spiritual conditions of the time in which he lived" (*Essential Shakespeare*, p. 14). Sisson found reassurance in a Shakespeare who, "as a man and as artist, . . . experienced and faced the twin problems of pain and evil in no spirit of petulance, but with an insight into immanent good" ("Mythical Sorrows," p. 32). Frye, concerned to establish the autonomy of literary structures, produces a Shakespeare whose chief merit is not to have obstructed the mirror he held up to art— with an unexplored concession to the "anxieties of his time." But each of these critics—whether comprehending Shakespeare as a by-product of seeing the plays in a certain way or as the chief goal of reading the plays—is in some way caught up in a circular process in which Shakespeare and Shakespeare's plays are read in terms of each other. Frye's Shakespeare who writes independently of psychic conflict, as much as the Shakespeare of spiritual unrest or the Shakespeare of Christian piety, seems to confirm Frank Cioffi's claim that "there is an implicit biographical reference in our response to literature. It is, if you like, part of our concept of literature." [24]

According to Cioffi, "a conviction that a poet stands in a certain relation to his words conditions our response to them"; our sense of the author will "throw a 'field of force' round the work" (pp. 106, 102). Cioffi constructs his argument against Wimsatt and Beardsley's claim to have dispensed with the "intentional fallacy" in order that criticism may properly concern itself with "the text itself." "But," asks Cioffi, "what is the text?"

> If you remind yourself of how questions about what is "in the text" are settled you will see that they involve a great deal which is not "in the text." . . . Where an interpretive issue has already arisen, the use of a distinction between internal, licit considerations, and external, illicit ones is just a form of question-begging. (p. 101)

The problem comedies are conspicuous instances of how difficult it is to determine what Frye calls "dramatic function and context" on the basis of what is "in the text." In order to resolve the intricate critical debate over what is in the text of these plays, critics have turned up an astonishing variety of external contexts. In this turning to external materials—philosophical ideas, dramatic conventions, political convictions, biblical stories, mythical patterns, literary sources, even the anxieties of the age—"Shakespeare" tends to become that entity through which these materials pass, either greatly

---

24. "Intention and Interpretation in Criticism," *Proceedings of the Aristotelian Society*, new series, 64 (1963–1964): 98. A striking instance of how easily—and how fruitfully—considerations of the "man" and the "work" may blur into each other is provided in T. S. Eliot's discussion of Shakespeare's development in the 1932 essay on John Ford:

> The standard set by Shakespeare is that of a continuous development from first to last, a development in which the choice both of theme and of dramatic and verse technique in each play seems to be determined increasingly by Shakespeare's state of feeling, by the particular stage of his emotional maturity at the time. What is 'the whole man' is not simply his greatest or maturest achievement, but the whole pattern formed by the sequence of plays; so that we may say confidently that the full meaning of any one of his plays is not in itself alone, but in that play in the order in which it was written, in its relation to all of Shakespeare's other plays, earlier and later: we must know all of Shakespeare's work in order to know any of it.
>
> ("John Ford," in *Selected Essays*, new ed. [New York: Harcourt, Brace and World, 1950], p. 170)

modified or simply duplicated, to emerge in the plays themselves.

But how are such conceptualizations related to the Shakespeare who produced those texts that bear his name? Does the Shakespeare that any one critic posits—explicitly or implicitly—reflect anything more than that critic's theoretical or personal need to find such a Shakespeare? Norman N. Holland, noting that psychological critics necessarily proceed from literary texts to the workings of a mind, is, in *Psychoanalysis and Shakespeare*, skeptical of criticism that claims to offer any insight into the mind of Shakespeare. Holland argues that psychoanalytic criticism must both find a "congruity between the literary work and some psychoanalytic description of the mind in general" and relate that general description to "some mind in particular."[25] But speculation about Shakespeare's mind, Holland concludes, is greatly limited by the paucity of relevant biographical data: "any conclusions we reach about him by reading through his works to his personality must remain highly interesting, perhaps highly useful, but ultimately unprovable: a Shakespeare-in-the-works who is as different from the Shakespeare one might actually meet as an X ray is from a portrait" (p. 295). Holland's preference is for a criticism that "deals with an audience's mind, as opposed to Shakespeare's" (p. 310). This preference he has put at the center of more recent theoretical work, which makes the reader's response to the literary text the basis of critical inquiry.[26]

Certainly, as Holland and others have emphasized, the critic's own experience of a text is the only experience he or she can know directly. What I say about Shakespeare's art is shaped and limited by what I bring to it; my characteristic style of responding to the world I inhabit will shape that part of the world I encounter through reading or seeing a play. In formulating what I find in *All's Well* or *Measure for Measure*, there is no way for me to efface the "I" that shapes both my direct responses to the plays and my attempts to locate them in larger Shakespearean contexts. But I will have failed in my effort if I cannot bring what I have to say into relation with the responses of other readers of Shakespeare, whether or not they have

25. *Psychoanalysis and Shakespeare* (New York: McGraw-Hill, 1966), pp. 293–94.
26. See *Poems in Persons* (New York: Norton, 1973); *Five Readers Reading* (New Haven: Yale University Press, 1975); and "Unity Identity Text Self," *PMLA*, 90 (1975): 813–22.

experienced a comparable uneasiness with the dramatic resolutions of the problem comedies. For the purposes of this study, I will use my responses to these plays as instruments of criticism, not as its objects of study. Like all investigative instruments, these will affect the field they survey—probably in many ways that will be more apparent to others than to me.

Holland is surely correct, however, in arguing that a critic's responses to a play by Shakespeare will not lead to a verifiable understanding of "Shakespeare's personality." The plays simply do not supply the kind of information we ordinarily use to understand the "personalities" of persons that we know as family, friends, colleagues, or whatever, and the available biographical materials are hardly adequate for reaching such an understanding either. But if we cannot know as much about Shakespeare the person as we can, say, about Keats or Lawrence or Joyce or any other modern writer who has left an extensive biographical record, does this dispense with the role of Shakespeare in Shakespearean criticism? I think there are several contexts in which we habitually read Shakespeare's works that make it impossible to answer that question with a clear negative.

For instance, my responses to *The Comedy of Errors* and *The Winter's Tale* will shape what I can say about each of these plays and what I can say about their relationship to each other. So long as what I want to do is interpret one of these plays or compare and contrast the two of them with each other, I can base my discussion on what I find in the two texts—their different ways of dramatizing family bonds, or mistaken identities, or situations of separation that lead to reunion, or the culminating importance of the recognition scene. But the interacting elements of this hypothetical discussion—my responses and the texts as they shape each other—are no longer sufficient as soon as I start to pose other questions: What are the relations of these two plays to their known sources? How does it happen that the figure of a mother as reconciling agency, important in both these plays, drops out of Shakespearean comedy between *The Comedy of Errors* and the late romances? How does it come about that Shakespeare is able to produce, near the end of his career, a play so much richer in poetry and characterization and dramatic power than the early, much more derivative comedy? And within these extraordinary changes, what is it that lets me think of both plays as equally Shakespearean?

I will not, of course, be able to come up with conclusively verifiable answers to these questions (what questions of interpretation
have ever yielded such answers?). But I cannot address such questions at all so long as I restrict myself to a consideration of my responses to the formal properties of two literary texts. Another entity, implicit in the questions themselves, must be added to this
discussion if such questions are to be pursued, and that entity can
conveniently be called Shakespeare. But if such a Shakespeare is not
"Shakespeare's personality," what is it? Holland, in more recent
work, argues persuasively that within the context of "our interaction
with the work" we can find "unities between the work and its author" (*Poems in Persons*, p. 142).[27] What can we say about such an
author?

Questions regarding the author's identity are taken up with special
rigor by Michel Foucault in an essay entitled "What Is an Author?"[28] Foucault identifies an important source of "the specific difficulties attending an author's name" and the way that name functions
in criticism: "the link between a proper name and the individual being named and the link between an author's name and that which it
names are not isomorphous and do not function in the same way;
and these differences require clarification" (pp. 121–22). A proper
name, Foucault observes, "moves from the interior of a discourse
to the real person outside who produced it," but "the name of the
author remains at the contours of texts—separating one from the
other, defining their form, and characterizing their mode of existence" (p. 123).

Foucault's exploration of "the 'author' as a function of discourse"

27. "The making of poetry," Holland writes, "is simply one ego's solution to the demands set by inner and outer reality," and that "solution" is
necessarily continuous with, and expressive of, the "personal style" of the
poet (*Poems in Persons*, p. 57). A writer's work, like every other activity he
undertakes, will express variations on an "invariant identity theme" ("Unity
Identity Text Self," p. 815), a concept for specifying the radical unity of
the individual self Holland borrows from the psychoanalytic writings of
Heinz Lichtenstein. Although I will not attempt to formulate an "identity
theme" for Shakespeare, much of what I say in this book will be consistent
with Holland's call for criticism that seeks out the ordering principles in an
author's work.

28. *Language, Counter-Memory, Practice: Selected Essays and Interviews*,
ed. Donald F. Bouchard (Ithaca: Cornell University Press, 1977), pp. 113–
38.

(p. 124) is part of a vast project extended in his questioning of the traditional "unities of discourse" in *The Archaeology of Knowledge*.[29] My own modest purpose is simply to clarify what is constructed in that endlessly circular process in which my reading of Shakespeare's plays leads toward a conception of Shakespeare that in turn influences how I read Shakespeare's plays. Foucault's essay helps to clarify the conditions of this circularity. Foucault notes that the "aspects of an individual, which we designate as an author (or which comprise an individual as an author), are projections, in terms always more or less psychological, of our way of handling texts" ("What Is an Author?" p. 127). The author thus produced is not identical with the person who produced the texts. It is "false to seek the author in relation to the actual writer," Foucault observes; "the 'author-function' arises out of their scission—in the division and distance of the two" (p. 129).

But the distance Foucault recognizes between the "author" and the "actual writer" is not simply dead space; this space is charged with what Cioffi calls a "field of force" that conditions how we interpret the works that bear an author's name. What enters into this "field of force"? Foucault uses Shakespeare to introduce a significant distinction regarding how we construct the authors of literary texts:

> The disclosure that Shakespeare was not born in the house that tourists now visit would not modify the functioning of the author's name, but, if it were proved that he had not written the sonnets that we attribute to him, this would constitute a significant change and affect the manner in which the author's name functions.
>
> (p. 122)

This distinction is deceptively neat, however; our understanding of the author is shaped by a vast number of materials that could be inserted between the two instances Foucault cites.

The particular house Shakespeare the "real person" was born in may, indeed, be of no importance to Shakespeare the "author"—though if it were shown that Shakespeare was born in a hovel or a castle, would this not affect how we respond to hovels or castles (or even to the whole issue of class structure and feeling) as they appear in the plays? But even without such a discovery, that Shakespeare was born in a small town and did his work in a large one, that he was

29. Trans. A. M. Sheridan Smith (New York: Harper and Row, 1972).

born into an aspiring middle-class family and wrote mostly about the aristocracy and the nobility, that he was born in the sixteenth century and not the thirteenth or the eighteenth, these and many other items of information circulate through our perceptions of the works whether or not they are explicitly acknowledged. The Shakespeare I find/fabricate in the drama is necessarily and obviously affected by this body of information that exists apart from the texts of the plays. Such information—which is only pertinent because we assume the existence of a "real person" who produced Shakespeare's plays—penetrates our understanding of the "author" Shakespeare, affects "the manner in which the author's name functions."

But information of this sort enters from the outside into the circular movement from plays to author to plays. My own effort to understand the problem comedies in relation to Shakespeare will not make explicit use of biographical data (except for the chronology that has been established with relative precision by modern scholarship);[30] I will neither seek corroboration for statements about the plays in biographical details nor move from such details to speculations about the drama. I will not attempt, as Chambers did, to speculate about the "puzzled and disturbed spirit" of a Shakespeare independent of the art he produced, or to show, in the manner of Dover Wilson, that Shakespeare was once brought to the edge of madness. Nor will I speculate about the order Shakespeare imposed on his life or his art at the level of personal belief. Even the most thorough reconstruction of the Elizabethan world picture, carefully correlated with ideological statements made in the plays, will not provide a reliable way of knowing what beliefs—religious, moral, political, social, or even artistic—Shakespeare would have been willing to acknowledge as his own. But it is doubtful that such knowledge, were it available, would be of decisive importance in understanding his art. Beliefs in themselves, as often instruments of self-deception as self-awareness, and ordinarily a mixture of both, simply do not provide a conclusive index to the ordering principles of a person's life or art.

30. For the purpose of my argument, no more chronological certainty is required than seems to be available. Much of what I say assumes that *All's Well* was probably written slightly earlier than *Measure for Measure* and that both plays were written in a four- or five-year period at the beginning of the 1600s that also includes *Hamlet, Troilus and Cressida,* and *Othello;* it is not important to my argument that any of these plays be dated with complete precision.

It seems likely to me, for instance, that Shakespeare believed marriage to be a proper and necessary and morally valid institution, an essential structure in the social and perhaps the religious order. Marriage in itself is important in the drama, however, not as an indicator of the dramatist's belief, but as a source, and a resource, of comfort and tension, strength and vulnerability, concord and violence, life and death, as the relation that at once perpetuates the family and exists in ineradicable tension with familial bonds. Such tensions, which animate the drama, manifest the larger psychological context in which beliefs function, not as ideological affirmations of the artist, but as codified reflections, or secondary resolutions, of deeply ambivalent attitudes doubled and redoubled in the multiple perspectives of drama.

In trying to clarify elements of that larger psychological context, however, I will assume that Shakespeare was once a child, and that his childhood, in itself irrecoverable, had a formative impact on later experience, including the writing of poems and plays. I will assume that Shakespeare responded to the world around him and to conflict within him, and that these responses produced characteristic attitudes toward experience that shaped the writing of his texts. And I will assume that these characteristic attitudes were not static, but that, within an underlying continuity, they developed. I know I cannot in my reading recover the "person" who underwent such development, but my assumption of his existence will shape how I imagine an "author" who shares his name, and who also exhibits patterns of psychological development. In short, although the "Shakespeare" I thus conceptualize exists only, in Foucault's language, "at the contours of texts," his attributes are not those of texts but those of persons—they exist in the same continuum of human possibility that I would bring to bear on the understanding of persons.[31]

31. While acknowledging that the author I place "in a certain relation" to his works is not identical with the actual person who produced them, it is well to remember that my neighbors, my colleagues, and my children are also not identical with my understanding of them. Reuben Brower points out that, even in lyric poetry, "the poet is always wrapping himself up in some guise, if only the guise of being a poet" (*Fields of Light* [London: Oxford University Press, 1951], p. 20). But a person I encounter in conversation or in the classroom or across the backyard fence is "wrapping himself up in some guise" as well; there can be no human exchange, literary or personal,

My concern in this book is with how the drama presents shifts in
relations to deep sources of psychic conflict that can only be explored by assuming the interpenetration of literary form and the
evolving temperament of an author. Despite their always precarious,
sometimes outrageous, speculations about Shakespeare's life apart
from the drama, Dowden, Chambers, Wilson, and others who are
often repudiated together as fanciful pseudo-biographers point suggestively in this direction. Chambers saw in the problem comedies
"the singularly interesting record of a particular phase in the poet's
shifting outlook on humanity and the universe to which humanity
is bound" (*Survey*, p. 210). The drama does present such shifts.
Wilson found in the drama of this period a "strain of sex-nausea"
that exceeded the "dramatic reason for it" (*Essential Shakespeare*,
p. 118); though there are often "dramatic reasons" that Wilson did
not recognize, the force of deeply sexualized conflict shaping these
plays does call for an interpretive context that attempts to account
for it.[32] My aim is to understand developments specific to the prob-

---

not mediated by such guises. The way we conceive of authors as manipulators
of literary conventions cannot be totally separated from, nor can it escape
the limitations of, the way we conceive of persons who present their individualized identities to us through the conventions of culturally codified behavior. We know persons, as well as authors, through constructions based on
codified information that partly reveals them, partly hides them from us. If
the Shakespeare I construct from the texts is as different, as Holland suggests,
"from the Shakespeare one might actually meet as an X ray is from a portrait," it is worth noting that we know very little about most people we actually meet and that an X ray can reveal a kind of truth that a portrait cannot.

32. Other critics, who have found more subtle and persuasive ways than
Chambers and Wilson of addressing problematic qualities in the problem
comedies, and who have been more restrained in speculating about Shakespeare's spiritual disposition, have also related their observations on these
plays to implied stresses in the life of their creator—even if the only evidence
for these stresses is provided by the plays themselves. Salinger, for instance, in
order to clarify the structural indebtedness of *All's Well* and *Measure for
Measure* to their probable sources, assumes a "personal tension fundamental
to Shakespeare's comedies" that reshapes source materials. Salinger argues
that in the problem comedies Shakespeare "was looking for a new way of
working out dramatically the emotional tension behind the complex of the
judge and the nun" (*Shakespeare and the Traditions of Comedy*, pp. 306,
313). At the heart of A. P. Rossiter's vigorous readings of *All's Well* and
Measure for Measure as tragi-comedies in *Angel with Horns* is his perception
of an unpurged tension between limitations in the comic conventions that
structure these plays and the force of turbulent moral and psychological pressures Shakespeare brings to them. My purpose has been to make more explicit

lem comedies and psychological trends that animate the overall development of Shakespeare's drama in the context of each other, with particular emphasis on shifting attitudes toward the interdependence of identity, family, and sexuality. I think this effort can disclose patterns that place Shakespearean drama within the frame of what we can know generally about psychological development, and can acknowledge the depth and intensity of conflict this development entails for Shakespeare in particular.

All's Well That Ends Well and *Measure for Measure*, because they cannot totally accommodate in comic form pressures released during a phase of heightened intensity in Shakespeare's development, offer unique vantage points from which to view larger trends in that development. Freud likened disclosures about the self made possible by investigations of certain neurotic disturbances to the lines of a crystal that are revealed when the crystal, under unusual pressure, has been split:

> If we throw a crystal to the floor, it breaks; but not into haphazard pieces. It comes apart along its lines of cleavage into fragments whose boundaries, though they were invisible, were predetermined by the crystal's structure.[33]

The "lines of cleavage" were there, potentially, all the time, but hidden in the perfect clarity of the whole. I do not wish to argue that the problem comedies are neurotic disturbances, but I think Freud's analogy can be adapted to include my view of these plays and their place in the development of Shakespearean drama. The relative failure of the problem comedies to achieve the level of dramatic integration that is attained in earlier comedies, as they are subjected to pressures that are mastered in tragedies written at nearly the same time, can provide valuable perspectives on those disruptive psychological tensions that Shakespeare's art exists to shape and control and understand in the symbolic action of drama.

---

the implications of such intuitive gestures toward placing Shakespeare in relation with the plays.

33. *New Introductory Lectures on Psychoanalysis*, in *Standard Edition of the Complete Psychological Works of Sigmund Freud*, ed. James Strachey, vol. 22 (London: Hogarth Press, 1964), p. 59.

II

<hr style="width:30%" />

Imperial Love and the Dark House:

All's Well That Ends Well

SHAKESPEARE'S decision to base a comedy on Boccaccio's story about a young man who flees rather than pursues his eventual wife, despises rather than adores her, creates for *All's Well That Ends Well* an altered set of comic conflicts.[1] Instead of accommodating the marital aspirations of a Bassanio or an Orlando, the play's action must bring Bertram to accept Helena as his wife. Before this action is completed, the young count is identified at various moments as a nobleman of great promise, an object of adoration, a complete fool, a snob, an ungrateful son and subject, a whimpering adolescent, a warrior of heroic stature, a degenerate rake, a liar, a moral coward, a suspected murderer, and, perhaps, a regenerate husband. Few characters in Shakespeare's comedies are called upon to fit so many different images, certainly none of Bertram's more compliant comic predecessors. Partly because he has often been seen through responses he generates in other characters, who repudiate him as son, subject, and comrade, Bertram has long held a reputation among critics as a "thoroughly disagreeable, peevish and vicious person."[2] Recent attempts to brighten Bertram's character

1. The source story of *All's Well, Decameron,* Day 3, Story 9, was adapted by William Painter as the thirty-eighth novel in *The Palace of Pleasure* (1566–1567, 1575). Geoffrey Bullough reprints Painter's story from the 1575 ed. in *Narrative and Dramatic Sources of Shakespeare,* vol. 2 (London: Routledge and Kegan Paul; New York: Columbia University Press, 1958), pp. 389–96.
2. W. W. Lawrence, *Shakespeare's Problem Comedies* (New York: Mac-

34

have often accompanied attempts to salvage the play from a long tradition of critical discontent, to demonstrate "that *All's Well* is a good play," that in fact, "All does end well."[3] I think instead that a close look at *All's Well* as it is experienced by Bertram can help identify unresolved tensions that not only define his position in the action but that shape the play as a whole and indicate the place it occupies in Shakespearean comedy.

Bertram, Marriage, and Manhood

KING   *Youth, thou bear'st thy father's face.*
Frank nature, rather curious than in haste,
Hath well composed thee. Thy father's moral parts
Mayst thou inherit too!   (I.ii.19–22)

Dr. Johnson's indictment of the young count can speak for many:

I cannot reconcile my heart to Bertram; a man noble without generosity, and young without truth; who marries Helen as a coward, and leaves her as a profligate: when she is dead by his unkindness, sneaks home to a second marriage, is accused by a woman whom he has wronged, defends himself by falsehood, and is dismissed to happiness.[4]

Johnson's denunciation seems to be exactly the response to Bertram that the moral context of the play demands. But Sir Arthur Quiller-Couch remarked, introducing his edition of *All's Well*, that Bertram "has something to say for himself against the moralizers":

There is nothing in him, until we come to the final scene, that we cannot find it in our hearts to forgive, if only he will give us the right excuse. . . . For, consciously or not, we have felt Helena's love pleading his cause with us all the while. The follies of youth—"lusty juventus"—come of nature and mettle, and arrogance of birth may be a fault well on this side of sin. There *must* be some attractiveness

millan, 1931), p. 61. Lawrence regarded the "blackening" of Bertram's character from Painter's presentation of Beltramo as "one of the most sweeping changes made by Shakespeare in the story as a whole" (p. 62).
    3. Albert Howard Carter, "In Defense of Bertram," *Shakespeare Quarterly*, 7 (1956): 21, 31.
    4. *Johnson on Shakespeare*, ed. Arthur Sherbo, in *The Works of Samuel Johnson*, vol. 7 (New Haven: Yale University Press, 1968), p. 404.

in Bertram to justify such devotion, and this will surely reveal itself, to satisfy us or nearly, before the curtain falls. But the final scene destroys our hope.[5]

The contrast between Quiller-Couch's tolerant view of Bertram and Dr. Johnson's severe indictment is present in the play, without seeming to come under the control of dramatic irony. The tension between these two perspectives, and between each of them and Helena's adoration of the youthful count, can be used to clarify the problem that Bertram poses, not only for *All's Well*, but for the development of Shakespearean comedy.

The first scene reveals little of Bertram directly beyond the impatience of an "unseasoned courtier" (I.i.66) anxious to realize the promise of manhood in the service of aristocratic ideals. The initial image of Bertram is focused chiefly through Helena's extravagant praise as she celebrates the "bright particular star" (I.i.82) of her imagination. Again at the French court, there is a strong trend to assimilate Bertram to identities that others impose upon him. In his first encounter with the king, Bertram plays an entirely passive role as the king weaves into rambling speeches wistful recollections of the old Count Rossillion, sober thoughts on his own approaching death, and impatient reflections on his youthful courtiers. As the king moves toward a nostalgic identification with the dead count, Bertram, by his mere presence, comes to be invested with a double, partially contradictory role. Bertram becomes, in the eyes of the king, a son ("Welcome, count; / My son's no dearer" [I.ii.75–76]) who represents both the promise of vicarious fulfillment through identification with his youthful promise and the threat posed by a younger generation unworthy of the tradition it inherits. Both of these projected identities become actively important in Bertram's subsequent meetings with the king.

Bertram begins to appear defined by his own presentation of self through action and sentiment in II.i. The young count watches the king issue an official farewell to the lords bound for the wars in Italy, which "may well serve / A nursery to our gentry, who are sick / For breathing and exploit" (I.ii.15–17). The king's speech is rich in the idealized rhetoric of ennobling war:

5. Introduction, in *All's Well That Ends Well* (Cambridge: Cambridge University Press, 1929), pp. xxvii–xxviii.

> Farewell, young lords.
> Whether I live or die, be you the sons
> Of worthy Frenchmen. Let Higher Italy
> (Those bated that inherit but the fall
> Of the last monarchy) see that you come
> Not to woo honor, but to wed it, when
> The bravest questant shrinks: find what you seek,
> That fame may cry you loud. (ii.i.10–17)

The king pronounces an ideal of honorable combat that promises self-fulfillment, liberation, and fame. These young lords may prove themselves worthy sons, brave men, and esteemed comrades. Opposed to the warlike courtship of honor are the snares of Italian women:

> Those girls of Italy, take heed of them.
> They say our French lack language to deny
> If they demand; beware of being captives
> Before you serve. (ii.i.19–22)

The king presents his lords with a world of masculine activity familiar to our culture and our poetry.[6] War offers sexualized aggressive release, idealization through the commitment to honor, and affectionate communion among men; heterosexual activity brings the threat of emasculation and is to be shunned or carefully subordinated to the masculine ideal. "Our hearts receive your warnings" (II.i.23), the lords reply, while Bertram eagerly looks on.

But Bertram must remain at court: "I am commanded here and kept a coil with / 'Too young,' and 'The next year,' and ' 'Tis too early' " (II.i.27–28). Denied access to heroic masculine endeavor by the king who has just exalted it, Bertram's forced stay at court takes its shape from his frustration:

> I shall stay here the forehorse to a smock,
> Creaking my shoes on the plain masonry,
> Till honor be bought up, and no sword worn
> But one to dance with. By heaven, I'll steal away!
> (ii.i.30–33)

Encouraged by Parolles and the other lords, who join for a moment in the masculine camaraderie from which Bertram is about to be

6. See the discussion of Lovelace's "To Lucasta, Going to the Warres" in Norman N. Holland, *The Dynamics of Literary Response* (New York: Oxford University Press, 1968), pp. 206–11.

severed, Bertram bristles with resentment toward the court life he now regards as effeminate. Bertram, who went to court to realize himself as a man, as a seasoned courtier, is treated as a boy, a condition Parolles uses to put salt into his barbed advice: "An thy mind stand to't, boy, steal away bravely" (II.i.29). Confined to the court he perceives as womanly, where the sword, the virile means to honor, merely adorns ballroom apparel, Bertram makes his first, precocious, gesture toward rebellion.

Bertram's implicit son relationship to the king—who tells him how to be a man and tells him also that he cannot be one yet—and his festering resentment at being "kept a coil" at court furnish essential background for the conflict shortly to develop when, after the king's mysterious cure, Bertram is appointed husband to Helena. His confrontation with the king in II.iii toughens and deepens the presentation of a Bertram just beginning to emerge as a character whose youthful ambitions seem destined for frustration. The scene appears to be heading for a triumphant culmination in Helena's selection of Bertram as husband. Helena's almost coquettishly ritualistic rejection of the other prospects lends comic momentum to her final decision. "This is the man," Helena announces, and the king sanctions the choice: "Why then, young Bertram, take her; she's thy wife" (II.iii.104–5). Because Bertram is caught off guard, and because he in turn catches the king off guard, the intensity now injected into the scene has a special emotional authority. Bertram's immediate response is astonishment: "My wife, my liege?" But he is quickly able to channel the logic of his position into a plea for freedom of choice: "I shall beseech your highness, / In such a business give me leave to use / The help of mine own eyes." The king seems a bit bewildered, but counters with a question that implicitly develops the authoritarian logic of his own position: "Knows't thou not, Bertram, / What she has done for me?" Bertram in turn challenges this argument: "Yes, my good lord, / But never hope to know why I should marry her" (II.iii.105–9).

As this exchange becomes increasingly heated, Bertram fights for his autonomy and the king insists on his own absolute power in a struggle that pits demanding father against rebellious son. The king identifies phallic mastery with honor and power: "My honor's at the stake, which to defeat, / I must produce my power" (II.iii. 148–49). Either Bertram bends before the all-powerful father or the king's restored virility is invalidated. Lafew has already comically injected the castration theme into the scene when, standing apart from the ritual elimination of all suitors but Bertram, he thinks that the courtiers Helena passes over have instead refused her: "Do all they deny her? An they were sons of mine, I'd have them whipped, or I would send them to th' Turk to make eunuchs of" (II.iii.85–87). But in the struggle of wills between Bertram and his king, this anxiety is developed into irreconcilable conflict. When Helena suggests that the marriage be waived, the king erupts in rage at the threat reluctant Bertram poses to his own restored manhood:

> Here, take her hand,
> Proud scornful boy, unworthy this good gift, . . .
> Check thy contempt.
> Obey our will, which travails in thy good.
> Believe not thy disdain, but presently
> Do thine own fortunes that obedient right
> Which both thy duty owes and our power claims;
> Or I will throw thee from my care forever,
> Into the staggers and the careless lapse
> Of youth and ignorance, both my revenge and hate
> Loosing upon thee, in the name of justice,
> Without all terms of pity. Speak! thine answer!
> (ii.iii.149–50; 156–65)

Under the shaming force of the king's violent anger, Bertram relents: "Pardon my gracious lord; for I submit / My fancy to your eyes" (II.ii.166–67). Bertram not only is the submissive son viewed from the lofty position of a towering king: he literally sees, for the moment of surrender, the situation through the king's eyes. He becomes, through a radical, forced suspension of self ("Believe not thy disdain"), an extension of the king's person. The validity of his own experience is defined by the king's imperative: "As thou lov'st her, / Thy love's to me religious; else, does err" (II.iii.181–82).[7]

7. The force of the king's confrontation with Bertram, and the broader importance of the king's role in Shakespeare's conception of the play, are accented by setting this long and intense exchange against the analogous scene in Painter. In that story, when Giletta (Helena) asks for Beltramo (Bertram) in marriage,

> the king was very loth to graunt him unto her: but for that he had made a promise which he was loth to breake, he caused him to be called forth, and said unto him: "Sir Countie, knowing full well that you are a gentleman of great

This submissive attitude toward the king must be abandoned, however, largely because the pressures that force Bertram to succumb to him are further complicated by conflict aroused by Helena herself. On the surface, Helena exacerbates Bertram's already expressed resentment at being confined to the effeminizing court. But this, too, builds on deeper dangers that Bertram has no means of understanding or adequately expressing:

> KING   Thou know'st she has raised me from my sickly bed.
>
> BERTRAM   But follows it, my lord, to bring me down
> Must answer for your raising? I know her well;
> She had her breeding at my father's charge.
> A poor physician's daughter my wife? Disdain
> Rather corrupt me ever!   (II.iii.110–15)

Bertram interprets his abhorrence of Helena in social terms, but his snobbery covers deeper fears. Helena has raised the king from his sickbed, cured him, and, symbolically, restored his virility, made him erect. But, asks Bertram, must this woman therefore "bring me down" to the marriage bed?

The forced marriage to Helena deflects him from his quest for a masculine identity and toward a sexuality he fears. "Undone, and forfeited to cares forever!" (II.ii.263), he whines, sounding like a little boy because he has been made a little boy through submission to the king. He can reopen future potentialities of manhood only by fleeing the sexual union forced upon him: "Although before the solemn priest I have sworn, / I will not bed her" (II.iii.265–66). Parolles' defensive rhetoric in counseling flight brings to the surface the unsavory resonance of debasing sexual anxiety, and opposes to it the ideal of war. "France is a dog-hole," advises Parolles, speaking not only to Bertram but for him,

> To th' wars, my boy, to th' wars!
> He wears his honor in a box unseen
> That hugs his kicky-wicky here at home,

---

honour, oure pleasure is, that you returne home to your owne house to order your estate according to your degree: and that you take with you a Damosell which I have appointed to be your wife."
(*Narrative and Dramatic Sources of Shakespeare*, vol. 2, p. 391)
Painter's king then insists, firmly but politely and perhaps even a little apologetically, that the reluctant Beltramo accept Giletta, arranges the marriage, and is never heard from again.

> Spending his manly marrow in her arms,
> Which should sustain the bound and high curvet
> Of Mars's fiery steed. To other regions!
> France is a stable; we that dwell in't jades.
> Therefore to th' war!   (II.iii.268; 272–79)

Marriage, from such a view, means dishonor and emasculation, a symbolic mode of castration ("A young man married is a man that's marred" [II.iii.292]); it drains off "manly marrow" better expended in the field of war than in "the dark house and the detested wife" (II. iii.286). Bertram's horror of marital sexuality, his fear of having his precarious masculinity overwhelmed by his wife, drives him to "those Italian fields / Where noble fellows strike" (II.iii.284–85).

The tensions provoked by this marriage are realized dramatically in Bertram's painfully dishonest parting from Helena, a scene brought to an anxious climax when his "clog" desires a farewell kiss. This is only the second time Bertram has spoken to Helena in the play, and the second time he says farewell; he is unable to speak to her at all in the scene in which the marriage is arranged. As he repeatedly bids a persistent Helena to go home without further ado, a squirming Bertram resorts for the first time to the lying that will characterize his behavior in relations to women henceforth. But within the lie he tells Helena, Bertram obliquely expresses a deeper truth about his situation:

> Prepared I was not
> For such a business; therefore am I found
> So much unsettled. This drives me to entreat you
> That presently you take your way for home,
> And rather muse than ask why I entreat you;
> For my respects are better than they seem,
> And my appointments have in them a need
> Greater than shows itself at the first view
> To you that know them not.   (II.v.60–68)

Bertram's options are to lie to Helena or lie with her, and the latter is unacceptable to him for reasons he is powerless either to alter or to articulate fully, to Helena or to himself.

All's Well That Ends Well, through those relationships centered subjectively in Bertram, deals with a young man's inevitable problem of freeing mature sexuality from threats that originate in the mutual development of family ties and infantile sexuality. Bertram's exchanges with Parolles and Helena as he prepares to flee France demonstrate how far he falls short of having won that freedom midway through the play. The "need / Greater than shows itself at the first view" that makes the prospect of marital sexuality intolerable is the unconscious dimension of his association of Helena, who "had her breeding at my father's charge," with his own family.

In I.iii, just after Bertram has gone to the French court, Shakespeare suggests the incestuous context of this relationship when the countess teases Helena into acknowledging her love for Bertram: "You know, Helen, / I am a mother to you" (I.iii.130–31). For the two women, Helena's pained protest in this prolonged exchange gives way to a simple resolution:

> HELENA   You are my mother, madam. Would you were—
> So that my lord your son were not my brother—
> Indeed my mother! or were you both our mothers,
> I care no more for than I do for heaven,
> So I were not his sister. Can't no other,
> But I your daughter, he must be my brother?
> COUNTESS   Yes, Helen, you might be my daughter-in-law.
>
> (I.iii.154–60)

But the countess jests with the very association of Helena with the Rossillion family Bertram fears, and which he cannot so easily resolve.

Bertram mentions his mother nearly every time he talks to or about Helena, casually at first (I.i.71–72), but more compulsively in the press of emotionally intense occasions later on (II.iii.272; II.v.69: IV.iii.85–86). A son's affection for a mother is directed by Bertram toward the countess; a son's fears of female domination and of his own oedipal wishes are aroused in Bertram by Helena. The situation builds on but complicates childhood circumstances in which an incestuous object-choice must be abandoned, for Bertram is forced to accept a woman unconsciously associated with the object of repressed incestuous impulses. Instead of allowing Bertram to find a sexual love removed from infantile conflict, the forced marriage reopens and concentrates the hazards of an oedipal relationship that has undergone repression. The marriage to Helena means for Bertram accepting a sexual bond made repugnant by its incestuous associations and abandoning the possibility of achieving a masculine identity independent of infantile conflict. In the typical oedipal situation, the son protects his own developing autonomy by relinquishing, through repression, the incestuous object to the father; in Bertram's situation, the father's power both transgresses the son's effort to achieve manly autonomy ("It is in us to plant thine honor where / We please to have it grow" [II.iii.155–56]) and compels the son to act out incestuous impulses made intolerable by repression ("I cannot love her, nor will strive to do't" [II.iii.145]).

In the Italian war Bertram finds release from the paralyzing force of this situation:

> This very day,
> Great Mars, I put myself into thy file.
> Make me but like my thoughts, and I shall prove
> A lover of thy drum, hater of love.   (III.iii.8–11)

He serves heroically, realizing in action the masculine ideal held up earlier by the French king to his restless courtiers. In place of the overpowering king, Bertram finds in the duke of Florence a family romance father whom he serves and saves, and who rewards him for conduct the king of France has forbidden. The comic exposure and renunciation of Parolles as a "counterfeit module" indicate further Bertram's escape from conflicts that beset him in France, for Parolles, however obviously bogus to others in the play, has been a necessary ally in bolstering the young count's courage at court. No longer in need of Parolles' assistance, Bertram can afford to recognize his duplicity. Among men and the affairs of war, Bertram in Italy becomes "the general of our horse," a "most gallant fellow" who has "done most honorable service," "taken their great'st commander," and who "with his own hand . . . slew the duke's brother" (III.v.).

In affairs of women and sexuality, Bertram also finds a strategy for evading conflict in Italy. Once he has located matters of honor, loyalty, and affection in a context independent of heterosexuality, he attempts to establish a sexual relationship with Diana that is independent of honor, loyalty, affection, and the conflicted impulses that have driven him away from Helena. Bertram attempts to escape infantile undercurrents of sexual inhibition by letting them rise to consciousness in a depersonalized context. He appeals to Diana: "And now you should be as your mother was / When your sweet self was got" (IV.ii.9–10). Here the maternal association emerges, not as a hidden inner block against marital sexuality, but as Diana's mother, a woman doing the universal, necessary—and therefore justified—act for begetting children. In Florence, Bertram can perform the act he has fled in disgust because he has—or, rather, he thinks he has—removed himself from conditions responsible for his fearful loathing. In his attempted seduction of Diana, however, Bertram is forced to use a symbol that binds his sexuality to his place in a family tradition, a ring that, as Helena explains to Diana, "downward hath succeeded in his house / From son to son some four or five descents / Since the first father wore it" (II.vii.23–25). Bertram relates to Diana his full awareness of the ring's significance, but he soon hands it over: "Here, take my ring! / My house, mine honor, yea, my life be thine, / And I'll be bid by thee" (IV.ii.51–53). In this impulsive gesture, Bertram completes the logic of his rebellion; he repudiates in an instant the inheritance leading back to "the first father" who wore this very ring. Bertram can win a measure of sexual freedom only by symbolically forfeiting his place among those familial bonds that have complicated his relation to Helena.

In Bertram Shakespeare invests in embryonic form the essential components of a romantic rebel who can only thrive by rejecting the society that has shaped him. Bertram has written this note to his mother on leaving France:

> I have sent you a daughter-in-law. She hath recovered the king, and undone me. I have wedded her, not bedded her, and sworn to make the 'not' eternal. You shall hear I am run away; know it before the report come. If there be breadth enough in the world, I will hold a long distance. My duty to you.
>
> Your unfortunate son,
> Bertram
> (III.ii.19–26)

Geographical distance here corresponds to the psychological distance Bertram must put between action and inner conflict if he is to pursue a desired identity. To preserve the purity of his deepest loyalty, that to his mother, Bertram must escape the marital claim of her surrogate Helena. He must find a new father, seek action in a land far removed from France, win a woman he can isolate from an unconscious dread of incest. Bertram's disillusionment at court; his flight from France and an unwanted marriage; his success among men at war in a foreign country; his cavalier attempt to seduce Diana; his symbolic repudiation of patriarchal loyalties in giving up the ring—these are gestures belonging to the Don Juan story, which Bertram brings into a comic art deeply committed to the family.

The problem Bertram puts to Shakespeare resides in the nature of the solution Bertram finds for his own intolerable situation at court. Bertram must be reinstated, for he threatens precisely those social and domestic values celebrated in the festive comedies. Although Shakespeare sketches out the logic of romantic flight in Bertram, the young count is released, ultimately, in order to be retrieved. Every step Bertram takes toward seducing Diana is a step toward the bed, and finally the household, of Helena, Shakespeare's chief agent for reclaiming him. But the effort to reassimilate Bertram further intensifies the pressures on comic form in this play. The nature of these pressures becomes clearer if *All's Well* is understood as a development out of earlier comedies.

All's Well as Comedy

LAVATCH *That man should be at woman's command, and yet no hurt done!* (i.iii.87–88)

Northrop Frye, in "The Argument of Comedy," called attention to the unusual turn Shakespeare gives the typical comic pattern in *All's Well*:

> The normal comic resolution is the surrender of the *senex* to the hero, never the reverse. Shakespeare tried to reverse the pattern in *All's Well That Ends Well*, where the king of France forces Bertram to marry Helena, and the critics have not yet stopped making faces over it.[8]

In Shakespeare's comedies, however, the *senex* is rarely a competing suitor, and never is this role of central importance. Although the aged and wealthy Gremio courts Bianca in *The Taming of the Shrew*,

8. *English Institute Essays 1948*, ed. D. A. Robertson, Jr. (New York: Columbia University Press, 1949), p. 59.

Petruchio has his future wife's father—a more typical role for old men in Shakespearean comedy—on his side in courting Kate. Shakespeare regularly takes pains to see to it that loving couples will not have their love excessively obstructed or compromised by the jealous claims of fathers on their daughters. Once, with Oberon's help, love has worked itself out in the forest of *A Midsummer Night's Dream*, the obstructive Egeus is superseded by higher authority when Theseus sanctions the marriage of Hermia to Lysander. Egeus's role, though essential to the plot, is of minor significance in the drama of discordant love. When Bassanio solves the riddle of the caskets in *The Merchant of Venice*, that obstacle to marriage reveals itself as a symbol of protective paternal wisdom rather than unwarranted intrusion. Often the heroines have dead and esteemed fathers, like Portia or Viola or Beatrice, or loving and compliant ones like Rosalind, who in *As You Like It* succinctly expresses the liberation from paternal ties that facilitates romantic triumph in the comedies: "But what talk we of fathers when there is such a man as Orlando?" (III. iv. 34–35). Villainous fathers, when they are central to comic plots, do not stand directly in the way of the principal loving union, nor do they effectively block the marriages of their own daughters. Shylock, for all the power he exerts in *The Merchant of Venice*, is easily evaded by Jessica; in *As You Like It* Celia marries a man whose lands have been seized by her father, the usurping Duke Frederick.

Comic heroes, like Orlando in *As You Like It*, also often have dead and esteemed fathers—when their parentage is mentioned at all. Living fathers of heroes appear on stage only in the first three comedies Shakespeare writes (Egeon in *The Comedy of Errors*; Vincentio, Lucentio's father in *Shrew*; and Antonio, father to Proteus in *The Two Gentlemen of Verona*), where the indebtedness to Terentian and Plautine models is strongest. Dead fathers who are mentioned do not reach out from the grave to obstruct the love plot. Indeed, Petruchio seems to feel liberated by his father's death in *Shrew*; Sir Rowland de Boys not only lives in spirit in Orlando, but his past friendship with the duke is instrumental in sealing Orlando's match with Rosalind in *As You Like It*.

But perhaps more significantly for understanding *All's Well* in relation to earlier comedies, no comic hero or heroine has a mother whose presence, either as memory or as living person, is of central importance (a curious exception occurs when the mother of the twin Syracrusians appears in the final scene of *The Comedy of Errors*). The mother, often the "son's ally" in New Comedy (Frye, "Argument," p. 58), is virtually omitted from Shakespearean comedy, until she becomes a significant figure, first Bertram's ally, then Helena's, in *All's Well*. In those comic actions that dramatize the renewal of the family and the transmission of family heritage, Shakespeare, through the virtual elimination of mothers and the minimization of roles traditionally played by fathers in New Comedy, carefully plays down the potential for disruption in relations across generations.

With what Frye calls the reversal of the usual comic pattern in *All's Well*, such disruptions are introduced directly into the play. Conflict in *All's Well* invariably occurs in contexts that include a parent or surrogate parent, the countess, the king, or Diana's mother, all of whom are present and important in the final scene. *All's Well* begins with a potential loosening of family ties as Bertram prepares to leave home for the court. Like many comparable characters in the festive comedies, both Bertram and Helena have recently lost to death worthy fathers. The value of each of them is understood in relation to that father; Helena "inherits" her father's disposition, Bertram his "father's face," and, the king hopes, his "moral parts" as well. Like Viola and Olivia in *Twelfth Night*, each has the task of going beyond mourning to find his or her own place in life, and each has a plan for doing this. But the movement outward into adult identities is greatly complicated in *All's Well* by developments that relate the younger generation to the old.

These complications consistently redefine the young characters in their roles as children—Bertram as promising then as rebellious son, Helena as virtuous and increasingly beloved daughter. Bertram will find at court a "father" in the king, who will also serve, in Lafew's explanation, as a "husband" to the countess. The countess also becomes a mother to Helena: "If she had partaken of my flesh and cost me the dearest groans of a mother, I could not have owed her a more rooted love" (IV.v.9–11). Family bonds are not severed by death, but reconstructed and rescued from death. The countess, who often talks about dying, is greeted by Helena in the final scene: "O my dear mother, do I see you living?" (V.iii.316). The king, rather than die from his fistula, becomes through Helena's cure "of as able body as when he numbered thirty" (IV.v.75–76). This play, which begins with the separation of children from parents, ends when Diana's mother brings Helena on stage, to be presented to the king and the countess as well as to Bertram. The final union of the young couple is defined, not by its liberation from ties of family, but by parental sanction retrieved from the threat of parental repudiation and punishment.

These altered conditions radically change the comic spirit of *All's Well* from that of earlier comedies. But perhaps they represent less a reversal of Shakespeare's usual comic pattern than a forcing into the action of conditions latent in previous plays. Shakespearean comedy, like New Comedy, dramatizes the cultural crisis perpetually reenacted when bonds of family and friendship must yield to sexual passion and the bond of marriage. The movement through and beyond friendship plays a prominent role, often more visible than the movement beyond family, in these plays. In *The Merchant of Venice*, Bassanio must be freed from the binding power of Antonio's love, as in *Much Ado About Nothing* Benedick must be freed from his self-identification as soldier and comrade, if the key marriages of these plays are to be completed. In *Merchant*, a crisis in the friendship of Bassanio and Antonio temporarily disrupts the marriage of Bassanio and Portia; the disrupted wedding of Claudio to Hero forces a crisis in Benedick's friendship with Claudio in *Much Ado*. In *As You Like It*, Rosalind exploits her disguise as Ganymede by forming a friendship with Orlando. As Ganymede, and as Ganymede pretending to be Rosalind, Rosalind uses the familiarity of friendship Orlando grants her as a boy to bring his naive love a step closer to an awareness of the human properties of his exalted beloved. In each case, a liberation from or a movement through and beyond friendship is performed that is consistent with the capacity Bertram develops to free himself from Parolles, although this friendship is unusual among the comedies in being presented as a bogus relationship in and of itself. More important, however, for understanding *All's Well* in relation to earlier comedies are complications in the comic movement beyond family ties.

Frye suggested that New Comedy dramatizes a "comic Oedipus situation" in which a young man (the son in the Oedipus triangle) outwits a father or father-figure to win the love of a young woman

("Argument," p. 58).[9] Such a heroine presents an image of the youthful mother that a son loved and thought himself to possess as a child. In this framework, the comic movement toward marriage builds on fantasies of triumphant return to a time in which a boy thought himself in complete possession of a mother's love, and the father could still be regarded as an unwelcome intruder, susceptible, at least in the child's imagination, to magical exclusion. The cunning slave, so often the young hero's ally in New Comedy, and the "efficient cause" (p. 59) in Frye's analysis, perhaps represents an extension of this magical resourcefulness, serving the son's sexual aspirations, and yet independent enough of him to preserve his innocence in the contest with the father. The "material cause," Frye argued, is the "young man's sexual desire," which may be fulfilled when "it turns out that she [the young woman, "usually a slave or courtesan"] is not under an insuperable taboo after all but is an accessible object of desire, so that the plot follows the regular wish-fulfillment pattern" (pp. 58, 59). In Shakespearean comedy, however, the young man rarely seems to be driven by overpowering sexual longing, and the women are typically high-born daughters of noble fathers, suggesting that the Oedipus situation stands in a very different relation to the comic action than in Plautus or Terence.

Freud has shown that a typical result of the incest barrier formed by repression is to deflect the feelings of young men for women along two different paths: toward sexual relations with women who are in some way degraded, and toward idealized and sexually inhibited relations with women chosen after the model of the mother.[10] The device in New Comedy by which the sexually desired young woman often turns out to be nobly born after all is a way of synthesizing in drama these two separate paths, so that they ultimately converge on the same woman. But in the two comedies that seem most closely to resemble *All's Well*, particularly in the characterization of the heroine, Bassanio's love for Portia and Orlando's love for Rosalind fol-

9. For a more rigorously psychoanalytic consideration of this comic pattern, see Ludwig Jekels, "On the Psychology of Comedy" (1926), tr. I. Jarosy, in *Theories of Comedy*, ed. Paul Lautner (New York: Doubleday, 1964), pp. 424–31.

10. "On the Universal Tendency to Debasement in the Sphere of Love," in *Standard Edition of the Complete Psychological Works of Sigmund Freud*, ed. James Strachey, vol. 11 (London: The Hogarth Press, 1957), pp. 179–90.

low the idealization pattern from the beginning. Bassanio loves a Portia of "wondrous virtues" (I.i.163), Orlando the "fair, the chaste, and unexpressive" (III.ii.10) Rosalind; neither expresses nor demonstrates compelling sexual ardor. And very little happens in these plays to suggest that either Bassanio or Orlando has been liberated significantly from the "aim-inhibited," idealizing trends in their loves.

Orlando and Bassanio are less driven by a desire to possess their women sexually than to be possessed by them, and the possession they long for seems to exclude or minimize sexual desire. Orlando, for instance, associating Rosalind with the chaste goddess Diana, longs to surround himself with a forest in which every tree will bear "thy huntress' name that my full life doth sway" (III.ii.4). The heroines seem to be attractive to these men because of their susceptibility to idealization and their practical strength and resourcefulness in creating conditions that make the marriage arrangements possible.

Sexual desire for men in such comedies tends to be deflected away from the hero into the language, and sometimes the actions, of secondary figures, especially clowns or fools. Touchstone, for instance, wittily deflates romantic love to mere sexual desire, both in his bawdy recasting of Orlando's poetry and in his pursuit of the country wench Audrey. C. L. Barber catches exactly the dramatic purpose Touchstone serves in relation to the "play's romance": "the fool's cynicism, or one-sided realism, forestalls the cynicism with which the audience might greet a play where his sort of realism has been ignored." [11] But the separation of "instinct" in Touchstone from idealizing sentiment in Orlando suggests psychological necessity as well as dramatic strategy in *As You Like It*. Orlando fills perfectly the role Shakespeare gives him, but that role reflects constraints essential to Orlando's relation to the psychological base of comic form in the festive comedies, which demands that ardent sexual longing and idealizing love be kept separate. Touchstone's function is not only to counterpoint the hero's idealizing love, but to protect it. The force of sexual degradation and the threat of sexual anxiety are released through the fool's bawdy wit without invading the hero's love; but the full integration of sexual desire and serious love remains a promise, not an achieved dramatic reality, at the play's end.

11. *Shakespeare's Festive Comedy* (Princeton: Princeton University Press, 1959), p. 232.

Bassanio and Orlando pursue an image of the beloved that builds on a child's need to inhabit a world presided over by a benevolent, powerful mother, a need strong enough that a boy sacrifices his sexual claim on a mother to it when desire and dependence come into conflict with each other. This need is vital particularly at those moments when a child relinquishes his precarious autonomy for a reassuring maternal presence able to supplant threatening reality with magically protective intimacy. The dramatic resolutions of *Merchant* and *As You Like It* are curiously akin to such moments. Portia presides over the end of *Merchant*, teasing and generous, seductive and aloof, furnishing from within her position of complete control a wife for Bassanio and "life and living" for Antonio. Rosalind, as she accepts in the last scene of *As You Like It* her womanly positions as daughter and wife, provides magical dispensations of happiness through union and reunion that suggest the intervention of a generous mother to put things right. Indeed, Rosalind has overseen the boyish tribulations of Orlando, and of Silvius as well, with the playful, semi-indulgent patience of a confident mother observing and directing the games of children. Lorenzo's closing remark to Portia and Nerissa assimilates them to the need for loving nurture that forms the first bond of love an infant experiences: "Fair ladies, you drop manna in the way / Of starvèd people" (V.i.294–95). Each of these plays culminates in a gesture of submission before the magical, maternal presence of a strong, wise, loving woman. In these plays, Shakespeare must deemphasize the potential for parental conflict and with it the sexual dimension of desire, because the hero's love includes within itself a need for maternal presence potentially disruptive of the movement into the sexual bond of marriage.

Bertram closely resembles such heroes as Bassanio and Orlando. All are young, inexperienced, eager, ambitious; each has less depth of characterization than the woman he marries. Each is intent on a course of self-fulfillment, which Bassanio and Orlando are able to achieve because of the actions of Portia and Rosalind. But Bertram is unable to achieve what he wants because of the actions of Helena. With the formidable backing of the king and the countess, characters who have no very exact predecessors in the festive comedies, Helena presses the comic hero for the first time to come to terms with a sexual bond within the play itself. Dramatically, the presence of the older generation intensifies the stress brought on by this alteration of the comic plot. Psychologically, however, the presence of the king and countess does not so much engender conflict as represent the unconscious association of sexuality and family ties forced into the action in *All's Well* when the marriage is pushed forward into the second act.

The clown's role in *All's Well* reflects the changes that occur in the main plot. Lavatch, whom Frye calls "the most mirthless even of Shakespeare's clowns," [12] and who is often regarded as a rather desperate departure from his predecessors, [13] can behave much like earlier clowns, as when he wittily exposes Parolles as a fool (II.iv.) or plays on the sexual connotations of his "bauble" (IV.v.). When he first appears, Lavatch seems to be a nearly direct descendant of Touchstone, who in *As You Like It* justifies his marriage to Audrey as a necessary accommodation to the constraints and liabilities of sexual drives: "As the ox hath his bow, sir, the horse his curb, and the falcon her bells, so man hath his desires; and as pigeons bill, so wedlock would be nibbling" (III.iii.69–71). Lavatch would marry Isbel because "my poor body, madam, requires it." Like Touchstone, he is "driven on by my flesh," though he introduces a rather darker association than Touchstone's analogies from the animal kingdom: "he must needs go that the devil drives" (I.iii.28–30). But instead of resigning himself to cuckoldry in marriage (like Touchstone: "As horns are odious, they are necessary" [III.iii.45–46]), Lavatch welcomes it,

> for the knaves come to do that for me which I am aweary of. He that ears my land spares my team and gives me leave to in the crop; if I be his cuckold, he's my drudge.   (I.iii.40–43)

By the time he returns from court, bringing Bertram's letter instead of Bertram himself, "your old ling and your Isbels o' th' court" have led Lavatch to forgo sexual desire altogether: "The brains of my

12. *A Natural Perspective* (New York: Columbia University Press, 1965), p. 105.

13. Lawrence found Lavatch "a thoroughly unsavory fellow" who ordinarily provides "rather poor comic relief"; like Parolles, he has "none of the geniality with which Shakespeare often endows his depraved characters" (*Shakespeare's Problem Comedies*, pp. 64–65, 66). E. M. W. Tillyard saw in Lavatch "the Clown who hates being such" (*Shakespeare's Problem Plays* [Toronto: University of Toronto Press, 1949], p. 111).

Cupid's knocked out, and I begin to love, as an old man loves money, with no stomach" (III.ii.14–16).

When he declares that he has lost his stomach for passion, Lavatch parodies and generalizes Bertram's response to marital sexuality; each response serves, in a different way, a common purpose. Lavatch makes the connection between the two when he comments on Bertram's flight. Since her son has run away, Lavatch tells the countess, Bertram "will not be killed so soon as I thought he would. . . . The danger is in standing to't; that's the loss of men, though it be the getting of children" (III.ii.36–37; 40–41). Lavatch here identifies sexuality and emasculation in precisely the way Bertram identifies them when he rejects his marriage to Helena. Bertram's flight from marital sexuality, from "the dark house and the detested wife," is matched by his flight into licentious sexuality apart from marriage; both flights reflect his vulnerability in relations to women, and both are related to the more general rejection of sexual desire expressed by Lavatch.

"A shrewd knave and an unhappy," Lavatch remains at Rossillion by the authority of Bertram's dead father, who "made himself much sport out of him" (IV.v.59–61). Although he is not a member of the Rossillion family, part of his role is to articulate tensions generated by the pervasive concern with family bonds in this play. Lavatch is like a child who endures all the inhibiting force of parental constraints, and who exchanges the right to grow beyond them into manhood for the clown's privilege of expressing with witty aggression the child's anxieties in an adult world that is both his home and his confinement. When he recounts his withdrawal from sexual desire, Lavatch expresses the most primitive, infantile level of Bertram's response to marriage with Helena. But that response, like the sexual anxiety that engenders it, threatens the effort to affirm a masculine identity. Bertram's compulsive effort to seduce Diana in Florence suggests that his seductive ardor is a means of defending himself against complete surrender to sexual inhibition so that he may prove to himself that his potency has survived the threat aroused by the incestuous dimension of his marriage.

Earlier, when Lavatch is accused by the countess of corrupting a song, he claims to have accomplished a "purifying" of it, for he has sung the prospect of "one good woman in ten. . . . Would God would serve the world so all the year! . . . An we might have a good woman born but or every blazing star, or at an earthquake, 'twould mend the lottery well; a man may draw his heart out ere 'a pluck one" (I.iii. 78–84). Here Lavatch does not speak the bawdy raillery of earlier clowns but an ironically detached version of the misogyny that torments Hamlet and Iago. *All's Well* belongs to a phase of Shakespeare's development when the forceful presence of a woman is often perceived, or misperceived, as a deep threat to a tragic hero's manhood. Lavatch gives comic voice to a mistrust of women as potential destroyers of manhood tragically present in *Hamlet* and *Othello*. When the countess commands him to "be gone," Lavatch responds: "That man should be at woman's command, and yet no hurt done!" (I.iii.85; 87–88). Lavatch's droll, ironic astonishment, if expressed in a more desperate vein, would indicate that point at which Bertram's experience breaks with that of earlier comic heroes and links up with the world of *Hamlet* and the tragedies. When Parolles counsels flight for Bertram, he speaks to a center of anxiety in the young count analogous to the vulnerability Iago exploits when he urges Othello to "be a man" (IV.i.65) by destroying the unsettling sexual presence of Desdemona. Bertram's flight, indeed, is a comic version of such destruction, completed symbolically by Helena's apparent death, by Bertram's relief that she is dead, and by the king's suspicion in the last act that Bertram may have been directly responsible for killing her.

In both Bassanio's high-spirited journey to Belmont and Orlando's venture to find "some settled low content" (II.iii.68) in Arden, the young hero's effort to set out for himself is inseparable from his effort to court the heroine. Each of these young men pursues his own ends within relationships that come under the pervasive control of the heroine, until his own adventure of self-definition is absorbed into a comic movement that culminates when the heroine puts every one in place, including the hero, in the festive community she has created. The ready compliance of earlier comic heroes gives way to recalcitrance in *All's Well* when Bertram encounters the demand that he submit himself sexually to a woman he sees as part of his family, and who is backed by a king whose manhood nullifies his own. But when the force behind his aversion to Helena is acknowledged, Bertram's actions seem less those of a uniquely reprehensible character than those of a typical comic hero who finds himself at the center of deep psychological conflict from which his predecessors have been carefully protected.

Bertram's response to Helena creates for Shakespeare an unprecedented conflict between the inner dimension of Bertram's experience and the demands of comic form. This conflict expresses the tension between comic form as Shakespeare has used it up to this point and developments that have recentered his art in tragedy. Bertram's flight from Helena and his quest for autonomous selfhood develop in embryonic and ultimately aborted form psychological issues dealt with masterfully and sympathetically in the tragedies; the form of the play extends the movement toward marriage, often presided over by a strong, active woman, which works out happily in the festive comedies. This tension between the play's design and its psychological content can only be intensified by efforts to resolve it. Helena can meet Bertram's mocking conditions for accepting the marriage only by becoming more powerful and sexually aggressive. But her efforts exaggerate conditions responsible for his initial flight. Whatever Bertram's accomplishments in Italy (and no other comic hero can offer comparable achievements), from the perspective of his home and the French court Bertram becomes increasingly boyish and dependent, Helena increasingly a woman of exceptional strength and virtue, until they almost seem to parody the subtler mismatches of Bassanio with Portia, Orlando with Rosalind.

It could be argued that the completion of their sexual union in Florence exorcises incestuous associations that have interrupted their marriage; Bertram does have intercourse with Helena, and makes her pregnant, even though he thinks she is someone else. But the play does little to suggest that the bed trick, which allows the comic plot to be completed, significantly alters the psychological conditions that have made it necessary. The integration of sexuality and the marriage bond thus accomplished seems to be almost purely contractual, a near fulfillment of the terms Bertram has expressed in his letter to Helena:

> When thou canst get the ring upon my finger, which never shall come off, and show me a child begotten of thy body that I am father to, then call me husband; but in such a 'then' I write a 'never.'
>
> (III.ii.56–59)

When Bertram receives news that Helena is dead, he tucks his hasty grief among the "sixteen businesses" he transacts in his busy last night in Florence, including his apparent seduction of Diana and his witnessing of Parolles' exposure. Helena's death fulfills a wish generated by his position in the play; as the king later says, "thou didst hate her deadly, / And she is dead" (V.iii.117–18). With Helena dead, Bertram can return home to "my lady mother." But the strongly developed movement toward illicit sexuality for Bertram is never countered by a comparable movement toward acceptance of the marriage to Helena. The brief exchange between Helena and Bertram when they are united in the final scene, though it can be bolstered by theatrical production, hardly seems substantial enough to provide a fully dramatic resolution of the complex psychological conflict that has led into it. Bertram briefly acknowledges that Helena is a wife both in name and substance: "Both, both; O, pardon!" (V.iii.304). When presented with his ring and his letter, "doubly won" Bertram responds with this rather dismal and curiously conditional couplet—addressed not to Helena, but to the king: "If she, my liege, can make me know this clearly, / I'll love her dearly—ever, ever dearly" (V.iii.312–13).

Bassanio is not much more, and Orlando even less, loquacious when, the complications of their plays finally resolved, these men are united with their spouses. But in both *Merchant* and *As You Like It*, these inevitable unions, unobstructed by any reluctance on the part of the comic heroes, are carried by the sweeping force of festive celebrations of marriage and community. Instead of dramatizing conditions that facilitate a completed union between Bertram and Helena, the last scene of *All's Well* emphasizes Bertram's place in the social and moral world of the king—first by the effort to find a marriage that the king can newly sanction and then by the considerable energy expended in showing how badly Bertram has behaved, and continues to behave, as his new beginning in France inaugurates a new set of lies on his part. I have suggested that Bertram's flight from Helena reflects anxieties expressed more fully in tragedies written at about the same time as *All's Well*. The effort in the last scene to settle Bertram's marital status in a manner suitable to the king, the countess, and Lafew points beyond the problem comedies to the late romances, and I will consider the relationship of *All's Well* to those plays in the last section of this chapter. The relentless exposure

of Bertram's shortcomings in the last scene points to earlier developments in Shakespeare's art, but not so much in the comedies as in the
Sonnets.

"Lascivious grace"
in the *Sonnets* and *All's Well*

PAROLLES   *Who cannot be crushed with a plot?*   (VI.iii.302)

The moral condemnation of Bertram—first for his rebellious
flight, later for his lust and his lies—and the king's "conjectural
fears" that Bertram's "deadly" hate of Helena has been responsible
for her death, are virtually unprecedented in earlier Shakespearean
comedy. Even Claudio in *Much Ado About Nothing* is let off rather
easily for his reprehensible shallowness and its near tragic consequences, as if the form of that play is unable to admit into itself
morally pertinent gestures of judgment. The increased prominence
of moral feeling in *All's Well* accompanies an intensified expression
of love on the part of the heroine. In Helena's love, the ironic and
high-spirited playfulness of earlier heroines gives way to compulsively devoted and anguished adoration. Both Helena's devotion and the
expression of intense moral feeling have Bertram as their object,
and both may be explored in the context of G. Wilson Knight's
claim that *All's Well* "recalls the Sonnets more nearly than any other
play." [14]

14. *The Sovereign Flower* (London: Methuen, 1958), p. 95. Knight argues
that *All's Well* "comes from the same intimate centre of the poet's creating
soul as do the sonnets" (p. 157), and finds Helena's love "characterized less
by desire and possessiveness than by service and adoration, reminiscent of
the Sonnets" (p. 134). M. C. Bradbrook points out that Helena's "three
great speeches . . . have a number of parallels with the sonnets," and relates
these connections to what she argues is the source of the play's dramatic dis-
unity, a conflict of "personal and impersonal theme" (*Shakespeare and
Elizabethan Poetry* [London: Chatto and Windus, 1957], pp. 169, 162).
Roger Warren also finds that Helena's love recalls the love for the friend and
bases his reading of *All's Well* on its affinities to the *Sonnets* in "Why Does It
End Well? Helena, Bertram, and the Sonnets," *Shakespeare Survey*, 22
(1969): 79–92. Emphasizing the "intensity of heartbreak" in *All's Well*,
Warren links "the curiously unsympathetic portrait" of Bertram with the
young man of the *Sonnets* and observes that the "mature, melancholy poetry"
of the king in the last scene "echoes those images in the Sonnets by which

Roger Warren, in his persuasive account of Shakespeare's "uncompromising treatment of Helena and Bertram," finds that the condemnation of Bertram "corresponds with even the details of the suggested 'fault' of the friend of the Sonnets"—a " 'sensual fault' " that contradicts "outward show."[15] Helena's love, Warren argues, survives trials forced upon it by Bertram, even as "Shakespeare's love in the Sonnets seems to have undergone similar trials and overcome them" (p. 92). I find convincing Warren's extensive parallels between Helena's love and that of the *Sonnets* poet, but two matters lead me to put the relationship of *All's Well* to these poems very differently. First, I do not find that Shakespeare in the *Sonnets* "overcomes" the many stresses that trouble his love for the friend, particularly those related to the young man's sensuality. Indeed, the last mention of the friend, in 144, expresses the poet's suspicion that his "better angel" may be "turned fiend," a speculation that will await the test of syphilitic "fire." However problematic the ending of *All's Well* may be, it is an ending, which imposes at least superficial order upon the relations of its characters. But no sonnet— either through the corroded but curiously intact ideal that survives in the cynicism of 144, or through the optimistic assurance of a poem like 116 ("Let me not to the marriage of true minds")—ever manages to bring stability, much less finality, to the strange and powerful love they together confront.[16] Second, the "fault" of the friend can be presented only from the perspective of his lover, who regularly draws back from pressing forcefully any judgment that could jeopardize his love. In *All's Well*, by contrast, Bertram is seen not only from Helena's perspective, but also from those of other characters whose moral judgment of him carries great dramatic force.

The effort in the *Sonnets* to celebrate the "external grace" and "constant heart" (53) of the beloved is often in conflict with reluc-

Shakespeare conveys his sense of loss and hence of love" (pp. 80, 84, 88). John Russell Brown sees a dark reflection of the *Sonnets* in Parolles, whose early remarks to Helena on virginity "mock and pervert the wisdom of the sonnets" (*Shakespeare and His Comedies*, 2nd ed. [London: Methuen, 1962], p. 186).

15. "Why Does It End Well?" pp. 79, 85.

16. Carol Thomas Neely expertly demonstrates that large gestures toward stabilizing the poet's relationship to his love in 94, 116, and 129 are in considerable tension not only with surrounding sonnets but with countertrends within these poems ("Detachment and Engagement in Shakespeare's Sonnets: 94, 116, and 129," *PMLA*, 92 [January, 1977]: 83–95).

tant recognitions that a lovely "mansion" may house "vices," or that "beauty's veil doth cover every blot" (95). The view of the friend that gradually emerges along with the image of a "beauteous and lovely youth" (54) is well described by W. H. Auden:

> As outsiders, the impression we get of his friend is one of a young man who was not really very nice, very conscious of his good looks, able to switch on the charm at any moment, but essentially frivolous, cold-hearted, and self-centered, aware, probably, that he had some power over Shakespeare—if he thought about it at all, no doubt he gave it a cynical explanation—but with no conception of the intensity of the feelings he had, unwittingly, aroused.[17]

But such a perspective ordinarily emerges only insofar as Shakespeare is unable to persuade us—and a usually silent part of himself —that the friend is identical with his exalted image of him, if only the angle of vision could be adjusted appropriately. Transgressions on the friend's part, rather than shatter that ideal, more typically provoke self-accusation on the part of the poet, as if Shakespeare is willing to forfeit all claims of the loving self in order to shore up the perpetually endangered image of the beloved.[18]

The *Sonnets* make effort after effort to close what seems to be an ever widening gap between Shakespeare's appropriation of the friend by adoration and the friend's mysterious, elusive otherness. Individual sonnets seem to be shaped from the outside by pressures alien to the longing that shapes them from within. In *All's Well*, written in the aftermath, or perhaps the last stages, of the experience reflected in the *Sonnets*, Shakespeare can create a young man wholly responsive to his own invention; he can express as many attitudes toward him as there are characters in the play, and let those attitudes jostle against each other in the temporal movement of a closed action he can control with his own imagination. The *Sonnets* begin, like a comedy, with pleas that the young man marry, but lead on into perilous intensities of devoted friendship transecting the intricacies of triangular sexuality involving the dark lady. The friend is carried by

17. Introduction, in *The Sonnets*, ed. William Burto (New York: New American Library, Signet ed., 1964), pp. xxxiii–xxxiv.

18. I discuss the tension between idealization and potential disillusionment in a series of poems marked by extreme contrasts in the poet's relation to the friend in "Poetry and Fantasy in Shakespeare's Sonnets 88–96," *Literature and Psychology*, 22 (November 1972): 151–62.

Shakespeare's expansive adoration beyond the early insistence that
he marry and have children. Bertram is not merely urged but commanded by the king to marry Helena. When instead of consum-
mating this marriage, he goes off with "my Parolles," Bertram's attempt to elude Helena leads him ultimately to his place as husband
and father. Bertram's friendship with Parolles is totally dishonored;
his effort at seduction returns him to his wife when Diana refuses
the dark lady role by pretending to accept it.

In the *Sonnets*, Barber writes, "Shakespeare turns injury into
poetry. The very act of writing about the betrayal is a kind of acceptance of it. . . . The poet's artistic sympathy encounters the ruth-
lessness of another living identity and remains open to it." [19] *All's
Well* imposes a rigorous, compensatory, even vindictive dramatic
structure upon a love that in the Sonnets repeatedly betrays the
dedicated idealization Shakespeare brings to it, that eludes and mocks
the poet's every attempt to seek self-definition through it. But what
makes this dramatic transformation of the *Sonnets* experience into
something much more complex than a kind of revenge comedy is the
extension into the play, through Helena's love for Bertram, of the
eloquent adoration that Shakespeare lavishes on the young friend.

Helena's first soliloquy, which celebrates Bertram and laments his
unattainability, closely recalls the love for the friend:

> I am undone; there is no living, none,
> If Bertram be away. 'Twere all one
> That I should love a bright particular star
> And think to wed it, he is so above me.
> In his bright radiance and collateral light
> Must I be comforted, not in his sphere.
> Th' ambition in my love thus plagues itself:
> The hind that would be mated by the lion
> Must die for love.   (1.i.80–88)

Helena expresses a love that, like the *Sonnets* poet's, is life-sustaining
and selfless, impeded by class distinctions, and tormented by the impossibility of a consummation. And, as often in the *Sonnets*, her
lines reveal more about her than about the beloved. Like Shakespeare, who takes precarious delight in recreating the "lines of life"

19. "An Essay on the Sonnets," in *Elizabethan Poetry: Modern Essays in
Criticism*, ed. Paul J. Alpers (New York: Oxford University Press, 1967),
pp. 316–17.

that define the young man's beauty in lines of verse drawn by his "pupil pen" (16), Helena dotes on Bertram with an artist's eye:

> 'Twas pretty, though a plague,
> To see him every hour, to sit and draw
> His archèd brows, his hawking eyes, his curls,
> In our heart's table—heart too capable
> Of every line and trick of his sweet favor.
>   (1.i.88–92)

The quality of religious devotion, which J. B. Leishman stresses in his discussion of the *Sonnets*,[20] finds cognate expression in *All's Well* when Helena confronts her apparent loss of Bertram: "But now he's gone, and my idolatrous fancy / Must sanctify his relics" (I.i.93–94).

> Religious in mine error, I adore
> The sun that looks upon his worshipper
> But knows of him no more.   (1.iii.198–200)

"My imagination / Carries no favor in't but Bertram's," Helena announces in her first soliloquy, and she is true to those words throughout the play, understanding even her cure of the king in the context of her love for Bertram. Her devotion to her truant mate leads through an emotional range comparable to that released by the strange turns taken in the *Sonnets*. Helena often expresses a logic of self-sacrifice characteristic of such sonnets as 49, where Shakespeare vows,

> And this my hand against myself uprear
> To guard the lawful reasons on thy part.
>   To leave poor me thou hast the strength of laws,
>   Since why to love I can allege no cause.

20. *Themes and Variations in Shakespeare's Sonnets,* 2nd ed. (London: Hutchinson University Library, 1963). Helena's adoration across a distance she herself articulates as absolute suggests a trend of feeling in the *Sonnets* that Leishman describes beautifully:

nowhere, one might almost say, in Shakespeare's sonnets is there unmistakable evidence that Shakespeare really believed that his friend, in any deep and meaningful sense of the word, loved him at all. . . . Saddest of all, I think, are those sonnets where Shakespeare speaks of their difference in rank, and sometimes of his own profession, as an insuperable barrier between them, for they suggest that he may actually have had to endure (and to forgive) just such slights and insults as Beethoven was always so groundlessly (and, I fear one must add, so ignobly) suspecting in his aristocratic friends and patrons. . . . (p. 226)

Helena's lovely lines as she prepares to give up her place in Rossillion similarly affirm her devotion through resignation and self-effacement:

> I will be gone.
> My being here it is that holds thee hence.
> Shall I stay here to do't? No, no, although
> The air of paradise did fan the house,
> And angels officed all. I will be gone,
> That pitiful rumor may report my flight
> To consolate thine ear. (III.ii.120–26)

In Sonnets 71 ("No longer mourn for me when I am dead") and 72 ("O, lest the world should task you to recite"), Shakespeare contemplates his own death as a means of freeing the friend from the shame of his overreaching love; Helena, in a sonnet, announces her impending death as a means of freeing Bertram from her "ambitious love": "He is too good and fair for death and me; / Whom I myself embrace to set him free" (III.iv.16–17).

In marked contrast to the indignation of other characters, Helena regards Bertram's Florentine escapade with lavish moral patience. Her imperturbable poise as she studies the course of Bertram's "idle fire" in Italy extends the willingness of the *Sonnets* poet to indulge in the friend "those pretty wrongs that liberty commits . . ." (41). Even her riddling consideration of "wicked meaning in a lawful deed, / And lawful meaning in a lawful act, / Where both not sin, and yet a sinful fact" (III.vii.45–47) suggests the curious playfulness often evoked in the *Sonnets* poet by morally ambiguous situations. Commenting on her night in bed with Bertram, Helena cuts across the morality of sexual conventions to put them in the perspective of their psychological consequences:

> But, O strange men!
> That can such sweet use make of what they hate,
> When saucy trusting of the cozened thoughts
> Defiles the pitchy night; so lust doth play
> With what it loathes, for that which is away.
> (IV.iv.21–25)

Helena's extraordinary detachment in commenting on a relation of absolute importance to her, as it is simultaneously violated and consummated, recalls the spiritual exercises of Sonnets 41 and 42, although Helena is keenly analytical where the *Sonnets* poet is will-

fully self-deceptive. Helena, who replaces Diana, retrieves her love
for Bertram from the apparent triangularity of 'I love him, he loves
her'; the *Sonnets* poet in 42 labors to undo loss to a third party
through identification with the friend:

> If I lose thee, my loss is my love's gain,
> And losing her, my friend hath found that loss:
> Both find each other, and I lose both twain,
> And both for my sake lay on me this cross.
> But here's the joy: my friend and I are one;
> Sweet flattery! then she loves but me alone.

Helena, though she gives voice to a love for Bertram that is humble,
adoring, and beyond consummation, acts resourcefully to get her
man anyway, with vigorous, cunning, determined pursuit. In the first
act Helena laments "that wishing well had not a body in't, / Which
might be felt" (I.i.165–66); in Florence she completes her wish and
literalizes her metaphor when she possesses the body of Bertram.
A. P. Rossiter, confronting this apparent contradiction, concluded
that "analysis of Helena's character only results in confusion."[21]
But the conflicting elements in her love for Bertram are found in
Shakespeare's love for the friend as well, which alternately relinquishes all claims for fulfillment and asserts itself as an unbreakable
bond. Like Helena, Shakespeare at times releases the beloved because
of his own lack of "deserving," as in 87:

> Farewell: thou art too dear for my possessing,
> And like enough thou know'st thy estimate.
> The charter of thy worth gives thee releasing;
> My bonds in thee are all determinate.

But elsewhere, as in 92, his claim on the beloved is affirmed as incon-
trovertible:

> But do thy worst to steal thyself away,
> For term of life thou art assurèd mine,
> And life no longer than thy love will stay,
> For it depends upon that love of thine.

Here the *Sonnets* poet provides a succinct sketch of the comic action
of love in *All's Well*, in which Helena's mock death becomes the
means for returning Bertram to France and to herself. What reads

21. *Angel with Horns* (New York: Theatre Arts Books, 1961), p. 106.

like rather desperate fantasy in the *Sonnets* is concretely realized in the action of the play.

In the opening scene of *All's Well*, Helena moves from a quiet, modest assumption of her place in the Rossillion household to a poignant description of her unattainable love for Bertram. She then must wittily fend off Parolles, whose lewd offer to "naturalize" her by disposing of her virginity presumes liberties that forcefully dramatize the social limitations of Helena's position. But their exchange on virginity also calls out Helena's extraordinary individual resourcefulness. When Parolles leaves the stage, she makes a preliminary dedication of herself to the "project" of winning Bertram—a project that will be successfully completed only when she is admitted into the aristocratic household as Bertram's wife. These remarkable shifts do not point to confusion of characterization but to a dramatic recasting of the exceptional elasticity Shakespeare brings to an aristocratic world he cherishes but cannot enter in the *Sonnets* experience. Indeed, Helena's comparatively low birth and her very high achievement mirror Shakespeare's own situation when, as a working playwright, he appropriates for his drama the world of royalty and aristocracy. "His stage world," Leo Salinger has observed, "gravitates toward the great house or the court,"[22] and Helena does likewise in *All's Well*. Her exertions in pursuing Bertram dramatize a successful quest for mastery that is continually frustrated in Shakespeare's love for the friend. Even the vicarious interest in the friend's procreative sexuality—"the tillage of thy husbandry" (3)—is brought in the play to a direct and socially acceptable consummation when Helena's body becomes the vehicle of Bertram's "sweet use" in Florence.

Within this dramatic world, however, Helena not only gets Bertram for herself, she also replaces him as a figure worthy of the love of others.[23] In the *Sonnets*, the aristocratic friend has magnetic powers of attraction, drawing to him the love of the poet, other poets,

22. *Shakespeare and the Traditions of Comedy* (Cambridge: Cambridge University Press, 1974), p. 255.
23. Carol Thomas Neely points out to me that what happens in this regard *in* the action of *All's Well* happens in responses of readers *to* the *Sonnets*, where sympathies are clearly with the poet and not the shadowy image of the friend.

the dark lady. *All's Well* strips Bertram of those characters close to him, turning them away from him and toward Helena. At the beginning of the play, Helena is an orphaned "physician's daughter," attached to an aristocratic household, but isolated by her hopeless love for the pride of the house. As Bertram is perceived as a "proud, scornful boy" (II.iii.150) and an "unworthy husband" (III.iv.26), Helena comes to be generally regarded as "the most virtuous gentlewoman that ever nature had praise for creating" (IV.v.8–9). Although Helena continues to express her love for Bertram, she draws onto herself the loving attention originally bestowed on him by other characters—his mother, the king, the French lords:

> COUNTESS There's nothing here that is too good for him
> But only she, and she deserves a lord
> That twenty such rude boys might tend upon
> And call her hourly mistress.   (III.ii.78–81)

Like the tension between Helena's adoration of an unattainable Bertram and her resourceful conquest of him, developments that lead other characters increasingly to admire Helena and scorn Bertram represent ways in which the play transforms elements of the *Sonnets* experience. Much of the power of *All's Well* derives from the release in its dramatic action of trends precariously held in check in the *Sonnets* by the idealizing love for the friend. Freud describes idealization in love as a process in which

> the ego becomes more and more unassuming and modest, and the object more and more sublime and precious, until at last it gets possession of the entire self-love of the ego, whose self-sacrifice thus follows as a natural consequence. The object has, so to speak, consumed the ego.[24]

This process is central to the *Sonnets*, where Shakespeare forfeits ordinary self-concern in the attempt to live through an identification with the young man endowed with the "seemly raiment" of his own heart. In what Shakespeare calls "sin of self-love" (62), he lavishes upon the beloved longings for unqualified adoration that derive from the early infantile experience of forming a self.

24. *Group Psychology and the Analysis of the Ego*, in *Standard Edition*, vol. 18, p. 113.

Such longings originate in the gradual development beyond what Freud calls "primary narcissism"—in which the infant as yet makes no distinction between the self and a world external to it—toward relations, still characterized by very fluid self-boundaries, with the first object of the infant's love and hate, the mother.[25] The tenderness at the core of the poet's love expresses the maternal solicitousness that goes with benign experiences of mother and child in early infancy, a quality Shakespeare catches as metaphor in Sonnet 22:

> O therefore, love, be of thyself so wary
> As I, not for myself, but for thee will,
> Bearing thy heart, which I will keep so chary,
> As tender nurse her babe from faring ill.

The explicit object of this love is the friend, but the friend as an idealized extension of the poet's self:

> But when my glass shows me myself indeed,
> Beated and chopped with tanned antiquity,
> Mine own self-love quite contrary I read;
> Self so self-loving were iniquity:
>   'Tis thee (myself) that for myself I praise,
>   Painting my age with beauty of thy days.   (62)

The love for the friend takes into itself the family context that, as social imperative, is abandoned after the very early sonnets. In the opening situation of *All's Well*, this internalized familial context is restored to its external status in Bertram's position as beloved son, both to his mother, the countess, and to his surrogate father, the king. Whereas the *Sonnets* release the friend from the obligation to his family and to himself to marry and bear children, Bertram's rejection of Helena as wife and mother to his children imports deep hostility into actual and symbolic family relations that define his position throughout the play. Upon Bertram's flight to Italy, the countess is ready "to wash his name out of my blood" (III.ii.66). The ailing king of the play's beginning recalls the "decrepit father" who in the simile of Sonnet 37 "takes delight / To see his active child do deeds of youth." But the king, restored to health and wholeness, hardly takes delight in those "deeds of youth" Bertram

25. See "On Narcissism: An Introduction," in *Standard Edition*, vol. 14, pp. 69–102.

performs in Italy. In a smouldering rage near the play's end, the king is ready to see Bertram punished for Helena's supposed death.

The rage provoked by Bertram's misdeeds brings into the drama elements of Shakespeare's love for the friend that are necessarily suppressed in the *Sonnets*. In his devotion, Shakespeare goes to the extremes of witty sophistry to authorize the "trespass" of the friend:

> For to thy sensual fault I bring in sense
> (Thy adverse party is thy advocate)
> And 'gainst myself a lawful plea commence.... (35)

Shakespeare is similarly eager to accept any valuation the young man would place upon him, sometimes taking pleasure in enlarging or confirming shortcomings the friend might suggest:

> Say that thou didst forsake me for some fault,
> And I will comment upon that offense;
> Speak of my lameness, and I straight will halt,
> Against thy reasons making no defense. . . .
> > For thee, against myself I'll vow debate,
> > For I must ne'er love him whom thou dost hate.   (89)

The need to sustain the identification with the adored image of the friend will not allow the poet to confront directly the hostility provoked by the beloved, or to make the friend accountable to any standard of action independent of his observed activity.

L. C. Knights once wrote that "in the Sonnets Shakespeare is working out a morality based on his own finest perceptions and deepest impulses."[26] I find it more plausible that in the devotion to the friend Shakespeare finds himself unable to articulate a moral perspective in which he can synthesize conflict within his own deepest impulses, in which he can reconcile the need for autonomous selfhood and the anger that attends its violation with unqualified devotion to the friend. The adoration of the friend carries the poet into a range of feeling essentially independent of morality. When trials in the relation seem to call for a voice of judgment, that voice is checked in order to protect the adoration: "So true a fool is love that in your will, / Though you do anything, he thinks no ill" (57). The hostility provoked by the friend, and the demand for a voice of judgment that

26. *Explorations* (1947; reprint ed. New York: New York University Press, 1964), p. 76.

could express that hostility and protect the claims of the loving self, create a powerful undercurrent in the *Sonnets*, but can never be brought into clear relation to the whole experience.

Even so powerful a sonnet as 94 ("They that have pow'r to hurt and will do none"), which seems to move toward a monumental standard of accountability, trails off into a slur in the couplet: "For sweetest things turn sourest by their deeds; / Lilies that fester smell far worse than weeds." A telling way of dealing with the nearly suppressed voice of judgment may be glimpsed in the paradoxical accommodation that culminates Sonnet 40: "Lascivious grace, in whom all ill well shows, / Kill me with spites; yet we must not be foes." Here the tension between the demand for judgment, based on the poet's perception of "love's wrong," and the more urgent need to sustain the relation is precariously resolved by incorporating the offending quality into the object of adoration. As in 96, "those errors that in thee are seen / [are] To truths translated and for true things deemed." In other sonnets, the hostility that cannot be focused as judgment in relation to the friend is typically turned back against the poet's self, leading to gestures of sheer self-negation:

> O, let me suffer, being at your beck
> Th' imprisoned absence of your liberty;
> And patience, tame to sufferance, bide each check
> Without accusing you of injury.   (58)

Again, a pattern of reversal links *All's Well* to the poems. Unlike the *Sonnets*, which only rarely and provisionally pass judgment on the friend, the play judges Bertram at every turn. Where the *Sonnets* poet is often eager to view himself according to the whim of the friend, the play exposes Bertram's own bad judgment repeatedly. It is the young man's "misprision" (87) once to have carelessly overrated the poet's worth; Bertram's "vile misprision" (II.iii.151) is to underrate the worth of Helena. Although the countess seeks to excuse Bertram's actions in Florence as "Natural rebellion, done i' th' blade of youth," her position soon shifts, when Bertram's activity in Florence comes to appear increasingly shameful, to an angry cry for justice: "Now justice on the doers!" (V.iii.6; 154).

In the *Sonnets*, expressions of shame, of being painfully exposed to the humiliating gaze of others, are often, and in mutually opposing ways, connected with perceptions of the friend's glory. In such

poems as 29 ("When, in disgrace with Fortune and men's eyes")
and 110 ("Alas, 'tis true I have gone here and there"), the friend
becomes a refuge from the "disgrace" the poet feels in the eyes of
others and of his own self-judgment. But in other poems, as in 72,
the well-born friend is himself the source of the poet's preoccupation
with a deep sense of shameful inadequacy:

> O, lest your true love may seem false in this,
> That you for love speak well of me untrue,
> My name be buried where my body is,
> And live no more to shame nor me nor you;
> > For I am ashamed by that which I bring forth,
> > And so should you, to love things nothing worth.

The poems of extreme prostration draw Shakespeare into expressions
of "vassal bound" devotedness that would be sources of deep humiliation in any context other than the insistent but precariously maintained devotion to the friend: "Being your slave, what should I do
but tend / Upon the hours and times of your desire?" (57).

Dramatic situations of shame or humiliation dispersed throughout
All's Well have a base of feeling in the ominously unstable acceptance of shameful self-regard in the *Sonnets*. Helena risks a "di-
vulgèd shame" (II.i.171) in curing the king, only to be humiliated
when Bertram abandons his low-born wife to join the "noble fellows" in war. In the sonnet she leaves behind when undertaking her
pilgrimage, however, she declares that she must atone for her own
shameful overreaching:

> Ambitious love hath so in me offended
> That barefoot plod I the cold ground upon,
> With sainted vow my faults to have amended.
> > (III.iv.5–7)

The tension between seeing Helena as the victim of shameful behavior on Bertram's part and her seeing herself as someone who has
acted with shameful ambition extends tensions that mark the poet's
love for the friend. But two extended rites of exposure in *All's Well*,
which do not have Helena as their object, transform the force of
shame in the *Sonnets* experience. The first of them, the unmasking
of Parolles, suggests a kind of cruelly cathartic, perhaps self-con-
scious, mockery of the *Sonnets* situation in the play.

Empson once wrote, in a stunning insight into the relation of the *Henry IV* plays to the *Sonnets*, that Falstaff serves Shakespeare as a "savage and joyous externalization of self-contempt." [27] If the force of this statement is muted, and the emphasis tilted toward savagery, Empson's suggestion will carry over to Falstaff's comic kinsman Parolles, who like Falstaff, and like the *Sonnets* poet, lives through his relationship to a high-born friend. The handling of Parolles— who finds dubious glory by attaching himself to a young aristocrat, who urges his "sweetheart" away from Helena and from the French court, who serves as a pander to Bertram in Florence, and who thrives on flattery within a relationship ultimately revealed to be as hollow as the drum that is his undoing—suggests a savage parody of the love expressed for the young friend in the *Sonnets*. There is even a broad burlesque of the triangular sexuality of the poet/friend/dark lady relationship when the poem is found on Parolles that would attempt to win Diana away from Bertram. The dramatization of Parolles' efforts "to beguile the supposition of that lascivious young boy" (IV.iii.278–79) places the "lascivious grace" applauded in the *Sonnets* in the perspective of contemptuous hindsight.

But within the mockery of Parolles, Parolles' own mockery of Bertram as "a foolish, idle boy, but for all that very ruttish" (IV. iii.200–201), suggests welcome comic release from the willful self-blinding of the *Sonnets* poet. In the extended comic ritual of ridicule and rejection in which Parolles is "crushed with a plot," Bertram's "devoted friend" is drawn deeper and deeper into incriminating falsehoods, paralleling the exposure of Bertram in the final scene. But Parolles in his fall lands on solid comic ground. He absorbs the attack with remarkable resilience, affirming a comic identity based on physical life itself rather than the social and moral conventions that complicate it:

> Yet am I thankful. If my heart were great,
> 'Twould burst at this. Captain I'll be no more,
> But I will eat and drink and sleep as soft
> As captain shall. Simply the thing I am
> Shall make me live.   (IV.iii.307–11)

27. William Empson, *Some Versions of Pastoral* (1935; reprint ed. New York: New Directions, 1960), p. 100.

Parolles' adaptation, as he descends from high-flown flattery to "live / Safest in shame" (IV.iii.314–15), parodies the movement in the *Sonnets* through lofty adoration toward the poet's accommodation to base desire in the poems to the dark lady.

Parolles survives his energetic shaming to assert a clownish durability that fits readily into a comic world: "being fooled, by foolery thrive. / There's place and means for every man alive" (IV.iii.315–16). The exposure of Bertram, however, introduces a new note into Shakespearean comedy. The last scene of *All's Well* is designed to bring out fully the force of suspicions and animosities toward Bertram that have accumulated in the play, particularly the king's festering resentment over Helena's death. "The nature of his great offense is dead," the king remarks, in a futile exercise of the will to forget, "And deeper than oblivion do we bury / Th' incensing relics of it" (V.ii.23–25). But the "incensing relics" will not stay buried. Although the king assures the countess:

> I have forgiven and forgotten all,
> Though my revenges were high bent upon him,
> And watched the time to shoot, . . .   (v.iii.9–11)

the last scene is dominated by remembering rather than forgetting, by the reanimation of vengeful feelings toward Bertram in the king, the countess, and Lafew. "Wrapped in dismal thinkings," the king's powerful, brooding presence comes to tower awesomely over an ever-shrinking Bertram, exaggerating further the confrontation between them in II.iii, when Bertram is compelled to marry Helena.

Helena's presence as sacred memory is evoked anew by each turn in the proceedings; against the ideal of her virtue is set the ever-darkening image of Bertram. In the movement toward judgment, Bertram himself is the chief party to his final defamation. The scorn this scene directs toward Bertram's cavalier defense of the "wanton way of youth" (V.iii.211) is intensified as he gets more and more caught in a web of distortion and evasion and in his own very real confusions about what is going on. As Quiller-Couch remarked, in a passage quoted earlier, the last scene "destroys our hope" that there "*must* be some attractiveness in Bertram to justify [Helena's] devotion. . . ." Shakespeare discards the earlier and potentially sympathetic dramatization of the psychological imperative behind Bertram's actions and manipulates the plot to make Bertram appear as reprehensible as possible.[28] "I will buy me a son-in-law in a fair, and toll for this," Lafew comments, as Bertram's position gets murkier, "I'll none of him" (V.iii.148–49). Bertram complies to make dramatically appropriate the moral aggression of proceedings that shatter his nerve: "You boggle shrewdly; every feather starts you" (V.iii. 232). One of the French lords has observed of Bertram in Florence: "The great dignity that his valor hath here acquired for him shall at home be encountered with a shame as ample" (IV.iii.63–65). A central purpose of the symbolic action of *All's Well*, that part of it completed in the exposure of Bertram, is to heap shame on Bertram, amply.

The rage expended on Bertram in the last scene suggests that *All's Well*, in transforming the experience of the *Sonnets*, embodies a process Freud found to be common to "mourning and melancholia." Freud described the "conflict due to ambivalence" as it operates in

> all those situations of being slighted, neglected or disappointed, which can import opposed feelings of love and hate into the relationship or reinforce an already existing ambivalence. . . . If the love for the object—a love which cannot be given up though the object itself is given up—takes refuge in narcissistic identification, then the hate comes into operation on this substitutive object, abusing it, debasing it, making it suffer and deriving sadistic satisfaction from its suffering.[29]

This account of hostile trends generated by loss of a love object describes a process complementary to the process of idealization; it recalls Freud's comments on idealization quoted earlier in exactly the way *All's Well* recalls the *Sonnets*. The love for the friend, which "gets possession of the entire self-love of the ego" in the *Sonnets*, gives way to the moral attack on Bertram as he is appropriated for the action of the play. The exposure of Bertram releases a righteous feeling of moral outrage, and with it a kind of vindictive

28. Tillyard argues plausibly that Bertram's behavior in the last scene is consistent with his characterization throughout: "Bertram's nerve has been thoroughly undermined by the events just related; he was frightened of Diana. When confronted with her, his nerve gives way still more and he resorts in panic to any lie that will serve his turn. The exhibition of human nature is ignoble and unpleasant to witness, but it is perfectly true to the facts" (*Shakespeare's Problem Plays*, p. 122).

29. "Mourning and Melancholia," in *Standard Edition*, vol. 14, p. 251.

pleasure that corresponds to the sadistic attack on the internalized object lost in reality described by Freud. The positive response to the loss of a love object is expressed in the play's explicit and extensive concern with mourning—first in the attempt to recover from death the aristocratic values of the dead Count Rossillion, then in the idealization of Helena when she is thought to be dead. But in the shaming of Bertram, moral condemnation expresses the hostile component of a deep ambivalence that in the *Sonnets* has been suppressed or turned back against the poet's self.

The shallow arrogance Shakespeare goes to such lengths not to describe directly in the fair friend is dramatized fully and punitively in Bertram's behavior; the poet's sense of personal unworthiness in relation to the idealized friend is reenacted in Helena's compulsion to love "where she is sure to lose" (I.iii.208), then gone beyond as she becomes the object of idealization by others and the actual winner of Bertram. As Bertram's lover, Helena extends the positive side of the ambivalent relation to the friend, but her adoration of Bertram is always in tension with the figure Bertram presents, and other characters condemn. In the play's action, the hostility toward Bertram must be released before Helena can return from her apparent death. But the play as a whole is not so easily released from a shift in comic attitude that accompanies responses to Bertram.

The stern morality that judges Bertram spreads into a whole way of looking at life. At the beginning of IV.iii, the two French lords, who have earlier supported Bertram's wish to leave the French court for the Italian wars, "dwell darkly" on Bertram's "unchaste" behavior:

> 1 LORD   He hath perverted a young gentlewoman here in Florence, of a most chaste renown, and this night he fleshes his will in the spoil of her honor. He hath given her his monumental ring, and thinks himself made in the unchaste composition.

They then proceed to generalize the implications of Bertram's activity:

> 2 LORD   Now God delay our rebellion! As we are ourselves, what things we are!
>
> 1 LORD   Merely our own traitors. And as in the common course of all treasons, we still see them reveal themselves till they attain to their abhorred ends, so he that in this action contrives

against his own nobility, in his proper stream o'erflows
himself.   (IV.iii.18–24)

Through the French lords, Shakespeare uses Bertram as a mirror of
inevitable human self-betrayal. "The web of our life is a mingled
yarn," the lords conclude, "good and ill together; our virtues would
be proud if our faults whipped them not, and our crimes would
despair if they were not cherished by our virtues" (IV.iii.66–69).

Just how radically this perspective departs from the *Sonnets* may
be seen by setting the ponderous worrying the French lords devote
to Bertram's wanton activity against the opening lines of Sonnet 96:

> Some say thy fault is youth, some wantonness;
> Some say thy grace is youth and gentle sport;
> Both grace and faults are loved of more and less:
> Thou mak'st faults graces that to thee resort.

But the gloss on fallen human nature provided by the French lords
also points to an important transformation in Shakespeare's uses of
comedy. As *All's Well* reworks in comedy tensions in the love for the
friend of the *Sonnets*, the play comes to convey attitudes toward experience different from either the *Sonnets* or the festive comedies.
Bertram's desperate effort to seek independence and elude submission
to Helena and the king; Helena's all-consuming adoration of Bertram,
and her use of her own sexuality to win him for herself; the austere
vision of sinning humanity the French lords articulate in Florence;
the prominence of the older generation in commenting on the action, and manipulating it whenever possible; all these trends dramatize attitudes toward love, sex, and society that are new or newly
intensified in *All's Well*. The effort in the *Sonnets* to celebrate a
love through which "all losses are restored and sorrows end" (30),
like the expectation in the festive comedies that young love will work
itself out and renew the social community in an inclusive action of
love, gives way in *All's Well* to a love that finds a precarious place
in a community centered in the moral authority of the older generation.

But Shakespeare's attempt to pull the play together with the reappearance of Helena, as if in miraculous recovery from death, ties
All's Well to yet another mode of Shakespearean comedy. He has
already brought Hero back from a deathlike state in *Much Ado*, but
in a way that is not quite at the center of feeling in a play much more

vitally engaged in the union of Beatrice and Benedick than that of Hero and Claudio. The dramatic importance of miraculous recoveries is, however, central to the comic mode developed in the late romances. Helena's role in *All's Well* not only points back to Portia and Rosalind, and to the *Sonnets* poet, but forward to Marina and Imogen, Perdita and Miranda. Many of the qualities that strain comic form in *All's Well* anticipate possibilities brought into the center of the altered comic form of the late romances.

All's Well and the Late Romances

HELENA *Then shalt thou give me with thy kingly hand*
What husband in thy power I will command.
(II.i.193–94)

The dying king, who has been pronounced beyond hope of recovery by the "most learnèd doctors," at first rejects Helena's promise of a cure; it would discredit the dignity of his position "to prostitute our past-cure malady" to further, futile efforts (II.i.116; 121). Lafew, however, in his praise of Helena's medical power, has already suggested qualities that set it apart from that of the typical physician:

> I have seen a medicine
> That's able to breathe life into a stone,
> Quicken a rock, and make you dance canary
> With sprightly fire and motion; whose simple touch
> Is powerful to araise King Pepin, nay,
> To give great Charlemain a pen in 's hand,
> And write to her a love-line.   (II.i.72–78)

erotic

What is remarkable about this account is the emphasis on erotic properties that indicate Helena's power not only to restore health but to arouse male sexual potency.[30] Such erotic suggestions are brought fully into play when Lafew, on leaving the king alone with Helena, likens himself to Pandarus: "I am Cressid's uncle, / That dare leave two together. Fare you well" (II.i.97–98).

The ensuing exchange with the king and Helena presents this

30. For the sexual suggestiveness of *stone, fire, motion, touch,* [a]*raise,* and *pen,* see Eric Partridge, *Shakespeare's Bawdy,* 2nd ed. (New York: E. E. Dutton, 1955).

eroticism in another mode, once removed from the openly sexual banter of Lafew. Helena's extraordinary confidence in her curative power, the king concludes, "must intimate / Skill infinite, or monstrous desperate" (II.i.183–84). The terms of his agreement to let her proceed take into account both possibilities: "Sweet practicer, thy physic I will try, / That ministers thine own death if I die" (II.i.185–86). Helena, however, provides an even more suggestive option, along with her possible death, should the medicine fail. "Upon thy certainty and confidence / What dar'st thou venture?" asks the king, and Helena replies:

> Tax of impudence,
> A strumpet's boldness, a divulgèd shame
> Traduced by odious ballads; my maiden's name
> Seared otherwise; nay, worse of worst, extended
> With vilest torture let my life be ended.   (II.i.169–74)

Her willingness to risk utter degradation and death prompts the king to think that in Helena "some blessèd spirit doth speak / His powerful sound within an organ weak" (II.i.175–76). Either Helena is the agent of a sacred power or she is a creature of shame, no maiden but a "strumpet" who deserves the notoriety of a convicted whore. Her future is settled in terms of sexual legitimacy: she will know either the fate of a prostitute or that of honored wife to Bertram.

The two possible outcomes dramatize a sexual trend in the king's regard for Helena and the defense against that trend through idealization and projection. The recovery of the king allows the idealized version of Helena to suppress the potentially "monstrous," degraded one. Sexual longings in the father/king's love are projected into the legitimate order of marriage, but a marriage arranged by the king. The elevation of the king's regard for Helena to an idealized plane allows the expression of his love; the projection of the sexual component of that love onto another assures paternal propriety. Lafew, however, reconfirms the sexual dimension of the cure when he watches the newly healed monarch enter with his "preserver":

> Lustick! as the Dutchman says. I'll like a maid the better whilst I have a tooth in my head. Why, he's able to lead her a coranto.
>
> (II.iii.40–42)

The tension between what is presented as a restoration of the king's potency and the paternal role the king assumes toward Helena—who derives her medical power from her own father—points toward a mode of comedy Shakespeare will not bring to completion until the very end of his preoccupation with tragic drama.

Helena's cure of the king suggests complex interconnections of power, sexuality, and trust, manifested in the relations of a fatherly king, a young virgin, and her potential husband, that are more characteristic of the romances that follow *All's Well* than of the earlier festive comedies. The king of France, like Pericles and Leontes, is restored fully to himself through the presence of a woman who has herself survived the threat of sexual degradation: Marina is sold to a brothel in *Pericles*; in *The Winter's Tale* Hermione is symbolically destroyed by Leontes' accusations of infidelity, Perdita is seen by Polixenes as a "fresh piece / Of excellent witchcraft" (IV.iv.416–17) unacceptable as wife for Florizel; Helena faces the fate of a strumpet should she fail to cure the king in *All's Well*. When the king offers Bertram to Helena, he anticipates the royal fathers of the late romances, who proceed from their recovery to sanction the marriages of their daughters to noble husbands. Restored to himself by Marina, Pericles in turn restores her to her birthright, and enables her to take a royal husband. The recovery of Perdita in *The Winter's Tale* enables Leontes to proceed to the further recovery of his lost wife, his lost friend, and his full kingly power; Leontes in turn sanctions the marriage of Perdita to Florizel. In *The Tempest*, Prospero, banished from Milan, finds in Miranda "a cherubin . . . that did preserve me!" (I.ii.152–53). Prospero in turn restores his child, now a woman, to her birthright, and presents her with a royal husband to confirm her new sexual and social status.

In relation to the drama centered in Helena's recovery of the king, Bertram too assumes a role that looks forward to the romances. The king welcomes the son of his dead friend to his court in the first act of *All's Well* much in the manner that Leontes will receive Florizel, the son of his lost friend, in the last act of *The Winter's Tale*. Although Bertram finds a father in the king, the marriage arrangements put the king in a father's relation to Helena as well. Without quite losing his own filial status, Bertram is placed, like Posthumus Leonatus, Florizel, and Ferdinand, in the position of one who would take the daughter in marriage. Posthumus is first exiled by Cymbeline for his marriage to the king's daughter, and later begs to be tortured because of his role in her apparent death, before he safely "anchors upon Imogen" (V.v.393). Florizel must endure the wrath of Polixenes, who is outraged that his son would do precisely what Bertram is compelled to do—marry a "low-born lass" whose natural grace "smacks of something greater than herself" (IV.iv.156, 158). Ferdinand, in order to win Miranda, must chop wood in ritual debasement before Prospero, while he is made to think his own father is dead. Bertram, like these figures from the romances, must withstand a stiff challenge to his own masculine autonomy when he is kept at court and further undergo humiliation and a father's rage, before he completes a marriage with a woman who has given new life to a powerful father.

The king's anger when Bertram refuses marriage with Helena suggests ambivalent paternal attitudes later sorted out differently in *The Tempest* in Prospero's mixed response to Ferdinand. Prospero controls the release of his resentment of a young suitor by imposing verbal abuse and ritual slavery upon Ferdinand before awarding him with the "rich gift" of Miranda. The king offers Bertram the "good gift" of Helena, and then is driven into resentful rage when Bertram declines. The embattled exchange in which Bertram is pressured to marry Helena anticipates a pattern of reciprocal powers linking fathers and daughters that will be more benignly embodied in the designs of the late romances. "If thou canst like this creature as a maid," the king argues, "I can create the rest" (II.iii.141–42). Bertram's acceptance speech confirms the king's capacity to balance the regenerative power of Helena with his royal power, much as Pericles, Leontes, and Prospero recompense the restorative powers of their daughters:

> When I consider
> What great creation and what dole of honor
> Flies where you bid it, I find that she, which late
> Was in my nobler thoughts most base, is now
> The praisèd of the king; who, so ennobled,
> Is as 'twere born so.   (II.iii.167–72)

Helena has restored the king to health, he has "ennobled" her in return, and awarded her with an appropriately noble husband of her choice; Helena's marriage to Bertram completes the pattern centered in her relation to the king and summarized in terms she has defined: "Then shalt thou give me with thy kingly hand / What husband in thy power I will command" (II.i.193–94).[31]

Were Bertram able to embrace this resolution in a stable way, the play would end here as a fragmentary first sketch of the late romances. But Bertram's flight subverts the reciprocity essential to relations of precious daughters and powerful fathers in the late plays, a reciprocity that balances a woman's power to give life against the authority of a king to give life structure. Rather than create a worthy noblewoman, duly rewarded with a noble husband, the king unwittingly sets Helena up to be insulted and abandoned, which in turn denies his own power. In one direction taken by the action, Helena, although she is freed from the potential for sexual degradation in her relation to the king, is forced to prostitute herself to her husband's desire for an illicit sexual union. In another direction, the nullification of the king's power contributes to the ominous force of his brooding in the final scene, as he attempts, with little success, to forget and forgive Bertram's flight. The king is still trying to recover his power to "create the rest" in his very last speech, when he turns to a woman of even humbler status than Helena, the Florentine Diana, and directs her to choose a husband: "If thou beest yet a fresh uncroppèd flower, / Choose thou thy husband, and I'll pay thy dower" (V.iii.323–24).

The pattern centered in the king's recovery by Helena, and completed in a marriage to Bertram sanctioned by the king's authority, cannot bring *All's Well* to a comic conclusion, but its insistent presence reflects the transitional position of *All's Well* in Shakespeare's development toward the late romances. C. L. Barber, in an essay on *Pericles* and *The Winter's Tale*, provides a framework that helps bring the transitional status of *All's Well* into focus. "In the festive comedies," Barber writes, "holiday liberty frees passion from inhibition and the control of the older generation." But in *The Winter's Tale*,

---

31. Note the progression *thou—me—thy—thy—I* as it leads into *command*—ordinarily the king's prerogative—as the verb to Helena's *I*. The tendency of the play's action to concentrate all available powers for promoting marriage in Helena is presented in small in this sentence, which itself ironically echoes Lavatch—"That man should be at woman's command, and yet no hurt done!"—in the previous scene.

the festive moment is included within a larger movement where the centre of feeling is in the older generation. The festive comedies move out to the creation of new families; *Pericles* and *The Winter's Tale* move through experiences of loss back to the recovery of family relations in and through the next generation. . . . One can put this in summary by saying that where regular comedy deals with freeing sexuality from the ties of family, these late romances deal with freeing family ties from the threat of sexual degradation.[32]

In the late romances, "fulfillment for the principal figure requires a transformation of love, not simply liberation of it" (p. 61). Barber argues that "the primary motive which is transformed in *The Winter's Tale*, as father-daughter motive is transformed in *Pericles*, is the affection of Leontes for Polixenes, whatever name one gives it. The resolution becomes possible because the affection is consummated, as it could not otherwise be, through Perdita and Florizel" (p. 65).[33]

Helena's resourceful maneuvering to retrieve Bertram as husband extends in alien circumstances an action that recalls the festive comedies. But its comic purpose, to free Bertram from anxieties that originate in family ties, is crossed by those trends in *All's Well* that anticipate the late romances. In a manner that looks forward to these later plays, family ties become increasingly important, especially as a fatherly king arranges the marriage of Helena to Bertram. Insofar as either Bertram or the king is a center of dramatic conflict, however, the action of *All's Well* dramatizes neither a liberation from nor a transformation of obstacles that obstruct the marriage to Helena. Where Leontes, as Barber observes, discovers "the Holy Mother in the wife" (p. 66), Bertram returns to France seeking "my lady mother" (IV.iii.83) and finds the wife whose apparent death has

32. "'Thou that beget'st him that did thee beget': Transformation in *Pericles* and *The Winter's Tale*," *Shakespeare Survey*, 22 (1969): 61.

33. Barber's view of Leontes' relation to Polixenes enlarges an observation first made by J. I. M. Stewart, who explores *The Winter's Tale* in terms of Freud's analysis of the relations of repressed homosexuality, delusional jealousy, and paranoia (*Character and Motive in Shakespeare* [New York and London: Longmans, Green, 1949]). Murray M. Schwartz has shown that "the rooted affection of Leontes and Polixenes is itself rooted ontogenetically in the mother-child relationship. . . . The myth of childhood affection . . . preserves in masculine form a narcissistic and idealized version of the mother's dual unity with the son" ("Leontes' Jealousy in *The Winter's Tale*," *American Imago*, 30 [Fall, 1973]: 256).

been a condition of his returning. Bertram's regard for Helena, as I tried to show earlier in this chapter, includes an incestuous dimension in it, which is partly responsible for his flight, which is in turn responsible for Helena's apparent death. But the threat of incest, as I suggest above, also enters into the action through the king's regard for Helena. The extreme intensity of the king's outburst when Bertram refuses Helena suggests that even more than his honor is "at the stake." The king does not relinquish Helena, he compels Bertram to take her, forcing the issue even after Helena has offered to withdraw her claim. Bertram becomes for the king a symbolic extension of his own potency, restored in the cure by Helena, which is threatened by the young count's refusal of the woman who "has raised me from my sickly bed."

In *Pericles* the "monstrous" potential in paternal love, displaced onto the incestuous union that Pericles flees, is symbolically reiterated in the attempt to prostitute Marina, which she must survive before she is reunited with her father. Prospero's love for his daughter is protected from its tabooed dimension by the presence of Caliban, who, in his attempt to rape Miranda, embodies repressed, degraded sexual impulses in the family bond.[34] Leontes looks on Perdita with an eye that has "too much youth in't" (*WT* V.i.224), but the ensuing recognition of her as daughter leads beyond her to the recovery of Hermione. Both Leontes and Pericles recover wives through their daughters; Prospero, with the release of his daughter, "a third of mine own life, / Or that for which I live" (*Tmp.* IV.i.3–4), looks beyond her to his own death. But for the king in *All's Well*, saved from death by Helena and restored to vigorous manhood, there is no wife to recover. Where the romances renew relations purged of unacceptable sexual content, the king enters into a new relation that renews his potency. The sexual trend in the king's regard for Helena is not transformed into a relation with a wife, or surrendered in a movement toward death, but expressed in the attempt to compel Bertram to marry her.[35] The union of Bertram and Helena, rather

34. Norman N. Holland reviews psychoanalytic commentaries that suggest "the imaginary figures, Ariel, Caliban, and Sycorax, are projections of unconscious aspects of Prospero's personality" (*Psychoanalysis and Shakespeare* [New York: McGraw-Hill, 1966], p. 274).

35. Lafew advises the countess that she will find a "second husband" in the king, but the king does not seem to find a second wife in the countess. Although the two of them symbolically complete families from the perspectives

than exorcise the threat of paternal sexuality, is forced to include it.

Those conditions that interrupt the transformation of love relations, as well as those that subvert the reciprocity of male and female powers, point to conflicting ways of dramatizing trust in *All's Well*. These conflicting ways reflect the different ways trust enters into the actions of earlier comedies and the late romances. Crises in the festive comedies challenge the confidence and the competence of hero and heroine, but do not shake that trust in the resources of human ingenuity and love in which comic action is grounded. Characters confront comic crises with reserves of strength and adaptability in themselves; their inner resourcefulness is supported by dramatic worlds protected from extreme catastrophe and often magically responsive to gestures of love and faith. The trust in human resources on which festive comic action is based becomes the locus of crisis in the late romances. Pericles is driven into stuporous withdrawal from life by the loss of his daughter to apparent death. Imogen, for all her resourcefulness, is rendered utterly helpless in *Cymbeline*. Leontes retreats into a self-created world of persecutory delusion in *The Winter's Tale*. Though we only see Prospero after he has supplanted lost political power with the power of magic in *The Tempest*, he and his infant daughter have been cast out of Milan to probable death as a result of his misplaced trust in Antonio. In each instance, the intensity of crisis challenges to the core what Erik Erikson calls "basic trust."

Basic trust, Erikson argues, is the "cornerstone of a vital personality";

> it arises out of the encounter of maternal person and small infant, an encounter which is one of mutual trustworthiness and mutual recognition. This, in all its infantile simplicity, is the first appearance of what in later reoccurences in love and admiration can only be called a sense of "hallowed presence," the need for which remains basic in man.[36]

The sense of trust established in this encounter must create, and in turn be sustained by, an image of a "reasonably coherent world" (p.

---

of both Helena and Bertram, their relationship in itself receives little dramatic emphasis. Unlike the king after his cure, the countess looks toward her own death in a manner that anticipates Prospero.

36. *Identity: Youth and Crisis* (New York: Norton, 1968), pp. 97, 105.

106) that makes meaningful actions and relations with others possible. But the encounter that provides the indispensable foundation for all ensuing growth provides the context for the deepest psychic hazards as well: "For along with a fund of hope, an inescapable alienation is also bequeathed to life by the first stage, namely a sense of threatening separation from the matrix, a possible loss of hope, and the uncertainty whether the 'face darkly' will brighten again with recognition and charity." [37]

The women of both the festive comedies and the late romances participate in the heritage of the first encounter with a "maternal person," but they serve different purposes in relation to the issue of trust in the two modes of comedy. Portia and Rosalind, as a part of their roles, order relations that presuppose an intact sense of trust in themselves and in characters who need them; part of their purpose is to see to it that crisis does not develop into catastrophe. In the late romances, catastrophic loss reenacts the loss in infancy of the maternal presence. The recognition scenes in the late romances dramatize the recovery of a lost sense of what Erikson calls "hallowed presence." This movement toward restored trust, dramatically central to *Pericles* and *The Winter's Tale*, and already partly accomplished in the past recounted by Prospero in *The Tempest*, is facilitated by and completed through relations to women who restore to the protagonists the core of the self that originates in relations to a trustworthy maternal presence.

In order to assume such roles in the romances, however, the women must first survive violent attacks on them. Destructive and sexual motives, which are included in the ambivalent, sensual relations of childhood, are woven into designs in which central female figures are the objects of fierce masculine aggression. The virginity of young women, the sexual fidelity of wives, and the lives of both are threatened by efforts to rape, seduce, prostitute, slander, and murder them. Cruel and deceitful women often participate in the violent aggression of these plays. Although in *The Winter's Tale* female destructiveness is confined to fantasy, Dionyza orders Marina murdered in *Pericles*, a wicked queen deceives the king and sponsers Cloten's sadistic aggression in *Cymbeline*, and the witch Sycorax has left behind her spell and her son Caliban on the island Prospero inhabits

37. *Insight and Responsibility* (New York: Norton, 1964), p. 154.

with Miranda. The real or imagined destructiveness of these women reflects fears of women that partly originate in infantile helplessness. But the good women who survive attempts to violate them redeem protagonists from the helplessness they bring upon themselves, and provide the sacred context in which the resolutions of these plays can take place.

Erikson connects religious feeling with the need to protect and renew the heritage of basic trust as it is threatened by disruptive motives that exist along with it:

> Primitive religions, the most primitive layer in all religions, and the religious layer in each individual, abound with efforts at atonement which try to make up for vague deeds against a maternal matrix and try to restore faith in the goodness of one's strivings and in the kindness of the powers of the universe.[38]

In what Barber calls "transformation in the direction of the sacred" ("Transformation," p. 60), this "layer" of need for atonement is embodied in the romances in dramatic designs that move through aggression directed against essential female presences and on to the restoration of a lost world and its apparently lost victims. In *The Winter's Tale*, for instance, "vague deeds against a maternal matrix" are particularized in Leontes' psychic assault on Hermione; the action of the play moves beyond this attack to an atonement completed when Leontes recovers Hermione as sacred presence, as faithful wife, as the actual mother of his children. Of these children, Mamillius is sacrificed to Leontes' assault on Hermione when he loses in actuality the mother Leontes loses in fantasy; Perdita makes possible the recovery of that mother in her role as wife.

The king in *All's Well*, like the protagonists of the late romances, recovers trust through his relationship to a woman: "More should I question thee, and more I must, / Though more to know could not be more to trust" (II.i.205–6). The king's trust in Helena is essential if the cure is to proceed; symbolically the recovery of the king's health and of his trust are identical. His recovery from a fatal disease parallels Pericles' recovery from his deathlike trance and Leontes' recovery through mourning for his apparently dead wife. The king's renewed health provokes Lafew's declaration of faith in a sacred world that transcends secular life yet can miraculously renew it:

38. *Childhood and Society*, 2nd ed. (New York: Norton, 1963), p. 251.

> They say miracles are past, and we have our philosophical persons,
> to make modern and familiar, things supernatural and causeless. ,
> Hence it is that we make trifles of terrors, ensconcing ourselves into
> seeming knowledge when we should submit ourselves to an un-
> known fear.   (II.iii.1–6)

This sacred realm is a source of "terrors" for Lafew, as it will be in
the late romances, when a great storm rocks Pericles' ship at Marina's
birth, for instance, or when Leontes, ensconced in "seeming knowledge," flaunts the oracle's truth in *The Winter's Tale*. But it is also
a miraculous source of trust for those who submit themselves to it.
The quality of sacred feeling Lafew invokes points forward to the
scene in which Marina makes available "another life / To Pericles
thy father" (V.i.209–10) and to the reunion of Leontes and Hermione in Paulina's chapel.

But Lafew's celebration of transcendent powers, itself quickly
ensnarled in a burlesque exchange with Parolles, describes a world
very different from the one Helena negotiates, not by means of
transcendent intervention, but by determined dedication of herself
to a single goal. The dramatic movement toward an individual restoration of trust that confirms the presence of sacred powers is out
of phase with the play's comic movement. The recovery of trust for
the king does not, as in the romances, exorcise the threats of hatred
and sexual degradation; rather it creates conditions that release Bertram's fearful mistrust of marital sexuality. The principal aggression
toward feminine goodness, which in the romances makes restoration
of trust necessary and gives atonement its dramatic power, is expressed in Bertram's rejection of his wife and her symbolic death—
after the king has been restored to health.

The dramatic world of miraculous powers suggested by Helena's
cure of the king will be completed in the whole designs of the late
romances; in *All's Well* it simply ceases to exist after the king's recovery. Before choosing a husband, Helena declares:

> Now, Dian, from thy altar do I fly,
> And to imperial Love, that god most high,
> Do my sighs stream.   (II.iii.73–75)

This movement from chastity to sexuality is accompanied by a movement from Helena's reliance upon the patriarchal god who has presided over the cure, "Him that all things knows" (II.i.149), to re-

sourceful, individual determination. Sacred Dian will reappear to intervene in the action of *Pericles*; the all-knowing patriarchal god will return as Jupiter to straighten out the complications of *Cymbeline*. But in *All's Well*, Dian will give way to Diana the Florentine maiden who conspires with Helena to trap Bertram; the benevolent masculine god will give way to the "auspicious mistress" Fortune; "imperial Love, that god most high," will serve at most as a metaphor for Helena's zeal, as she uses her disguise as a holy pilgrim and the complicity of the rector of Saint Jaques le Grand to secure Bertram for herself.

I have tried to show in this chapter that distinct modes of comic drama—one pointing back to the festive comedies, the other forward to the late romances—tend to interfere with each other in *All's Well*. Helena's resolution of the plot cannot fully resolve conflicts created in part by the responses of others to her. By contrast, Rosalind is clearly the character who focuses the experience of *As You Like It*, not at the expense of such divergent spirits as Jaques or Touchstone, but because her consciousness presents the most inclusive response to relations of love and life in that play, because her involvement in the action is what engages the play's audience most poignantly, and because she is able to bring dramatic mastery to a range of feeling she both provokes in others and knows in herself. Three of the late romances are centered in the experience of a father. Leontes' role contrasts sharply with Rosalind's; he never knows what is coming next, and until the very end he is never, except magically, in his delusion, in control of relations that matter most to him. But in his experience conflicts that animate the entire play are focused; both the catastrophic events and the ultimate resolution of *The Winter's Tale* spring from Leontes' needs and fears. In *All's Well* there is no comparable center that cumulatively integrates the play's action. Helena, the king, and Bertram, in their various roles, localize various ranges of conflict; each often seems to respond to situations never fully realized in the dramatic action of *All's Well*, but which look in to this play from other Shakespearean contexts. Rather than converge in an integrated comic resolution, potential centers of conflict and aspiration that conflict with each other push the play toward mutually antagonistic resolutions, each of which is more fully realized elsewhere: in the feminine resourcefulness that organizes the festive comedies, in the anguished adoration that suppresses potential outrage in the *Sonnets,* in the violent antagonism between trust and sexuality in the tragedies, in the sacred restoration of trust to an older generation purged of sexual anxiety in the late romances.

Directors who put *All's Well* on the stage are free to play down conflicting trends within it. Richard David describes a successful Old Vic production of *All's Well* (Winter 1953–1954) that worked in part because the director's "first step was to take the King and the Countess down a peg. The King became a figure of fun and the affairs of his court pure farce." [39] In this performance, according to David, Parolles, who was presented "as a sort of amateurish Mephistopheles," took over Bertram, and much of the play as well, while pressures on the main love plot were relieved by reducing "hero and heroine . . . to decorative pasteboard" (p. 136). What such maneuvering does, I think, is resolve the tension in *All's Well* between regular comic form and Shakespeare's development toward the late romances; the characteristic centrality of the older generation in the romances gives way entirely to an action of young love that, like the romances, emphasizes loss and recovery. It is easy to see that much is lost by such theatrical decisions, including the king's almost fierce dignity and his strong bond to Helena, Helena's own rich and complex characterization, and the importance of conflict inside Bertram and not just in his relation to Parolles. But the effect of the whole performance, for David, was a sudden revelation of the "kinship" of *All's Well* with the late romances:

> With these it shares the theme of paradise lost and paradise regained: the penitent Bertram recovers the wife he has cast off as surely as do Leontes and Posthumus, and his restoration to Helena makes her as much amends as the meeting of Ferdinand and Miranda does to Prospero. Here, however, it is themselves that the losers lose and find, and their redemption is their own and not the work of another more innocent generation.   (p. 136)

I quote at some length from David's concluding remarks because it seems to me that what he saw in Michael Benthall's production, apart from Parolles' scene-stealing inventiveness, is a shadowy image of the kind of comic resolution called for by the deepest developments in *All's Well:* the coming together of a young man and a

39. "Plays Pleasant and Plays Unpleasant," *Shakespeare Survey,* 8 (1955): 134.

young woman who "lose and find" each other in a sacred, sexual union that has moved beyond both idealization and sexual degradation, that integrates the need for autonomy with the need for trusting submission, and that is consummated in a world that reconciles a young generation seeking release from family ties with the necessary but threatening presence of an older generation that embodies cultural traditions. But this is a resolution Shakespeare can never fully dramatize: not in the festive comedies, where the role of parents and the potential conflicts in male sexuality are minimized; not in the tragedies contemporaneous with *All's Well*, where male protagonists recoil from female sexuality with fear and hatred; not in the late romances, where the principal figures find redemption in "another more innocent generation"; and not in *All's Well*, where every relationship is complexly overdetermined by contexts that derive from nearly every phase of Shakespeare's development. This chapter has been a study of that overdetermination. If the text of *All's Well* is taken in its entirety, and not shrewdly rewritten in the manner of Benthall's production, what one finds is a play that moves toward what for Shakespeare cannot be dramatized. As the play breaks against the hard impossibility of finding its ideal resolution, it shatters into fragmented pieces that can only be integrated in the shape of a long career.

"We may perhaps be forced to become reconciled to the idea," Freud wrote in a speculative mood, "that it is quite impossible to adjust the claims of the sexual instinct to the demands of civilization. . . ." [40] Whatever the validity of this statement in the whole context Freud addresses, it describes an antagonism that in Shakespeare's art is never fully reconciled. This antagonism enters into *All's Well* in the first scene.

> PAROLLES Are you meditating on virginity?
>
> HELENA Ay. You have some stain of soldier in you; let me ask you a question. Man is enemy to virginity; how may we barricado it against him? (1.i.106-9)

This puzzling exchange on virginity terminates when Helena returns the subject to the realm of her meditation ("Not my virginity yet . . ." [I.i.159]), where it will remain until she surrenders her

40. "On the Universal Tendency to Debasement in the Sphere of Love," in *Standard Edition*, vol. 11, p. 190.

virginity to Bertram's "wanton siege" (III.vii.18) of Diana, submitting to a conquest that makes her the victor. But in their opening exchange, Helena and Parolles initiate the play's troubled exploration of sexuality's essential and problematic place at the meeting point between human rule and the "rule of nature" (I.i.132). After Parolles has held forth at some length on the "sin" of virginity, Helena asks: "How might one do, sir, to lose it to her own liking?" (I.i.145–46). As the action proceeds, the question Helena asks opens out to the large problem taken on in *All's Well*: how can sexuality be made to serve love, pleasure, and social tradition, the needs of both the individual and the married couple, of both the children and the parents, who belong to both nature and society? The problem is not unique to *All's Well*; it is addressed to some extent by all the comedies before and after it. But in this play it creates difficulties from which the earlier comedies are protected.

The limitations of Parolles' response to Helena suggest limits that the action of *All's Well* is unable to surpass. Parolles' witty attack on virginity cynically justifies sexual activity ("Loss of virginity is rational increase, and there was never virgin got till virginity was first lost" [I.i.123–24]) quite apart from, and in a manner quite alien to, the prospect of human intimacy. But as Parolles' harangue continues, his mockery of virginity tends to conflate sexual desire with fear of and disgust for sexuality:

> Virginity breeds mites, much like a cheese, consumes itself to the very paring, and so dies with feeding his own stomach.
>
> . . . .
>
> Your date is better in your pie and your porridge than in your cheek; and your virginity, your old virginity, is like one of our French withered pears: it looks ill, it eats drily. Marry, 'tis a withered pear; it was formerly better; marry, yet 'tis a withered pear! Will you anything with it? (1.i.134–39, 153–58)

Parolles' advocacy of sexual license becomes a gross fantasy about the female genitals.[41] His lines provide a low comic defense by bravado against the fear of female sexuality that will form part of the movement toward madness for Othello, for Lear, and for Leontes, who seems to paraphrase from this exchange, complete with

41. Partridge: "Her virginity is localized in, and made synonymous with, the pudend . . ." (*Shakespeare's Bawdy*, entry under "withered pear").

military metaphor, in his recoil from Hermione: "No barricado for a belly. Know't / It will let in and out the enemy / With bag and baggage" (*WT* I.ii.203–5). Parolles, like Lavatch in later scenes, voices a distrustful attitude toward sexual intimacy that is focused dramatically in Bertram's flight from marriage but never resolved in the play's comic action.

The Winter's Tale, the late romance that most closely recalls *All's Well,* presents Shakespeare's most powerful dramatic movement through extreme sexual mistrust to a reconciliation of estranged partners when Leontes' recovery of Hermione as a work of art gives way to his further recovery of her as living wife. Murray M. Schwartz has shown that the restoration of Hermione emphasizes qualities that have made her "as tender / As infancy and grace" (V.iii.26–27), qualities that belong to the context of infantile relations transmuted into sacred feeling, and not the disturbing sexuality that has earlier pitched Leontes into jealous rage.[42] But the response to Hermione as a sacred presence includes a vital response to the living body Leontes has before recoiled from in fear. The younger Hermione, "not so much wrinkled, nothing / So aged as this seems," is present in the Hermione recovered by Leontes: "O, thus she stood, / Even with such life of majesty—warm life, / As now it coldly stands— when I first wooed her!" (V.iii.28–29, 34–36). Othello, when he murders Desdemona, seems to want to preserve a coldly statuesque image of the purity he has sought in her: "Yet I'll not shed her blood / Nor scar that whiter skin of hers than snow, / And smooth as monumental alabaster" (V.ii.3–5). Leontes, by contrast, urges the cold statue of Hermione toward living flesh:

> Would you not deem it breathed? and that those veins
> Did verily bear blood?
>
> . . . .
>
>   What fine chisel
> Could ever yet cut breath? Let no man mock me,
> For I will kiss her.   (v.iii.64–65, 78–79)

42. "Shakespeare has created the theatrical equivalent of our earliest responses to the image of the mother," Schwartz argues. "The statue provokes a constellation of associations related to the earliest provident relationship between self and other. . . . 'Infancy *and* grace.' The correspondence between childhood wish and religious fulfillment could not be more complete" (*"The Winter's Tale*: Loss and Transformation," *American Imago*, 32 [Summer 1975]: 195–96).

The ending of *The Winter's Tale* brings to exquisite dramatic realization the unstable mix of shame and renewed grief, of reunion and renewed life, of sexual degradation and marital intimacy, that troubles the ending of *All's Well*. Psychological determinants that overburden the role of Helena in her relations to other characters are sorted into three different characters who together make possible the "exultation" of union and reunion in *The Winter's Tale*. The maternal dimension that obstructs Helena's marriage to Bertram is reinvested and completed in Hermione, who is restored to her husband and who rejoices in the preservation of their "issue." Helena the young daughter who becomes a wife is reimagined as Perdita, whose union with Florizel seals out the threat of sexual degradation. Helena's role as patient overseer and manipulator of troubled love relations, associated with her disguise as a "holy pilgrim," is taken over by priestesslike Paulina, who, standing just apart from the main love plot, presides over its completion. Leontes then gives to Paulina a husband "by my consent, / As I by thine a wife" (V.iii.136–37). The uneasy sense in *All's Well* that the king's promise to find a husband for Diana repeats his troubled effort to provide a husband for Helena gives way in Leontes' gesture to the reassertion of kingly authority in final balance with the life-giving powers of the play's women. This "match" numbers Paulina among the "precious winners all" who have withstood the fierce conflicts of *The Winter's Tale*, and gone beyond them.

III

Vincentio and the Sins of Others:

The Expense of Spirit
in *Measure for Measure*

A s in *All's Well That Ends Well*, conflict converges most sharply in *Measure for Measure* on a sexually naive young man thrust
into a new relation to authority. Bertram's specific revulsion from
sexual longing in connection with Helena is generalized in Angelo's
attempt to lift himself above sexuality and in his disdain for the carnal
weaknesses of others. Both characters come to seek sexual release outside a morality the plays are concerned to enforce; each eventually is
brought to judgment before a powerful figure of authority who embodies that morality. Bertram, his own father dead, is initially appropriated as surrogate son by the king of France, but rebels against
that bond when he experiences it as coercive. Bertram's attempt to
seduce Diana is conducted away from the watchful eyes of the king,
but eventually comes to his outraged attention in the last scene.
Angelo is at first invested with both the love and the power of the
Duke of Vienna. But when abruptly commanded to exercise at the
highest level the autonomy denied to Bertram in *All's Well*, Angelo
finds his rigid sexual restraints exploded from within. Angelo, who
has no companion comparable to Parolles, must deal with his crisis
in isolation. His fall into sexual degradation is closely watched over,
however, by the Duke, who in disguise assumes another paternal role,
that of a friar, a "ghostly father." Angelo's humiliation in the last
scene culminates a scheme by which the Duke channels his deputy's

92

wayward, private longings into legitimate, public purpose. Following Angelo into and beyond his moral collapse can help focus issues of psychological and dramatic importance to *Measure for Measure*.

Angelo's Brief Authority

LUCIO   *They say this Angelo was not made by man and woman after this downright way of creation. Is it true, think you?* (III.ii.97–99)

Angelo begins the play with a fully developed idea of severe but equitable justice, a strong sense of personal piety, and a high disdain for "filthy vices" (II.iv.42) of the blood. But he seems to have had no experience in wielding authority, has never had his rigid, private morality tested by complex moral situations, and has never felt directly the force of urgent sexual arousal. His first act in office, decreeing the vigorous enforcement of a long dormant law that punishes fornication with death, reflects all these factors. Claudio, sentenced to die under this law, thinks Angelo puts it into practice to enhance his reputation, and perhaps Angelo is ambitious enough to give this claim some credibility. But if his inexperience is taken into account, along with pressures of responsibility that suddenly crowd in on him in his new role, it is clear that to establish himself in office Angelo relies upon the strict enforcement of measures most consistent with deep needs in his character. He governs Vienna with strictures that govern him.

That Angelo feels some insecurity in his new role is suggested by his initial, rather nervous response to being deputized:

> Now, good my lord,
> Let there be some more test made of my mettle
> Before so noble and so great a figure
> Be stamped upon it. (I.i.47–50)

This uneasiness is masked for a short time: it does not appear in the powerful defense of his severe measures that he offers Escalus, though it might be a factor in his irritability and impatience in hearing the case of Elbow vs. Pompey (II.i.). But the sudden collapse of Angelo's habitual defenses once he is in power demonstrates the brittleness that goes with their rigidity and the vulnerability his new office brings out in him. The very speed with which he is overwhelmed by desire after taking on the Duke's power emphasizes the unstable relation between sexuality and authority in Angelo's character.

Angelo's assumption of the Duke's political power is psychologically akin to taking over the familial role of the father. The extent to which Angelo is thrust politically into a position of paternal authority is accented by Vincentio's insistence that fatherly "old Escalus, / Though first in question," be made Angelo's "secondary" (I.i.45–46). Angelo's new position brings out in him conflicts engendered in a boy's relations to paternal authority. The typical resolution of oedipal conflict for a boy involves both repression of sexual longing for the mother and identification with the father—a preliminary internalization of what the boy apprehends as the father's prohibitions and strengths, while he remains in subservient relation to the father external to him. Angelo's character structure is like that of a person who prolongs an extreme version of this oedipal resolution into adulthood at the expense of never fully integrating into the self the ideals that shape it. His habitual denial of his own sexuality—his effort to "rebate and blunt his natural edge / With profits of the mind, study and fast" (I.iv.60–61) as Lucio neatly puts it—suggests an unstable over-identification with paternal authority stabilized by his service to lofty ideals and authority outside himself: "It is the law, not I, condemn your brother" (II.ii.80). He generalizes the repression of incestuous desire into a repudiation of all sexual longing, and he serves a man who takes over the authoritarian role of father: "Always obedient to your grace's will, / I come to know your pleasure" (I.i. 25–26). Angelo, virtuous in the extreme, but inclined to keep his virtue to himself, is responsible to a severe but insufficiently internalized superego; he is secure only so long as he remains in subordinate relation to a readily available figure of paternal authority and does not enter into a fully independent relation with the world around him.

When Vincentio's departure puts Angelo in power, his precarious inner restraint is stripped of its external sanction. This new situation, away, he thinks, from the observation of higher authority, makes Angelo susceptible in a new way to that "prone and speechless dialect, / Such as move men" (I.ii.178–79), which underscores Isabella's plea to spare Claudio's life. Furthermore, the very nature of Isabella's argument, which exposes as a "glassy essence" (II.ii.120)

the authoritarian ideal upon which he has based his life, contributes
to the shattering of Angelo's inner barricade against sexual desire.
Isabella's initial appeal to mercy, to a compassion based on common
bonds of humanity, has little effect: "Were he my kinsman, brother, or my son, / It should be thus with him: he must die to-morrow"
(II.ii.81–82). But her eloquent commentary on authority in men—
"a little brief authority" that makes proud man "most ignorant of
what he's most assured" (II.ii.118–19)—produces perceptible results. "O, to him, to him, wench; he will relent," urges the observant
Lucio: "He's coming, I perceive't" (II.ii.124–25). It is when Isabella
argues that authority can "err like others," that the figure of authority harbors within his heart "a natural guiltiness" like that of
Claudio, that Angelo finds himself irrevocably caught up in sensual
desire: "She speaks and 'tis / Such sense that my sense breeds with
it" (II.ii.134, 139, 141–42).

The dense ironies of *sense*, explored so perceptively by Empson
as the key word in *Measure for Measure*,[1] here cluster around *sense*
as meaning or rationale and *sense* as sensuality. The passion with
which Isabella throws herself into her appeal can arouse Angelo's
desire in part because her argument undermines the meaning he has
found in the elevation of authority beyond sensuality. She subverts
his characteristic effort to idealize authority, and to identify himself
with that ideal in its inner and outer manifestations, just after the
Duke has removed himself, and Angelo has been placed in his position. Isabella pleads with him:

> go to your bosom,
> Knock there, and ask your heart what it doth know
> That's like my brother's fault; . . .   (II.ii.136–38)

Angelo need not go far. Impulses long held in check by his inner and
outer relations to images of authority forcefully assert themselves.
Angelo rightly observes of himself:

> Never could the strumpet
> With all her double vigor, art and nature,
> Once stir my temper; but this virtuous maid
> Subdues me quite.   (II.ii.183–86)

---

1. William Empson, "Sense in *Measure for Measure*," in *The Structure
of Complex Words* (London: Chatto and Windus, 1951), pp. 270–88.

His repudiation of his own sexuality has been sustained in part by a deep contempt for the sexual treachery he associates with women. Nothing has happened to weaken this. But Angelo's disgust with female sexuality and those victimized by it is only half of a total attitude completed by his readiness to acknowledge Isabella's saintly virtue. Even the jesting Lucio seems to be struck by a sacredness in Isabella's presence when he visits her in the convent, and finds her "a thing enskied and sainted" (I.iv.34). No one acknowledges Isabella's purity more fully than Angelo, who laments: "O cunning enemy that, to catch a saint, / With saints dost bait thy hook" (II.ii.180–81). It is clear that Isabella's saintliness does just what an open sexual appeal to Angelo could not do. Although Angelo is aware of this, he is profoundly perplexed by his awareness:

> Can it be
> That modesty may more betray our sense
> Than woman's lightness? Having waste ground enough,
> Shall we desire to raze the sanctuary
> And pitch our evils there? O fie, fie, fie!   (II.ii.168–72)

Just as Angelo's self-proclaimed purity dramatizes a son's effort to repudiate sexual longings extended into an entire style of life, his acknowledgment of Isabella's sacred virtue builds on a complementary tendency to deny the mother's sexuality because it represents an intolerable provocation. Angelo's ideal of feminine purity and his equation of sexuality with evil originate together; they are polarized derivatives of the preoedipal union of infantile sexual desire and tender regard. Contempt for sexual desire and idealization of the incestuous object, the divergent routes leading Angelo away from their common origin in his own sexual nature, suddenly reverse directions to provide unwelcome, converging thoroughfares back to it:

> What dost thou? or what are thou, Angelo?
> Dost thou desire her foully for those things
> That make her good?   (II.ii.173–75)

Angelo is forced into a crisis that approximates the childhood situation from which ideas of what is good and foul emerge to be institutionalized as conscience. Angelo's separation of what is foul from what is good, upon which his whole moral style rests, generalizes a rigid resolution of oedipal tension in which the sexual bond to the mother is repudiated and the repressed incestuous drives are bound through a process of idealization. When he perceives Isabella as both sacred and sensuous, the self that has been organized around the separation of the ideal from the sexual collapses. He is unable either to give up this distinction or maintain it, and he cannot evade the desire that makes it a source of torment for him.

Quiller-Couch characterized Shakespeare's concern with "lechery" in the "work of the period to which *Measure for Measure* belongs" as a "biting upon it as upon a wound. . . ."[2] The expression well describes Angelo's tormented obsession with lust once it has been aroused by Isabella. Angelo's brutal assault upon Isabella's virtue includes a vindictive attack upon the moral temperament that has suddenly failed him. It is an action of perverse self-hatred, an attack upon his own moral core—as if daring it by his outrageous conduct to show again its might, possibly in the expectation that it will—as much as an attack on Isabella. That battered moral core does reassert itself, in a manner consistent with its earlier instability, precisely when Angelo's inner awareness is again matched with the awareness of the authoritarian Duke. The erring son whose conscience has been overpowered in the absence of external, paternal support, submits himself fully to judgment before Vincentio:

> O my dread lord,
> I should be guiltier than my guiltiness
> To think I can be undiscernible,
> When I perceive your grace, like power divine,
> Hath looked upon my passes.   (v.i.362–66)

There is a strong feeling of release and a curiously compelling dignity in Angelo when the chaos that has taken over his life is suddenly resolved into a stable sense of acknowledged shame and the expectation of a quickly ensuing death:

> Then, good prince,
> No longer session hold upon my shame
> But let my trial be mine own confession.
> Immediate sentence, then, and sequent death
> Is all the grace I beg.   (v.i.366–70)

2. Introduction, in *Measure for Measure*, ed. A. Quiller-Couch and J. Dover Wilson (Cambridge: Cambridge University Press, 1922), pp. xii–xiii.

Angelo finds in the shaming presence of the Duke—the restored image of external, paternal authority—the strength to snap even the durable thread of self-preservation that has led him to compound his corruption.

Shakespearean comedy moves into a denser range of feeling than it has before approached with the relation *Measure for Measure* develops between Angelo's surrender to compulsive lust and the crises it generates in other characters. Not until the very end of his career, when Shakespeare perfects a new comic mode in *The Winter's Tale* and *The Tempest*, will comedy again engage deep conflict so fully. As Angelo finds himself helpless before "the strong and swelling evil / Of my conception" (II.iv.6–7), he moves into a region that overlaps with the experience of the *Sonnets* poet confronting humiliation in his relation to the dark lady:

> Th' expense of spirit in a waste of shame
> Is lust in action; . . .
> Past reason hunted, and no sooner had,
> Past reason hated as a swallowed bait
> On purpose laid to make the taker mad: . . .
>   (*Son.* 129)

But in the very different circumstances of the late sonnets, with their very different woman, various accommodations to the "sensual feast" are to be found. If the *Sonnets* poet never is completely at ease with any of the postures he brings to his compulsion, he is remarkably flexible in moving from one to another. Angelo, once he gives his "sensual race the rein," finds nothing that can supplant his accustomed rigidity: "This deed unshapes me quite, makes me unpregnant / And dull to all proceedings" (IV.iv.18–19).

Angelo's collapse before sexual drives he cannot integrate connects with tragic actions in which unsubdued longings and unstable resolutions from the infantile past override moral, familial, and political orders of the dramatic present. The deep sense of inner division as Angelo discovers a previously unsuspected dimension of himself is in many ways close to Macbeth's astonished response to

> that suggestion
> Whose horrid image doth unfix my hair
> And make my seated heart knock at my ribs
> Against the use of nature. . . .   (I.iii.134–37)

When Angelo commands Isabella to put on "the destined livery"
of frail woman, he argues from an attitude toward womanhood and
sexuality that, experienced in a different way, is the source of Hamlet's self-torment and abuse of Ophelia:

> God hath given you one face, and you make yourselves another.
> You jig, you amble, and you lisp; you nickname God's creatures and
> make your wantonness your ignorance. Go to, I'll no more on't;
> it hath made me mad.   (III.i.143–46)

Iago's misogyny, in a manner related to Angelo's need to debase
Isabella once she has provoked his desire, is strangely threatened by
the possibility of a virtuous Desdemona when he does acknowledge
it:

> For 'tis most easy
> Th' inclining Desdemona to subdue
> In any honest suit; she's framed as fruitful
> As the free elements.
>
> . . . .
>
> So will I turn her virtue into pitch,
> And out of her own goodness make the net,
> That shall enmesh them all.
> (*Oth.* II.iii.322–24; 343–45)

For Iago to be successful in this effort, he must rely on a latent connection in Othello that leads from the general's doting devotion to
a fearful distrust of female sexuality:

> O curse of marriage,
> That we can call these delicate creatures ours,
> And not their appetites!   (III.iii.268–70)

It is striking that Angelo, unlike Hamlet, Iago, or Othello, is not
led away from sexual engagement but toward it, and does not so
much project the collapsing split between the ideal and the sexual
onto a woman, or a generalized conception of women, as suffer its
destructive force within himself:

> O place, O form
> How often dost thou with thy case, thy habit,
> Wrench awe from fools, and tie the wiser souls
> To thy false seeming! Blood, thou art blood;

> Let's write "good Angel" on the devil's horn,
> 'Tis not the devil's crest.   (II.iv.12–17)

When he would compel Isabella to "lay down the treasures of your
body" (II.iv.96), he entertains no delusion that at bottom she is a
whore anyway:

> The tempter, or the tempted, who sins most?
> Ha!
> Not she, nor doth she tempt; but it is I
> That, lying by the violet in the sun,
> Do as the carrion does, not as the flower,
> Corrupt with virtuous season.   (II.ii.163–68)

Angelo would force her, cunningly, and with a sense of getting even,
to conform to the degradation ("We are all frail" . . . "Nay, women
are frail too" [II.iv.121, 124]) he has submitted to in himself.

   The way Angelo's sexual fall is bound up with the authority of his
office suggests the link between sexuality and "the great image of
authority" made by the raging Lear:

> Thou rascal beadle, hold thy bloody hand!
> Why dost thou lash that whore? Strip thy own back.
> Thou hotly lusts to use in that kind
> For which thou whip'st her.   (IV.vi.155, 157–60)

The physical cruelty that Lear's whipper substitutes for lust parallels
the psychic cruelty unleashed by Angelo as part of his coercion of
Isabella:

> Fit thy consent to my sharp appetite,
> Lay by all nicety and prolixious blushes,
> That banish what they sue for; redeem thy brother
> By yielding up thy body to my will,
> Or else he must not only die the death,
> But thy unkindness shall his death draw out
> To ling'ring sufferance.   (II.iv.161–67)

The moral sadism earlier rendered impersonal in his enforcement of
the law here hones the edge of Angelo's terrible pleasure in assault-
ing Isabella. He releases into this perverse intimacy both the sexualized rage accumulated in his service to a tyrannous conscience and his
rage against Isabella for undermining its power: "Answer me to-

morrow, / Or, by the affection that now guides me most / I'll prove a tyrant to him" (II.iv.167–69).

Lear, however, understands the connection that he makes between lust and justice only at a certain distance. He fulminates at the sadistic hypocrisy of the "rascal beadle," but keeps that awareness isolated from an understanding of how helplessly bound he is himself to a violent, fearful hatred of the power of female sexuality:

> But to the girdle do the gods inherit,
> Beneath is all the fiend's.
> There's hell, there's darkness, there is the sulphurous pit; burning,
> scalding, stench, consumption. Fie, fie, fie! pah, pah! Give me an
> ounce of civet; good apothecary, sweeten my imagination!
> (IV.vi.125–30)

Angelo, a smaller person, bears the full burden of recognizing his own smallness, its contemptibility, and his helplessness before compelling demands that issue from within him. As he grossly subverts justice, he suffers full awareness of the motives and the implications of his acts:

> He should have lived,
> Save that his riotous youth with dangerous sense
> Might in the times to come have ta'en revenge,
> By so receiving a dishonored life
> With ransom of such shame. Would yet he had lived.
> Alack, when once our grace we have forgot,
> Nothing goes right; we would, and we would not.
> (IV.iv.26–32)

Nowhere in Shakespeare is the disruption of the precarious balance through which individuals living in society organize competing claims for self-preservation, for self-esteem, for instinctual gratification, and for moral coherence experienced more directly than when the moralist Angelo watches himself travesty morality, first to serve desire, then to save his skin. Even Othello, when he prefaces his suicide with a last effort to restore an image of his heroic, honorable self, in effect refuses to look squarely at the shameful, belittling implications of his actions; he would rather die a hero than recognize in himself a living fool. Like Othello, Angelo craves "death more willingly than mercy" (V.i.472), but only after having absorbed fully the shame from which that death would deliver him, and without compensatory fantasies of restoring forfeited honor.

By bringing the problem of sexual degradation clearly into the foreground, not only through Angelo's experience but in all the play's major crises, *Measure for Measure* confronts in a comic action pressures that underlie the whole development of Shakespeare's tragic art. That action, like those of the festive comedies, is driven forward by the need for sexual release intersecting social conventions and individual inhibitions. The exquisite opening speech of *Twelfth Night,* for instance, identifies the erotic potential deflected into narcissistic passion that Orsino mistakenly understands as love for Olivia. *Twelfth Night* is propelled by the need to focus and release the energies both bound and diffused in Orsino's polymorphous sentimentality. But Orsino's elegant sensuality, Petruchio's lusty opportunism in *Shrew,* the dignity of virility that goes with Theseus and Oberon in *Dream,* Rosalind's rich expression of urgent desire in *As You Like It,* these and kindred attitudes basic to earlier comedies are no longer accessible in *Measure for Measure.* The threat of sexual degradation, deflected by wit and subordinated to the larger movements of the festive comedies, in *Measure for Measure* is moved toward the very center of the comic action. In *As You Like It* love must be rescued from romantic illusions that distort the conditions in which intimacy can occur; intimacy is virtually crowded off the stage in *Measure for Measure* by a background of seething corruption and a foreground of anxiety, terror, and shame.

Measure for Measure proceeds from attitudes that imply an ineradicable tension between moral aspiration and an inherently debasing sexual nature. Lucio, the most vigorous advocate of sexuality in the play, thrives on precisely this tension. A. P. Rossiter has shown how Lucio's jesting "turns on the incongruity of men's dignified pretensions and their animal behaviour; and on the latter's usual consequences: sexual scandal and venereal disease (as a kind of cruel practical joke which makes the sufferer ridiculous)." Lucio " 'stands for' sex intellectualized as witty smuttiness, stripped of emotion and therefore debased. . . ."[3] Lucio jests at scars to protect himself from wounds, trivializes sexuality and morality to keep at a

3. *Angel with Horns* (New York: Theatre Arts Books, 1961), p. 155.

distance anxieties that go with the effort to integrate instinctual and moral obligations. Lucio's witty isolation of sexuality from emotional involvement and moral propriety is his way of dealing with a problematic relation that all major characters in the play must face.

Only among the regulars of the brothel underworld, for whom the degradation of sexuality is, so to speak, both institutionalized and outside the acceptable social order, is there consistent relief from the chorus of voices unnerved in one way or another by the "resolute acting" (II.i.12) of the blood. No one places Angelo's effort to legislate sexual morality in sharper perspective than the tapster/bawd Pompey:

> Does your worship mean to geld and splay all the youth of the city? ... If you head and hang all that offend that way but for ten year together, you'll be glad to give out a commission for more heads.
> (II.i.217–18; 225–27)

The play does not, of course, "approve" of Pompey's vocation or his outlook; Vincentio himself finds Pompey's livelihood particularly loathsome:

> Fie, sirrah, a bawd, a wicked bawd!
> The evil that thou causest to be done,
> That is thy means to live. (III.ii.17–19)

But the indignant rhetoric of Vincentio's moral outrage does not entirely escape irony when set beside Pompey's earlier, disarming statement of his own effort simply to survive—"Truly, sir, I am a poor fellow that would live"—or beside his declaration of vocational loyalty against the threat of a whipping—"Whip me! No, no, let carman whip his jade. / The valiant heart's not whipped out of his trade" (II.i.210; 241–42). In a play in which loyalty to principle, when not betrayed, is most often experienced in painful conflict with personal allegiances, the heartening assurance Pompey gives Mistress Overdone holds a special place: "I'll be your tapster still. Courage, there will be pity taken on you; you that have worn your eyes almost out in the service, you will be considered" (I.ii.105–7). His moral status apart, Pompey is the character who has adapted most comfortably to the world Shakespeare creates in *Measure for Measure*.

Leo Salinger has observed: "To pass from *Twelfth Night* to *Measure for Measure* is somewhat like passing from the Renaissance to the Reformation."[4] Those who belong to or oversee the central action inhabit what Salinger calls the "Reformation" world of the play. They represent a spectrum of attitudes characterized by an uneasy mistrust of sexual impulses and a preoccupation with the problem of what to do with them. Cynical utterances about man the animal are, of course, nothing new to Shakespeare's comedy: "As horns are odious, they are necessary" (AYL III.iii.45–46). But rather than take such perspectives in stride, as Touchstone's witty mockery is caught up in the larger movement of *As You Like It*, Shakespeare consistently brings the characters of *Measure for Measure* up against the task of pondering what to do with a sexual nature repeatedly seen as "filthy vice," "sweet uncleanness," "abhorred pollution," "dark deeds," "most offenseful act," and the like. Such expressions all refer explicitly to sexual transactions outside moral and legal codes, but the play offers no significant counterpoise to the attitudes they convey. There is little to suggest that the social institution of marriage can, like Lear's apothecary, sweeten the sexual imagination expressed in this play. *Measure for Measure* makes the problem of illicit sexuality the focus for anxieties seemingly based on the whole of man's sexual nature.

Claudio's death sentence provides the occasion for many of the play's reflections on sexuality. Despite much consternation that Claudio should die according to the law against fornication, there is little questioning of the assumptions upon which this law rests by those in the play who think seriously about justice. When Lucio urges that "a little more lenity to lechery would do no harm," Vincentio responds: "It is too general a vice, and severity must cure it" (III.ii.92, 94). Isabella launches her plea to save Claudio's life by setting up her defense against her deeper feelings about such matters:

> There is a vice that most I do abhor,
> And most desire should meet the blow of justice,
> For which I would not plead, but that I must, . . .
>   (II.ii.29–31)

4. *Shakespeare and the Traditions of Comedy* (Cambridge: Cambridge University Press, 1974), p. 322.

The most tolerant position is that of the provost, who laments that Claudio should die for committing a sin so general that it should simply be accepted as a part of human nature:

> Alas,
> He hath but as offended in a dream.
> All sects, all ages smack of this vice—and he
> To die for't!   (ii.ii.3–6)

But even kindly Escalus, for all his compassion, finds himself trapped into admitting to himself that justice will be served, and must be served, by Claudio's death:

> It is but needful.
> Mercy is not itself, that oft looks so;
> Pardon is still the nurse of second woe.
> But yet poor Claudio; there is no remedy.
>   (ii.i.267–70)

How difficult and problematic Shakespeare's typical comic task— that of finding and celebrating the appropriate meeting place of sexual drives and social forms—has become in this play, which Coleridge found "the most painful—say rather, the only painful—part of his genuine works,"[5] and which L. C. Knights considered "the play of Shakespeare's that has caused most readers the greatest sense of strain and discomfort."[6] Psychological circumstances that contribute to this problematic turn can be made clearer by following the complex interrelations, with each other and with the world they inhabit, of Claudio, Angelo, Isabella, and Vincentio, especially through the dense and explosive drama of the first two and one-half acts. The special qualities in Angelo's character are implicated in more general patterns. I think it is possible, and necessary, both to grant considerable autonomy to these characters, as each responds to situations of crisis with an identifiably individual style, and to recognize how each is part of a larger response, organized at a different level of psychic engagement, to a common core of conflict.

5. *Shakespearean Criticism*, ed. Thomas Middleton Raysor, 2nd ed., vol. 1 (London: J. M. Dent and Sons, 1960), p. 102.
6. "The Ambiguity of *Measure for Measure*," in *The Importance of Scrutiny*, ed. Eric Bentley (New York: G. W. Stewart, 1948), p. 141.

Sexuality, Life, and Death
in *Measure for Measure*

DUKE   *Reason thus with life:*
            If I do lose thee, I do lose a thing
            That none but fools would keep.   (III.i.6–8)

Claudio, sentenced to die, is eager to defend himself on legal, moral, and practical grounds:

> upon a true contract
> I got possession of Julietta's bed.
> You know the lady, she is fast my wife. . . .
>   (I.ii.140–42)

But at a deeper level than self-justification, and along with his anger toward Angelo, is a disgust he has come to feel for the "most mutual entertainment" that "with character too gross is writ on Juliet" (II.i.149–50). Explaining to Lucio why he is imprisoned, Claudio records his fate in lines that recall, like Angelo's lust, the "swallowed bait . . . A bliss in proof, and proved a very woe" of Sonnet 129:

> From too much liberty, my Lucio, liberty.
> As surfeit is the father of much fast,
> So every scope by the immoderate use
> Turns to restraint. Our natures do pursue,
> Like rats that ravin down their proper bane,
> A thirsty evil, and when we drink we die.
>   (I.ii.121–26)

Of course, it is not surprising that being sentenced to death for any activity should affect one's attitude toward it for the worse. Claudio's lines nonetheless suggest the almost infectious quality in the debased imaging of sexual activity in *Measure for Measure*. Once his activity is forcibly called to his attention as sinful and self-debasing, he cannot help acquiescing in that perspective. Claudio's image of sexuality as a "thirsty evil" shares common ground with Angelo's longing for the "sweet uncleanness" of bedding Isabella. Each sees himself as having taken sexual bait and been contaminated by it. However vigorously Claudio may resent Angelo's law, an element of guilty self-accusation clearly colors his response to it; the rat poison metaphor compromises the very intimacy he is otherwise concerned to justify.

Claudio's association of sexuality with inner contamination through ingestion reflects anxieties shaped by infantile levels of the psyche. In the earliest stage of infantile development, taking nourishment is the paradigmatic mode of sexual gratification as well as survival. The deepest threats to the emerging psyche result from stresses on the bond to the mother, which for the infant is organized chiefly around the rhythms of seeking and taking nurture, of desire that culminates in satiation. Disturbances of these rhythms may lead to crises of various sorts. Violent rage against the source of frustration may lead to attacks of biting and to fantasies of destroying the maternal world by devouring it. When such aggression in turn begets fear of retaliation in kind from a source of greater power, the infant may turn this rage against itself, internalizing the attack on the external world in order to preserve a relation to it. The shattering of psychic equilibrium in this infantile battleground may lead to a fear of being overwhelmed by the very impulses that keep the child alive or to a deep distrust of what may be offered to it for ingestion by the external world. The overriding threat is that impulses originating within the emerging self may lead to abandonment by a nurturing environment gradually recognized as separate from the self but essential to its survival. In extreme instances, when such disturbances are not contained within an environment that encourages the development of basic trust, these crises can become prototypes for disorders that radically inhibit or even preclude further development. But such disturbances are inevitable within the ordinary processes of infantile maturation and leave behind in the psyche what Erik Erikson describes as a permanent residue of basic mistrust.

In earlier comedies, where that residue of mistrust in instinctual impulses is carefully held in check (I discuss some of the conditions that make this possible in the second sections of chapter 2 and chapter 4), image patterns often establish benign associations between the processes of loving and feeding, as in As You Like It, where "the sight of lovers feedeth those in love" (III.iv.52). In Twelfth Night, where festive comic poise regarding sexuality wavers before the swerve into the darker regions of the problem comedies and the tragedies, a more ambivalent attitude to desire is expressed in the food imagery of Orsino's first speech:

> If music be the food of love, play on,
> Give me excess of it, that, surfeiting,
> The appetite may sicken, and so die.
>   (I.i.1–3)

It is hard to tell from Orsino's lines if he longs more to release sexual desire or to be released from it, though he clearly finds in both notions a source of self-indulgent pleasure. His entire speech is framed by the tension between the "spirit of love" as something "quick and fresh" and as a vast sea that devours and devalues the energies it releases:

>   Nought enters there,
> Of what validity and pitch soe'er,
> But falls into abatement and low price
> Even in a minute.   (I.i.9, 11–14)

The action of *Twelfth Night* is a search for a way of understanding love that can avoid this fall into "abatement and low price" that Orsino at first seems half to fear, half to crave.

Little of what is "quick and fresh" in love survives in *Measure for Measure*, a play in which mistrust has taken over the dramatized attitudes toward sexuality. Its imagery repeatedly connects debased sexual desire with eating, as when Lucio explains to the disguised Duke: "Yes, in good sooth, the vice is of a great kindred; it is well allied, but it is impossible to extirp it quite, friar, till eating and drinking be put down" (III.ii.95–97). Lucio would, indeed, put himself on a severe diet as the only way to curb his own lechery: "I am fain to dine and sup with water and bran; I dare not for my head fill my belly; one fruitful meal would set me to't" (IV.iii.150–52). In Lucio's imagination, good food leads to debasing sexuality, which for Claudio is in turn imagined as a taking in of poisonous food. To feed on love in *Measure for Measure* is to experience it as an internally corrupting agency, like Claudio's "proper bane," or even to be eaten by it: "Thy bones are hollow; impiety has made a feast of thee" (I.ii.53–54), Lucio observes of the first gentleman, who is being devoured by venereal disease.

Viennese authority counters the threat posed by self-devouring and self-contaminating inner impulses with the aggressive imposition of external controls. Appropriately, Vincentio uses the image of a child attacking its source of nurture to describe the chaos into which civil order has been driven:

> And Liberty plucks Justice by the nose;
> The baby beats the nurse, and quite athwart
> Goes all decorum.   (I.iii.29–31)

To check such unrestrained appetites, the Duke explains to Friar Thomas, requires the renewed enforcement of brutal laws long unused, "Even like an o'ergrown lion in a cave, / That goes not out to prey" (I.iii.22–23). Vincentio's image of the stilled but potentially ferocious lion is restated by Lucio, who notes that sexual offenses "have long run by the hideous law, / As mice by lions" (I.iv.63–64). Later the disguised Duke will complain that "the strong statutes / Stand like the forfeits [extracted teeth] in a barber's shop, / As much in mock as mark" (V.i.318–20). Psychologically, the effort to send the lion after its prey, to put teeth back into the old law that will devour sexual offenders, renews an unconscious threat of retaliation against aggressive sexual impulses; it turns back against the source of desire the aggressive component within it that leads to its being perceived as threatening. This turning back is conveyed tersely in Vincentio's conviction that Vienna must enforce "most biting laws" that will provide "the needful bits and curbs to headstrong jades" (I.iii.19–20).

Angelo exercises these "needful bits and curbs" on Claudio, then goes on to give his own "sensual race the rein." Indeed, Angelo's degradation of sexuality can be charted through images that intensify its connections with both insatiable eating and aggressive, external coercion. "We must not make a scarecrow of the law," he argues in defense of Claudio's death sentence,

> Setting it up to fear the birds of prey,
> And let it keep one shape, till custom make it
> Their perch and not their terror.   (II.i.1–4)

But in response to Isabella, Angelo quickly becomes one of these birds of prey, whose travesty of the law is a source of terror for his victim. After he takes the hook baited with Isabella, Angelo longs to "feast upon her eyes" (II.ii.179). He imagines sexual activity as "saucy sweetness" and as "sweet uncleanness," and would force Isabella to "fit thy consent to my sharp appetite" (II.iv.161).

When Angelo's assault prompts Isabella to condemn those who make the law pawn to their lust, she associates the treacherous mouth of corrupt authority with willful sexual appetite:

> O perilous mouths,
> That bear in them one and the selfsame tongue,
> Either of condemnation or approof,
> Bidding the law make curtsy to their will,
> Hooking both right and wrong to th' appetite,
> To follow as it draws.   (II.iv.172–77)

But Angelo's soliloquy before Isabella enters in this scene reveals the emptiness created in him when his bond to sacred authority is sacrificed to his appetite for sexual satiation:

> When I would pray and think, I think and pray
> To several subjects: heaven hath my empty words,
> Whilst my invention, hearing not my tongue,
> Anchors on Isabel: heaven in my mouth,
> As if I did but only chew his name,
> And in my heart the strong and swelling evil
> Of my conception.   (II.iv.1–7)

For Angelo, to succumb to the "swelling evil" of phallic sexuality is to lose the nourishment he seeks in prayer; he can only "chew" the name of God in spiritual impotence, without partaking of its sacred substance. Lever notes in the Arden edition "the suggestion of a sacreligious communion" in these lines, but the essence of this communion is sterility not blasphemy. For Angelo, neither the "empty words" of prayer nor the conquest of sexual prey will lead to peace or fulfillment.

The mistrust of sexual impulses expressed most directly in the complex of images that link them to eating or biting extends to other image patterns as well, which recapitulate and intermingle the oral, anal, and phallic stages of infantile sexual development. Sexuality in *Measure for Measure* is an appetite that must be checked by a law that devours sexual offenders, but it is also a "filthy vice," an "abhorred pollution," a source of "shame," and, in Pompey's words: "Indeed, it does stink in some sort . . ." (III.ii.26). The release of sexual drives in phallic activity, Lucio would like to think, is intrinsically as harmless as "filling a bottle with a tun-dish" (III.ii.161), but in *Measure for Measure* phallic sexuality, as I will try to show, typically leads to self-alienation and emasculation. Phallic sexuality carries the burden of deeper levels of conflict expressed both through the play's imagery and through its action. The familial contexts out of which these layers of conflict emerge become apparent in the relations among characters brought into crisis by that action.

Isabella relies on the purity of family bonds to relieve her of the burden of Angelo's sexual attack: "I'll to my brother" (II.iv.177). When Claudio seems adamant in his resolve to face death—before he knows the conditions for reprieve Angelo has offered—Isabella sees his resolution as an expression of ideal, patriarchal family bonds: "Thus spake my brother; there my father's grave / Did utter forth a voice" (III.i.86–87). But when Claudio pleads that his life be saved by the only means possible, Isabella responds, as Rossiter has aptly observed, with a terror that matches her brother's fear of death, "and with an analogous cry of the reluctant flesh" (*Angel with Horns*, p. 160):

> Wilt thou be made a man out of my vice?
> Is't not a kind of incest, to take life
> From thine own sister's shame?   (III.i.138–40)

The anatomical pun on "vice"[7] (Shakespeare's, I assume, and not, at least by conscious intention, Isabella's) catches exactly Isabella's deep physical revulsion from Angelo's sexual design, and assimilates her brother to the crime. It is a "kind of incest" that would allow Claudio to be reborn—fathered and mothered anew—through Isabella's intercourse with Angelo.

Isabella gives voice to an association of sexuality and incest implicit in Angelo as well. This association informs not only their direct responses to sexuality, but also their attempts to evade or control it. Initially for both of them, sexual drives are active only behind a barrier of repression that, when it functions effectively, not only prohibits direct release of sexual desire, but also makes alternative activity serve as disguised metaphor for repressed longings. In serv-

7. Eric Partridge cites *Ado* V.ii.18–24 to connect *vice* with *pudend and closed thighs* (*Shakespeare's Bawdy*, 2nd ed. [New York: E. E. Dutton, 1955]).

ing his severe superego, as I tried to show earlier, Angelo serves internalized paternal prohibitions against incestuous sexual desires.
Like Angelo's self-imposed chastity, Isabella's desire to enter the
convent perpetuates an infantile resolution of the oedipal situation.
Isabella, about to join a religious sisterhood that institutionalizes the
familial taboo on sexuality, would make a gift of her virginity, her
sexual potentiality exalted and desexualized as worship, to God.
But everything desexualized for these characters at one level is re-
sexualized at another. Angelo falls prey to his own erotic nature precisely through the appeal of Isabella's saintliness. Isabella's repudiation of Angelo's advances is in turn strangely, masochistically
eroticized in a vivid fantasy that expresses her own tormented image
of sexual contact:

> were I under the terms of death,
> Th' impression of keen whips I'ld wear as rubies,
> And strip myself to death as to a bed
> That longing had been sick for, ere I'ld yield
> My body up to shame.   (ii.iv.100–104)

Angelo's enforcement of the law against fornication projects and
transforms an unconscious stricture that punishes incestuous sexuality with castration into a legal stricture that punishes illicit sexuality with beheading. "Beheading," Freud observed, is "well-known
to us as a symbolic substitute for castrating."[8] Isabella implicitly

8. "The Taboo of Virginity," in *The Standard Edition of the Complete
Psychological Works of Sigmund Freud*, ed. James Strachey, vol. 11 (London: Hogarth Press, 1957), p. 207. There is, perhaps, behind Isabella's
initial encouragement to Claudio to face death bravely, a kind of dream logic
that sets up there the analogy of beheading with castrating:

> O, I do fear thee, Claudio, and I *quake*,
> Lest thou a *feverous* life shouldst *entertain*,
> And six or seven *winters* more respect
> Than a *perpetual honor*. Dar'st thou *die?*
> The *sense* of death is most in apprehension,
> And the poor *beetle* that we tread upon
> In *corporal sufferance* finds a *pang* as great
> As when a *giant* dies. (iii.i.74–81)

I have italicized the words that suggest unconscious sexual content: *quake*
suggests bodily excitation as well as the fearfulness Isabella associates with
sexuality; *feverous* often, especially in the *Sonnets* (cf. 147: "My love is as a
fever, longing still, / For that which longer nurseth the disease"), carries a
sexual meaning for Shakespeare; *entertain* is opposed to *winters* as Claudio's
sexual indulgence is opposed to Isabella's own chilly response by denial of

accepts and extends the psychological basis for that law when she decides that Claudio, to pay for one sexual crime and to redeem family heritage by preventing a worse one explicitly associated with incest, should go willingly to the chopping block:

> Though he hath fall'n by prompture of the blood,
> Yet hath he in him such a mind of honor
> That, had he twenty heads to tender down
> On twenty bloody blocks, he'ld yield them up,
> Before his sister should her body stoop
> To such abhorred pollution.   (ii.iv.178–83)

Claudio is expected to prove himself a worthy son, to redeem paternal honor and heritage, by embracing a fatal extension of the paternal threat of castration.

Claudio casts his resolve to accomplish this in a way that further develops the paradox by sexualizing his own death:

> Think you I can a resolution fetch
> From flow'ry tenderness? If I must die,
> I will encounter darkness as a bride,
> And hug it in mine arms.   (iii.i.82–85)

When that element of his resolution that derives from his will to live leads him to choose life and the violation of family bonds over death, the pressure of conflict shifts squarely back onto Isabella. So long as Claudio is ready to die, Isabella finds that "there my father's grave / Did utter forth a voice." But in her outraged reaction to his broken resolution, Isabella calls her mother's reputation into doubt to preserve an image of a father too good to have produced a Claudio:

> What should I think?
> Heaven shield my mother played my father fair,

---

her sexuality. Against these terms is set *perpetual honor*, which desexualizes, idealizes, and stabilizes the impulsiveness of phallic sexuality. *Sense* here, as elsewhere, suggests sensuality (see Empson, *Complex Words*), a suggestion confirmed by *die*, which often carries the meaning of sexual consummation. The link of *beetle* to *giant* through *corporal sufferance* and *pang* gives a particularly sexual resonance to dying; *beetle* and *giant* suggest both the relation of the penis to the entire body (the equation essential to the symbolic identity of castration and beheading) and the relation of a boy's smallness to a father's largeness as perceived by a boy facing the paternal obstacle to his own sexual ambitions.

> For such a warpèd slip of wilderness
> Ne'er issued from his blood. (III.i.140–43)

Rather than the honorable son of the honored father, Claudio becomes in Isabella's mind the contaminated son of a wayward mother.

As Janet Adelman observes, in a fine introduction written to accompany the telecast of *Measure for Measure* in the BBC/PBS series of Shakespeare productions, "Isabella seems to believe that her nature as a woman ties her to sexuality, particularly sexual misbehavior," a " 'destined livery' " that she "hopes to escape by putting on the robes of a nun." [9] Isabella shares in the deep distrust of women, of female sexuality, diffused throughout the entire play in much the way it permeates *Hamlet* and *Othello*. As she responds to Claudio's plea, she also participates in the defense against sexual contamination through the ideal of male honor. Isabella calls for Claudio's death with a logic like that of Othello: [10]

> Yet she must die, else she'll betray more men.
> (*Oth.* v.ii.6)
> Thy sin's not accidental, but a trade;
> Mercy to thee would prove itself a bawd,
> 'Tis best that thou diest quickly. (III.i.150–52)

She resorts to a violence of feeling similar to Othello's:

> Take my defiance,
> Die, perish. Might but my bending down
> Reprieve thee from thy fate, it should proceed.
> I'll pray a thousand prayers for thy death,
> No word to save thee. (III.i.143–47)

The unbending rigidity of her moral stance extends to her bodily self-consciousness, reflected in lines that clearly call for Isabella to hold herself stiff and erect in outraged defiance. Having repudiated the sexual heritage she associates with her mother, Isabella, energized with outrage, becomes a metaphor for phallic uprightness; she embodies the potency of paternal heritage Claudio has forfeited.

But Isabella's angry appropriation of a paternal legacy denied by

9. "Mortality and Mercy in *Measure for Measure*," in *The Shakespeare Plays: A Study Guide* (Delmar, Ca.: University Extension, University of California, San Diego, and Coast Community College District, 1978), pp. 104–14.

10. I am grateful to C. L. Barber for pointing out to me this resemblance.

Claudio parallels precisely the precarious resolution of conflict between sexual drives and paternal authority presented by the chaste
and tyrannous Angelo. Angelo is the "ungenitured agent" (III.ii.
162–63) [11] Lucio finds in him to the extent that he imposes upon his
sexual self the psychic equivalent of castration. But Angelo had embraced such "continency" in order to embody desexualized phallic
authority. In the oedipal phase, "idealization of the parents . . .
becomes focused on their phallic attributes," [12] attributes internalized
in the moral force of Angelo's superego. In denying himself direct
sexual expression, Angelo displaces onto an authoritarian moral style
rigid, hard, upright qualities that metaphorically extend repressed
phallic drives. When desexualization fails, Angelo's whole person
becomes subject to the threat of castration that earlier held his sexual
impulses in check.

Freud, speculating about the interconnections of castration anxiety and the "dread of women" as reflected in primitive taboos of
virginity, wondered if "the effect which coitus has of discharging
tensions and causing flaccidity may be the prototype of what the man
fears . . ." ("Virginity," p. 199). This pattern of erectness, discharge,
and flaccidity describes exactly the curve of Angelo's development
as his moral resolution dissolves in its sexual base. His phallic character structure is suddenly charged with repressed sexual content:
when the sexual tension of that "swelling evil" is discharged in the
night he thinks he spends with Isabella, the "deed unshapes me
quite" (IV.iv.18), makes him "unpregnant"—emptied of his
strength, his virility—and "dull" (compare Hamlet to Ophelia: "It
would cost you a groaning to take off my edge" [III.ii.240]). Finally
he submits himself, in shame before Vincentio, to his apparent death
by beheading.

In the same essay, Freud describes circumstances that suggest that
in relations to a woman "the man is afraid of being weakened, in-
fected with her femininity . . ." (p. 199). The paradoxical nature
of this fear—men fear the power of women to make them powerless
like women—not only helps explain Angelo's fate, but does much to
account for the whole psychological orientation of *Measure for*

11. J. W. Lever's gloss for *ungenitured* in the Arden ed. of *Measure for
Measure* (London: Methuen, 1965) is "sterile, seedless; or without genitals."
12. John E. Gedo and Arnold Goldberg, *Models of the Mind: A Psychoanalytic Theory* (Chicago: University of Chicago Press, 1973), p. 85.

Measure. Shakespeare's reduction of virginal Isabella to a position of tormented, helpless victimization—until the masculine presence of the disguised Duke intervenes—represents a turning away, a recoiling from the power earlier accorded such resourceful young virgins as Portia and Rosalind in the festive comedies, and in particular Helena in *All's Well That Ends Well*. The subordination of Isabella, both to the sexual assault of Angelo and to the masculine protectiveness of Vincentio, expresses a fearful attitude toward female sexuality often dramatized in the tragedies—in Hamlet's paralyzed brooding over his mother's incest, in the failure of Othello's manhood before the fantasy of Desdemona's infidelity, in Roman speculation about the seductive evil of Cleopatra.

Measure for Measure expresses a deep mistrust of impulses within the self that are provoked in men through relations to women. I have discussed various, largely unsuccessful, defenses the play brings to this fear of masculine vulnerability—the generalized degradation of sexuality, the limitations imposed upon the power of the play's women, the idealization of male authority by Angelo and of paternal honor by Isabella, the law that would prevent illicit sexuality by punishing offenders with death. In the most radical strategy for dealing with the dangers of impulses that threaten to exceed the mastery available to the self, fear of sexual drives spreads into a generalized contempt for and repudiation of all life processes. This strategy is offered in the Duke's prison advice to Claudio: "Be absolute for death" (III.i.5).

The counsel Vincentio offers the condemned Claudio does not reflect the Christian context suggested by his disguise as a friar. J. W. Lever has shown that Vincentio's "description of the human condition eliminates its spiritual aspect and is essentially materialist and pagan."[13] Rossiter emphasized that the speech lacks precisely what would be at the center of a Christian homily on death:

> there is no hint of redemption, no hint of immortality in the whole. The only certainties are existence, uncertainty, disappointment, frustration, old age, and death. It mentions values only as delusions.
>
> (*Angel with Horns*, p. 166)

Nor does the speech make any explicit effort to put the condemned man into relation with the sin he has committed and for which he

13. Introduction to Arden ed. of *Measure for Measure*, p. lxxxvii.

has been sentenced to die. Despite the nature of Claudio's crime, Vincentio avoids any emphasis on the place of sexuality in life. "Be absolute for death," Vincentio begins: "either death or life / Shall thereby be the sweeter" (III.i.5–6). There is little in what follows, however, that could conceivably sweeten the experience of living. The Duke proceeds to a somber celebration of death as welcome relief from a life fraught with misery and discontent:

> What's yet in this
> That bears the name of life? Yet in this life
> Lie hid moe thousands deaths; yet death we fear,
> That makes these odds all even.   (III.i.38–41)

Vincentio offers an inventory, more fully developed than Hamlet's, of "the heartache, and the thousand natural shocks / That flesh is heir to" (*Ham.* III.i.62–63). His speech expresses a revulsion from life as it is enslaved to processes never halted, which make all experience subject to debasing contingencies, violating even the capacity to be oneself:

> Thou art not thyself,
> For thou exists on many a thousand grains
> That issue out of dust.   (III.i.19–21)

All relations—to property, to the various stages of life, to the quest for happiness, to other people—obliterate solidarity, none more than relations to family:

> Friends hast thou none,
> For thine own bowels, which do call thee sire,
> The mere effusion of thy proper loins,
> Do curse the gout, serpigo, and the rheum
> For ending thee no sooner.   (III.i.28–32)

The contemptuous reference to procreation in these lines conveys a disgust with the physical dimension of life implicit throughout the entire speech; the cynical summation of parental relations conveys the oedipal hatred that goes with the taboo on sexuality. The fear the Duke associates with the "soft and tender fork / Of a poor worm" (III.i.16–17), whether it refers explicitly to worms that devour the body after death or to the bite of a poisonous snake that would end life, carries a suggestion of impotence that links fear of death to sexual anxiety.

Nothing that urges the self toward gratification brings with it satisfaction, even when apparent aims are accomplished:

> Happy thou art not,
> For what thou hast not, still thou striv'st to get,
> And what thou hast, forget'st.   (III.i.21–23)

Vincentio's evocation here of impotent striving, like Angelo's and Claudio's earlier reflections on their own sexual drivenness, recalls Sonnet 129:

> Mad in pursuit, and in possession so;
> Had, having, and in quest to have, extreme;
> A bliss in proof, and proved, a very woe;
> Before, a joy proposed; behind a dream.

But in Vincentio's meditation, even the "joy proposed" has lost its lustre; his speech is a movement through and beyond the lament of the sonnet for the "expense of spirit" to a spirit that has nothing to expend. The speech would break the lure of "the heaven that leads men to this hell" (*Son.* 129) by self-willed oblivion. Even death is presented not so much as desirable in itself as simply negation of intolerable life, which in all its "accommodations" is "nursed by baseness" (III.i.14–15).

Vincentio's homily is an elegant refutation of hope, the expectation that desire will lead to gratification, which he sees not, like Claudio, as medicine for the miserable, but as the disease itself. In *Measure for Measure*, impulses that obey the pleasure principle—which seek gratification through a relation with the external world—invariably lead to conditions of heightened inner stress; Vincentio here offers the strategy of withdrawing oneself from those impulses altogether.[14] Shakespeare taps—and momentarily masters through

14. Psychoanalysis has shown that the "avoidance of the unpleasurable . . . is characteristic of the primary mental processes" that govern the actions of the self in its very early stages, and that are only gradually modified in the course of development. "The decathexis of endogenous stimuli [withdrawal of psychic investment from inner impulses] which produce unpleasure is the mechanism of primary repression." Gedo and Goldberg, the authors I am quoting, observe that primary repression, "passively experienced and unavoidable," is the typical adaptive strategy of early infancy, but "continues to be the defense which becomes operative in case of traumatic overstimulation throughout the life span . . ." (*Models of the Mind*, pp. 95–98). The danger averted by this defense is the direct experience of complete helplessness, of

the nihilistic dignity of the Duke's utterance, which accepts annihilation willingly and passively rather than encounter it as a danger—a reservoir of basic mistrust in which the self is so vulnerable to being overwhelmed by its own mixed and unmasterable demands that its only defense is to draw away from the sources of energy that keep it alive.[15] Vincentio's meditation, within its serenity, reveals an estrangement as thorough as Macbeth's chilling account of life as a "walking shadow, a poor player / That struts and frets his hour upon the stage / And then is heard no more" (V.v.24–26).

As advice to the condemned man, however, its usefulness is quickly exhausted. When, in the same scene, Claudio enthusiastically resolves before Isabella to "encounter darkness as a bride," he already speaks from a psychological orientation very different from the passive resignation to death counseled by Vincentio. A few moments later, when Claudio perceives death as a "fearful thing," the situation of traumatic helplessness that Vincentio's speech attempts to short-circuit surfaces with astonishing power. In contrast to death as complete stasis as imagined by Vincentio, Claudio regards his impending death as the initiation of sustained, intolerable process, a savage, perpetual, and thoroughly sensual assault against the spirit:

> Ay, but to die, and go we know not where,
> To lie in cold obstruction and to rot,
> This sensible warm motion to become
> A kneaded clod; and the delighted spirit
> To bathe in fiery floods, or to reside
> In thrilling region of thick-ribbèd ice,
> To be imprisoned in the viewless winds
> And blown with restless violence round about
> The pendent world; or to be worse than worst
> Of those that lawless and incertain thought
> Imagine howling, 'tis too horrible.   (III.i.118–28)

Claudio fears a death so terrifying that "the weariest and most loathèd worldly life . . . is a paradise" (III.i.129–31) in comparison.

---

being overwhelmed or annihilated by impulses that exceed the reach of ego mastery. Within the sophisticated, artful advice offered by Vincentio, a process analogous to this primitive defensive response seems to be at work.

15. Erik Erikson associates basic mistrust, the necessary, negative counterpart to the establishment of basic trust in early experience, with "impressions of having been deprived, of having been divided, of having been abandoned . . ." (*Identity: Youth and Crisis* [New York: Norton, 1968], p. 101).

His horror of death elaborates a fantasy of eternal torments with the unchecked, "lawless" extremes of the infantile imagination. Although he knows that "this sensible warm motion" will rot in "cold obstruction," his imagination of death, flooded with fears of overwhelming sensual stimuli, extends his sensuality into the fate of the "delighted spirit." Claudio envisions an afterlife in which the howling spirit is passively subjected to extremes of physical torture—submerged in "fiery floods," lodged in ice, both imprisoned and blown violently about in "viewless winds." Death for Claudio is an eternity of traumatic helplessness and terror, a sensational extension of what Vincentio, in his meditation on death, fears in life. This imagination of "what we fear of death" exceeds in intensity even Hamlet's "dread of something after death." Claudio sketches a vivid map of that "undiscovered country" that "puzzles the will / And makes us rather bear those ills we have / Than fly to others that we know not of" (III.i.78–82). Together with the longing for release from shameful urgencies of life counseled by Vincentio (and later embraced by Angelo), Claudio's horror completes the divided relation to death expressed in Hamlet's "to or not to be" soliloquy. The longing for death Vincentio articulates includes the wish to be ultimately released from tensions that provoke intolerable anxiety and threaten to overwhelm the self's precarious mastery of its own impulses. Claudio projects these tensions into a fate of eternal torment, a terrifyingly passive recasting of his earlier brave resolve to "encounter darkness as a bride." The movement from the Duke's meditation on death as a release from sensuality to Claudio's fear of death as perpetual sensual torture is the most extreme form of an inescapable antagonism, worked out repeatedly in *Measure for Measure*, between intolerable instinctual demands and various unsuccessful strategies that oppose them. Vincentio imagines in death a region beyond the reach of disruptive impulses, but Claudio's imagination of an afterlife redramatizes the impasse of the entire play.

Deputation and the Sins of Others

DUKE *Wherein have I so deserved of you,*
      That you extol me thus? (v.i.498–99)

Understanding the Duke's meditation on death in this way, however, does little to account for its place, or that of its speaker, in the comic design of *Measure for Measure*. Nor does it explain how the advice the Duke offers Claudio fits into Shakespeare's characterization of the Duke. But both of these questions can provide suggestive keys to the problematic nature of *Measure for Measure*. Like Jaques's reflections on the world as a stage in *As You Like It*, Vincentio's darker observations vividly present a perspective that differs substantially from attitudes toward life suggested by the main comic thrust of the action. But Jaques's cynicism is brought into ironic relation with the whole movement of *As You Like It*; its impact is tempered by what we know of Jaques, and subordinated to the larger understanding of life provided by Rosalind. Vincentio, despite his repudiation of life's goals, becomes the chief agent of their comic achievement; he goes on to serve a purpose analogous to Rosalind's when he exploits "the love I have of doing good" to find a "remedy" (III.i.195). Vincentio's meditation on death as a release from life presents an antagonistic alternative to his own effort to bring comic unity into the world of *Measure for Measure*. Yet the play provides no effective ironic controls that can bring the longing for death into clear relation with the comic affirmation of life.

Despite the Duke's role as comic agent, the form of his speech on death tends to identify the content with the speaker in a curious way. Vincentio would present Claudio with an attitude toward life that he may imitate: "Reason thus with life: / If I do lose thee, I do lose a thing / That none but fools would keep. . . ." Within the first-person mode in which the advice is offered, Vincentio seems almost to be speaking for himself. The longing for death he expresses is not, I think, consistent with the characterization of the Duke that culminates in his position at the end of the play. But this speech does present a plausible response of a sensibility whose longing for dignified, rational control cannot be made to square with conditions of life as they are imagined in *Measure for Measure*. Does the Duke ever enter persuasively into a relation to life more compelling than that conveyed by this speech? Although spoken from behind the friar's disguise, apparently in response to the pressing need of another, the speech seems to be at least as much a gesture of self-definition as appropriate counsel for Claudio, who unlike Vincentio is enamored of "this sensible warm motion."

Vincentio uses a similar mode of giving advice when he schools Pompey on the shortcomings of his profession:

> say to thyself,
> From their abominable and beastly touches
> I drink, I eat, array myself, and live.
> Canst thou believe thy living is a life,
> So stinkingly depending? Go mend, go mend.
> (III.ii.21–25)

This exchange between characters at opposite ends of a spectrum of attitudes toward sexuality in *Measure for Measure* teasingly identifies the two for a moment when the Duke, addressing Pompey with fierce loathing, speaks for him in the first person. Through this expression of outrage, the raw-nerved outward venting of an attitude latent in his advice to Claudio, Vincentio obliquely participates in feelings of sexual parasitism much in the way he earlier appropriated for himself the feeling for imminent death. And Vincentio, in arranging for Mariana's night in bed with Angelo, does provide a service not altogether unlike that he abhors in Pompey. Is there a way in which opposites meet in or behind the character of Vincentio, as they meet when puritanical Angelo finds himself sexually coercing Isabella?[16] If so, what are the implications for the Duke's role in the comic design of *Measure for Measure*?

The troubled critical heritage of *Measure for Measure* reflects the difficulty of placing Vincentio as a character in consistent relation to the play's drama of sexual corruption. Assessments of the Duke range enormously. Is he a godlike figure of Christian providence[17] or a rather sinister, all-too-human manipulator "playing at being

16. It is interesting to compare Vincentio's admonishment of Pompey with the bedroom counsel Hamlet offers Gertrude:

> Not this, by no means, that I bid you do:
> Let the bloat king tempt you again to bed,
> Pinch wanton on your cheek, call you his mouse,
> And let him, for a pair of reechy kisses,
> Or paddling in your neck with his damned fingers,
> Make you to ravel all this matter out. . . .
> (III.iv.182–87)

Hamlet's message is framed with a negative that inverts it as advice, but allows him to express a desperate identification with Claudio's sexual prerogatives. His covert participation in this sexual fantasy brings to the surface with unsettling intensity repressed materials that lie at the heart of Hamlet's character and radiate outward into developments that animate the entire play.

17. Perhaps the chief proponents of this view are G. Wilson Knight, Roy Battenhouse, Neville Coghill (see note 23, ch. 1), and R. W. Chambers (*Man's Unconquerable Mind* [London: Jonathan Cape, 1939]).

God"? [18] Is he a kind of moral scientist conducting a "controlled experiment" [19] or a satiric butt exposed as imposter and fool? [20] Each of these views, I think, seeks an order of inner coherence in Vincentio as the dramatic center of *Measure for Measure* that is not fully realized in the play's comic movement. Harriet Hawkins puts the problem presented by the characterization of Vincentio aptly: "No matter how hard we try to incorporate the Duke's behavior into some over-all interpretation of the play, all the incorporation and all the interpretation appears to be ours—not Shakespeare's." [21] Hawkins concludes that Vincentio, "in the second half of *Measure for Measure*, remains outside any meaning, an external plot-manipulator, a dramatic engineer of a comic ending, who never sees beyond his theatrical goal" (p. 73). But perhaps the "meaning" of Vincentio's role can be approached precisely in the gap that separates his "theatrical goal" from the powerful drama of human conflict in *Measure for Measure*.

Rossiter described in a provocative and useful way tensions that go unpurged in the comic movement engineered by the Duke. He found "that *Measure for Measure* was *intended* to finish as a play of a higher ethic, and that ethic 'Christian,' " with Vincentio as the character who gives order to this design. "But," Rossiter continued,

> this remains largely an aim: achievable by manipulation of the plot (which is why you can take out "the moral fable" and talk about that), but carried out neither by character-development, nor (more important) by the texture of the writing. (*Angel with Horns*, pp. 168–69)

Rossiter found "an *imposed* quality" in the action: "There is a solution there: but the 'problem' is on one plane, the 'solution' on quite another" (p. 169). Conflicting trends in the characterization of Vincentio relate him to each of these "planes." A comic order that requires the elevation of Vincentio into a providential figure of

---

18. Empson, *The Structure of Complex Words*, p. 283.

19. F. R. Leavis, *The Common Pursuit* (London: Chatto and Windus, 1952), p. 170.

20. Howard C. Cole demonstrates how plausible the case for a satirized Duke can be in "The 'Christian' Context of *Measure for Measure*," *Journal of English and Germanic Philology*, 64 (1965): 425–51.

21. *Likenesses of Truth in Elizabethan and Restoration Drama* (Oxford: Oxford University Press, 1972), p. 72.

justice and authority encounters interference from psychological patterns that tend to submerge him in a region of unresolved conflict.

Vincentio is so taken up in the lives of others, and speaks so much through disguise and machination, that he himself often seems, like the generalized life he describes, to have "nor youth nor age, / But as it were an after-dinner's sleep, / Dreaming on both" (III.i. 32–34). He thrives best in mysterious circumstances he controls and yet from which he remains personally remote. He rarely talks about himself or how the action of the play bears on him. When he does, it often takes the form of disclaimer, as when he heatedly disavows Lucio's charges. Indeed, I.iii, the only scene in the play devoted at all extensively to Vincentio's motives, opens with a disclaimer. Apparently in response to a suggestion by Friar Thomas that he is leaving Vienna in Angelo's hands to pursue his own amorous inclinations, Vincentio insists on his aloofness from such matters:

> No, holy father, throw away that thought;
> Believe not that the dribbling dart of love
> Can pierce a complete bosom; why I desire thee
> To give me secret harbor hath a purpose
> More grave and wrinkled than the aims and ends
> Of burning youth.   (I.iii.1–6)

Set against a comic tradition that embraces the transforming power of erotic impulse, these lines seem to set Vincentio up for ironic deflation, like the king in *Love's Labors Lost*. Such an irony does not seem, however, to be effectively exploited, even when Vincentio abruptly proposes to Isabella in the last scene. More striking is a connection to a closely parallel passage lodged in the tragic ironies of *Othello*.

When Othello restates, in his own terms, Desdemona's argument that she go with him to Cyprus, Vincentio's "dribbling dart of love" is echoed in Othello's scorn for the "light-winged toys / Of feathered Cupid," paltry things compared to his "speculative and officed instruments" (I.iii.268–70). Like Vincentio, Othello is above the weaknesses of "burning youth":

> Vouch with me, heaven, I therefore beg it not
> To please the palate of my appetite,
> Not to comply with heat—the young affects

> In me defunct—and proper satisfaction;
> But to be free and bounteous to her mind;
> And heaven defend your good souls that you think
> I will your serious and great business scant
> When she is with me.   (ɪ.iii.261–68)

In the course of the play, Othello's protestation becomes ironic prophecy. Iago quickly shows him to be most vulnerable precisely where he declares himself beyond danger, in his relation to the sexual dimension of his marriage. Othello's breezy dismissal of "feathered Cupid" covers a latent core of fear and potential loathing in the relationship he has made the center of his being:

> there where I have garnered up my heart,
> Where either I must live or bear no life,
> The fountain from the which my current runs
> Or else dries up—to be discarded thence
> Or keep it as a cistern for foul toads
> To knot and gender in—. . . .   (ɪv.ii.57–62)

Othello and Vincentio have much in common. Both are figures of authority with troubled relations to younger officers who serve them. Each speaks and acts with great dignity and composure, and prides himself on a reputation for restraint and rationality he is deeply concerned to protect. Both are admired by others as emblems of mature manhood, although in each case the age is kept vague enough to make plausible a marriage to a young woman without making incongruous the speculations of Iago, that Othello is too old to satisfy Desdemona sexually, or of Lucio, that Vincentio is "now past it" (III.ii.170). Shakespeare exposes and exploits dramatically the vulnerability just below the surface of each of these qualities in Othello. The mix of awe and resentment provoked by authority in those who serve it, Othello's identification of himself with his "occupation," his need to live amid certainties, and his feeling that he has "declined / Into the vale of years" (III.iii.265–66), all become conditions of a tragic action that ends with murder and suicide. Once his trust in Desdemona is shaken, Othello is virtually defenseless against the world of adulterous deception imagined for him by Iago as the sexual norm of Venice. Iago's imagination of universal infidelity in Venice has its counterpart in the reality of sexual corruption in Vienna. But hazards that overtake the "free and open nature" (I.iii.393) of Othello are deflected away from Vincentio, who is kept always at least once removed from this corruption. The slanders of Lucio, in whom a sexual imagination akin to Iago's is rendered comparatively harmless, are turned back against him; Angelo's corruption ultimately hurts mainly himself; and instead of beginning the play with a potentially disastrous marriage, Shakespeare ends with Vincentio's proposal to Isabella.

The distance imposed between the Duke and those who participate directly in the force of conflict in *Measure for Measure* allows Shakespeare to develop a comic design presided over by judicious authority, by Vincentio presented as a wise, strong, merciful leader. I can find no reliable indication in the last act that the Duke, as he dispenses mercy and marriage and general order, is being deliberately undermined or ironically qualified. The central effort seems to go into dramatizing a Vincentio who, in Angelo's phrase, presides "like power divine" over the life of sinning Vienna. And yet, with many other critics of the play, I cannot find this effort fully convincing or satisfying as a culmination of the powerful drama that precedes it. The curious silence of those who benefit from Vincentio's mercy, for instance, suggests a kind of precariousness in these pardons as drama, as if the culmination of the action in mercy is too fragile to withstand the forceful recall of conflicted human feeling that has been released earlier. The four men pardoned from death sentences— Barnardine, an unrepentant murderer rather implausibly instructed to "provide / For better times to come" (V.i.480–81); Claudio, who has narrowly escaped the death sentence imposed by Angelo; Angelo, a double violator of "sacred chastity, and of promise-breech" (V.i. 401); and Lucio, who has grossly slandered the duke in his pretended absence—with the exception of Lucio say not a word to authenticate a movement into a new relation to life. And Lucio's pardon is dispensed as punishment.

Like the pardons, the marriages of the last act are attended by an almost pervasive silence. None of these marriages culminates a relationship given sustained attention throughout the play. The union of Claudio and Juliet claims at the outset a kind of centrality, but is soon subordinated to the intense drama surrounding Claudio's death sentence and Angelo's attempt to coerce Isabella. When his marriage is finally condoned, Claudio says nothing to Vincentio, who has saved him from death, to his now silent sister, with whom he has been brought into such violent conflict earlier, or to the equally silent Juliet, with whom he is reunited. Angelo gives no indication that he has shifted from his earlier scorn for Mariana, or that he is now ready to move beyond the shame that has led him to beg for immediate death. Isabella meets Vincentio's abrupt proposal with similar silence. Only Lucio comments on his impending marriage to the prostitute who has given birth to his child: "Marrying a punk, my lord, is pressing to death, whipping, and hanging" (V.i.517–18).

The completion of the comic design centered in the wise and benevolent Duke is made possible by theatrical maneuvers that limit its scope and blunt its force. They create a comic whole smaller than the sum of its parts. The idealization of the Duke is necessary in order to complete this design, but can only be accomplished by suppressing potential links between Vincentio and deep psychological conflict. But suggestive connections cut through the shield of idealization separating the Duke from the world he inhabits at precisely those points where Shakespeare most emphasizes difference. His exchanges with Claudio and Pompey as I have discussed them are relatively isolated instances that work against the effort to keep the Duke isolated from psychological circumstances that obstruct the comic movement. A more sustained instance of a psychological pattern in considerable tension with the comic design emerges in Vincentio's relation to Isabella.

The comic design of the play insists on the appropriateness of Vincentio's marriage proposal to Isabella, suggesting, perhaps, the symbolic "marriage of understanding with purity; or tolerance with moral fervour" that G. Wilson Knight saw in it.[22] From this vantage point the deception of Isabella regarding Claudio's apparent death ("His head is off and sent to Angelo") seems to be offered as a kind of moral test designed to develop attributes lacking in her fervent morality: "Show your wisdom, daughter, / In your close patience" (IV.iii.113; 115–16). But there also seems to be an element of gratuitous cruelty that overflows moral purpose in this scheme. Empson, indeed, found it a "peculiarly brutal flippancy that [Vincentio] should not only trick Isabella about Claudio unnecessarily but take pains to thrust the imagined death of Claudio upon her

22. "*Measure for Measure* and the Gospels," *The Wheel of Fire*, 5th ed. (New York: Meridian Books, 1957), p. 95.

mind" (*Complex Words*, p. 283). The aggression in this lie and in other aspects of Isabella's treatment in *Measure for Measure* can be brought into sharper focus by another glance at *Othello*.

Like Isabella, Desdemona encounters violently conflicted impulses to exalt and defile her. She provokes polarized tendencies to regard her, with Cassio, as the "divine Desdemona," and, with Iago, as a woman of threatening sexual appetites, "sport for Jove," but an awesome burden for an aging general who will come to see her as "that cunning whore of Venice" (II.i.73; II.iii.17; IV.ii.89). Freud has shown that such polar tendencies spring from an unstable attitude toward female sexuality, a failure to integrate sexual desire and tender regard in a single relationship.[23] In *Othello* these opposed attitudes are clarified as conditions of a troubled masculine response to women. Essential to this clarification is the realization of Desdemona as a woman independent of the images of herself she provokes in men who, as Carol Thomas Neely has shown, come to "see the women as whores and then refuse to tolerate their own projections."[24] The tragic action makes her its victim, but does not violate her characterization as a woman violently misperceived by men whose understanding of her veers away from her person toward mutually antagonistic modes of idealization and degradation.

In *Measure for Measure*, the saintly Isabella provokes Angelo's brutal assault upon her virtue; the collapsing split in Angelo's sensibility is akin to Othello's futile effort to separate the sexual from the pure Desdemona. The play sustains the aggression of Angelo's assault even as Isabella is delivered from its actual completion. The Duke's lie forcing her to understand Claudio's death as a real event is part of a pattern that extends Angelo's cruelty on a new, moralized plane, just as she seems to be released from it. Although she is spared the night in bed with Angelo because of the arrangement with Mariana, she is forced to accept publicly the shame of that experience in the last act. She must proceed, according to Vincentio's instructions, "with grief and shame to utter" the "vile conclusion"

---

23. See "On the Universal Tendency to Debasement in the Sphere of Love," in *Standard Edition*, vol. 11, pp. 179–90.

24. "Women and Men in *Othello*: 'what should such a fool / Do with so good a woman?'" *Shakespeare Studies*, 10 (1977): 148. Neely notes that critics of *Othello* often have tended to duplicate rather than recognize the divided impulse to idealize and degrade the play's women (pp. 133–34).

(V.i.95–96) of her negotiations with Angelo. In lines which complete in words an action averted in the flesh, Isabella explains:

> He would not, but by gift of my chaste body
> To his concupiscible intemperate lust,
> Release my brother; and after much debatement
> My sisterly remorse confutes mine honor,
> And I did yield to him. (v.i.97–101)

Isabella then undergoes the added indignity of having her claim regarded as criminal madness and conspiracy:

> By heaven, fond wretch, thou know'st not what thou speak'st,
> Or else thou art suborned against his honor
> In hateful practice. . . .
>   Someone hath set you on;
> Confess the truth, and say by whose advice
> Thou cam'st here to complain. (v.i.105–7; 112–14)

Even Escalus gets in on the sinister feeling provoked by Isabella's charges: "I will go darkly to work with her" (V.i.277).

The play labors to keep Isabella pure, a chaste figure worthy of marriage with the Duke. But Isabella is symbolically defiled, made to suffer for her sexual provocations, however unwitting, as a condition that makes this marriage possible. The scheme to test and verify her moral capacity also expresses and disguises the hostility she provokes in men capable of understanding women only in antagonistic contexts that deny each other. To prove her virtue she must accept symbolic degradation by falsely confessing that she has been dishonored. Where *Othello* moves toward a clarification of the origins of the fearful hostility provoked by Desdemona, *Measure for Measure* disguises the hostile impulse as moral testing. "Be thus when thou art dead," Othello utters, gazing tenderly at his sleeping wife, "and I will kill thee, / And love thee after" (V.ii.18–19). He would purge Desdemona of her dreaded sexuality in order to love a purified image of her. The split brought to the foreground in Othello's violence is, in *Measure for Measure*, obscured as a shaping force in the action. But a common psychological pattern governs both. Vincentio's procedures in the last act are a way of saying to Isabella: confess and suffer publicly for your powers of provocation, accept the shame of a degraded sexual liaison; I will then restore your purity by showing that the dreadful event never occurred; and I will marry you after.

Although designed to bring comic order into a troubled world, the union of the Duke and Isabella at the end of *Measure for Measure* includes within itself a deeply buried version of a disturbance that torments the marriage of the paternal, authoritarian Othello with the daughter of his friend. The proposed marriage of Vincentio and Isabella, who have known each other throughout the play as holy father and spiritual daughter, is at this level itself "a kind of incest." Their marriage brings unacknowledged into the center of the drama the disturbing familial context that edges into Shakespearean comedy in the king's regard for Helena in *All's Well*, that becomes tragedy wrought to its uttermost in *King Lear*, and that will later be resolved in the symbolic designs of the late romances, particularly in *The Tempest*, when Prospero, Vincentio's closest kin in Shakespeare's drama, bestows his daughter on a young suitor.

The tension between the idealization of Vincentio and latent connections that link him to deep conflict can help account for other puzzling developments in the play. One such development is the sudden eruption of Lucio's shrill attack on Vincentio's moral status. From the time he runs across the disguised Vincentio in prison, Lucio goes out of his way to slander "the old fantastical Duke of dark corners" (IV.iii.154–55). He constructs an image precisely opposite to the one the comic design of the play is concerned to establish. In Lucio's image, Vincentio has been "instructed" to the habitual leniency of his reign by a sympathy grounded in his own inclinations: "He had some feeling for the sport, he knew the service" (III.ii. 112–13). Lucio's invented duke "had crotchets in him" (III.ii.120), whims that led him to licentious degradation:

> The Duke, I say to thee again, would eat mutton on Fridays. He's now past it; yet and I say to thee, he could mouth with a beggar, though she smelt brown bread and garlic.
>
> (III.ii.169–72)

Because these accusations are made by a demonstrated liar, they cannot be taken seriously as conveying substantial truth about Vincentio's past. They are exploited for comic effect when the Duke triumphantly reappears in his own person. Lucio's charges do have, however, a peculiarly unsettling effect on Vincentio.

Although he is astonishingly calm in meeting the serious crises of the play, the Duke is quite exasperated by Lucio's slanders, and reacts to them with rare intensity:

> No might nor greatness in mortality
> Can censure 'scape; back-wounding calumny
> The whitest virtue strikes. What king so strong
> Can tie the gall up in the slanderous tongue?
>   (III.ii.174–77)

Vincentio is still brooding over Lucio's charges in the next scene, at Mariana's moated grange:

> O place and greatness, millions of false eyes
> Are stuck upon thee; volumes of report
> Run with these false, and most contrarious quest
> Upon thy doings; thousand escapes of wit
> Make thee the father of their idle dream,
> And rack thee in their fancies.   (IV.i.59–64) [25]

Does the Duke protest too much? Certainly his rancor is little diminished at the end of the play when he singles out Lucio:

> And yet here's one in place I cannot pardon.
> You, sirrah, that knew me for a fool, a coward,
> One of all luxury, an ass, a madman,
> Wherein have I so deserved of you
> That you extol me thus?   (v.i.495–99)

The Duke's response, when he is so offended by Lucio's inventions that the single rogue proliferates in his imagination into "millions of false eyes" and "volumes of report," is part of his broader concern with how he is observed by others. The plan to deputize Angelo includes the desire to keep his "nature never in the sight / To do it slander" (I.iii.42–43). This fear of being seen in an unfavorable

25. Most editors agree with Lever that this soliloquy completes the one quoted just above, and that it has been separated, perhaps by someone other than Shakespeare, from its "proper place in III.ii" (Introduction to Arden ed., p. xxi) to give the Duke something to say while Isabella and Mariana plan offstage their strategy for dealing with Angelo's lust. Lever notes that "the actor taking the Duke's part must have been required to deliver these lines with exceptional slowness and deliberation" (p. xxii). Whether this "crude attempt to fill up a gap" (p. xxi) is the work of Shakespeare or someone else, however, it is consistent with the Duke's response to Lucio that the concern expressed in these lines should come to mind when Vincentio finds himself alone.

light by his subjects is earlier explained as an aversion to public display altogether:

> I love the people,
> But do not like to stage me to their eyes;
> Though it do well, I do not relish well
> Their loud applause and aves vehement,
> Nor do I think the man of safe discretion
> That does affect it.   (1.i.67–72)

This declaration of modesty, however, which he restates a little later for Friar Thomas, is not substantiated by the Duke's subsequent activity, which culminates when he stages himself triumphantly before the people in the last scene. Here Vincentio's chief concern seems to be, not with avoiding public display, but with the need "to stage me to their eyes" in an image of himself over which he has full control.

Vincentio's sensitivity to how he is seen by others connects his love for "the life removed" (I.iii.8), his plan to hide behind the actions of Angelo, his disguise as a holy friar, his vehement response to Lucio's slanders, and his self-dramatization as benevolent ruler in the last act. The other side of this preoccupation with how he is looked at is his pervasive involvement in the play as a "looker-on" who not only watches but stages the actions of others. He participates in the action mainly as spectator and stage manager, hiding his own person in disguise while closely observing others as they respond to conditions of stress he has himself done much to create. I am not convinced that the play is designed to reveal the Duke as a character who manipulates "his subjects as puppets for the fun of making them twitch" (*Complex Words*, p. 283), although Empson makes that case persuasively. But I do think that in order to keep the Duke free of conflicts from which he will rescue his fellow characters, the comic design of the play adapts a psychological maneuver psychoanalysis has discovered in persons who live vicariously through the experience of others. Otto Fenichel writes that "the longing to substitute looking for acting makes persons who are in conflict about whether or not to follow some impulse long for someone else to perform the act." Such persons achieve a "release from responsibility" for actions they are themselves driven toward, but experience only through an identification with other persons whom they arrange to have perform the ambivalently regarded act for them.[26] In order to present Vincentio as the ideal ruler of Vienna, Shakespeare displaces conflict away from the central figure and into the world around him. Angelo, Claudio, Isabella, and other characters come to experience life within scenarios the Duke has arranged and which he closely observes. Vincentio is freed from involvement in, and personal responsibility for, motives realized in the actions of others.

Vincentio's role is remarkably like that of the dramatist who transforms his inner life into the action of his play. Francis Ferguson has persuasively argued that the Duke is a "figure for Shakespeare himself," who, like his creator, reveals "human life itself as a dream or masquerade."[27] But Vincentio, as a character in that play, is largely bereft of an inner life. It is as if the substantial life that might have been gathered into the conception of Vincentio's role is found unacceptable and emptied into his surroundings. If, with Ferguson, we grant that the Duke is in some sense a "figure for Shakespeare," we can get a glimpse of the mixed purposes served by the play for its author. In *Measure for Measure* Shakespeare conveys a deeply conflicted attitude toward sexuality comparable to those expressed in situations of crisis by Hamlet or Othello or Lear. But where Shakespeare uses the tragic hero to absorb the burden of that attitude through his catastrophic fate, he attempts in *Measure for Measure* to distance himself from conflict through the characterization of Vincentio.

Lucio's fanaticism for slandering Vincentio—"I am a kind of burr; I shall stick" (IV.iii.174)—fits with this as a kind of residual protest emerging from Shakespeare against his own dramatic strategies. So, perhaps, does Barnardine, whose drunken refusal to "consent to die this day" (IV.iii.52–53) represents the bottom line of human intractability before Vincentio's moralized comic goals. Lucio, who stridently insists that those qualities are in Vincentio that the comic design of the play is determined to keep out of him, attempts to serve Iago's purpose of cutting the larger-than-life figure of authority down to size. Although Lucio's charges are not in any ordinary sense true, his irrational tenacity in attacking the Duke suggests the dra-

26. *The Psychoanalytic Theory of Neurosis* (New York: Norton, 1945), pp. 348–49.

27. *The Human Image in Dramatic Literature* (New York: Doubleday Anchor Books, 1957), pp. 143, 141.

matic emptiness of Vincentio's characterization, as if through Lucio Shakespeare is obliquely trying to fill a void he has created at the heart of the play. In *As You Like It,* the disguised Rosalind looks out onto the lives of others in Arden forest and finds experience continuous with her own: "Alas, poor shepherd! Searching of thy wound, / I have my hard adventure found mine own" (II.iv.40–41). The disguised Vincentio becomes a "looker-on here in Vienna, / Where I have seen corruption boil and bubble / Till it o'errun the stew" (V.i.315–17). But his manipulation and his looking are the only links between that world he observes and his private experience the comic design can tolerate. The separation of the aloof Duke from his subjects seems to be necessary if deep conflict between sexual degradation and morality in *Measure for Measure,* a conflict rendered most sharply in Angelo's experience, is not to usurp entirely the possibility of establishing comic order. But this separation is a precarious one in relation to the powerful trend in this play to identify a shared core of human experience.

In reaching high and low into various sectors of Viennese life, *Measure for Measure* stresses qualities and interests linking all groups. An important way of dramatizing common bonds underlying divergent experience is deputation.[28] Angelo's authority substitutes for Vincentio's in governing Vienna; Mariana's body replaces Isabella's as the object of Angelo's lust; Barnardine's head is designated to substitute for Claudio's—"O, death's a great disguiser" (IV.ii.169)—and the head of Ragozine, who "died this morning of a cruel fever" (IV.iii.67), replaces Barnardine's to satisfy Angelo's desire to have Claudio's execution confirmed; even Elbow has been deputized to serve as constable for men in his ward with less "wit in such matters" (II.i.253). Deputation often suggests a common base of humanity in weakness before the power of the flesh. Escalus tries to persuade the still chaste Angelo to recognize in Claudio an image of his own suppressed "affections," and that recognition Angelo soon has forced upon him. But Vincentio's deputation of Angelo serves

28. Robert Rogers finds that the "substitution motif in the play points to the presence of doubles" (*A Psychoanalytic Study of the Double in Literature* [Detroit: Wayne State University Press, 1970], p. 74). "All things considered," Rogers concludes, "the Duke would seem to be the whole father, of which Escalus and Angelo and the Duke-as-Friar are but fragments" (p. 75).

the opposite purpose: to separate characters who at first seem in important ways to mirror each other.

The Duke's announcement that Angelo will replace him in his absence from Vienna includes an incongruously special intensity of expectation. He asks of Escalus:

> What figure of us think you he will bear?
> For you must know, we have with special soul
> Elected him our absence to supply,
> Lent him our terror, dressed him with our love,
> And given his deputation all the organs
> Of our own power. What think you of it?   (1.i.16–21)

He urges Angelo toward self-fulfillment in public service with an argument that recalls Shakespeare's plea in the early sonnets that his young friend should marry. In Sonnet 4, Shakespeare presents a metaphorical complex of images drawn from nature and usury typical of many of the sonnets that urge the friend to perpetuate his loveliness through children:

> Unthrifty loveliness, why dost thou spend
> Upon thyself thy beauty's legacy?
> Nature's bequest gives nothing but doth lend,
> And, being frank, she lends to those are free.

The same complex of images informs Vincentio's appeal that Angelo reinvest his virtue in public action:

> Thyself and thy belongings
> Are not thine own so proper, as to waste
> Thyself upon thy virtues, they on thee. . . .
>   Spirits are not finely touched
> But to fine issues, nor Nature never lends
> The smallest scruple of her excellence
> But like a thrifty goddess she determines
> Herself the glory of a creditor,
> Both thanks and use.   (1.i.29–31; 35–40)

In the *Sonnets*, Shakespeare's plea that the young man marry soon gives way to adoring identification with him. After urging Angelo to realize in political action the virtue he has kept to himself, Vincentio edges deputation toward identification:

> In our remove be thou at full ourself.
> Mortality and mercy in Vienna
> Live in thy tongue and heart.   (I.i.43–45)

The trust he invests in Angelo appears absolute, the basis for a thorough identification of his own person with Angelo's rule:

> Your scope is as mine own,
> So to enforce or qualify the laws
> As to your soul seems good.   (I.i.64–66)

Angelo is a "leavened and preparèd choice" (I.i.51), selected after scrupulous consideration because he is best equipped to govern the city in accordance with Vincentio's wishes and to be a fitting "figure" for the Duke himself.

In the Duke's next appearance, however, as he prepares to take on his disguise, Vincentio retracts this identification, distancing himself from Angelo's acts and their probable consequences. He explains to Friar Thomas that Angelo has been appointed so that his habitual severity will put force back into "strict statutes" (I.iii.19) that have been neglected during his own "permissive" (I.iii.38) rule. Rather than to provide a figure of the Duke's self, the substitution is designed to correct a "fault" (I.iii.35) in his own rule, and to protect Vincentio from the resentment he predicts will result from the harshness of Angelo,

> Who may, in th' ambush of my name, strike home,
> And yet my nature never in the sight
> To do it slander.   (I.iii.41–43)

Vincentio also reveals a keen interest in how the puritanical Angelo will bear up under his new responsibilities:

> Lord Angelo is precise,
> Stands at a guard with envy; scarce confesses
> That his blood flows, or that his appetite
> Is more to bread than stone. Hence shall we see,
> If power change purpose, what our seemers be.
> (I.iii.50–54)

These remarks are offered as a reason for the Duke's action, suggesting that Angelo is being set up for self-betrayal. Vincentio is expressly eager to catch Angelo out in a corruption of his lofty principles.

This scene begins, however, with remarks that link the Duke and his deputy in yet another way. In a passage quoted earlier for its relation to *Othello*, Vincentio assures Friar Thomas that his "complete bosom" cannot be penetrated by the paltry weaponry of love. Within his very different personal style, Vincentio's disdain for the "aims and ends / Of burning youth" connects with Angelo's reluctance to admit that his youthful blood flows. Both protestations, the one the Duke ascribes to Angelo and the one he offers for himself, serve the same purpose: they declare the man invulnerable to the "dribbling dart of love." Such a disavowal is precisely what leads Angelo into extraordinary confrontation with what seems to him an alien and terrible force within himself. He pays for his aspirations to asexual purity with a vengeance. But what about the Duke? How does the subsequent behavior of his deputy come to reflect on him?

After suggesting relations between Vincentio and Angelo that hold the promise of developing in several different directions, the play moves through an action that completes some possibilities by suppressing others. The tensions among the various ways Vincentio regards the deputation of Angelo create the possibility for a dramatic action generated by deeply conflicted impulses within the Duke. But the potential complexity of the Duke's characterization is sacrificed to the effort to affirm his moral purity.

The degradation of Angelo, like the humiliation of Bertram in *All's Well*, seems to include a kind of vengeful repudiation of the hold over Shakespeare's imagination exercised by the fair friend in the *Sonnets*. Empson connects Angelo's corruption, like carrion "lying by the violet in the sun," with the "lilies that fester" in Sonnet 94.[29] Early in the last act, with hidden mockery, Vincentio again addresses Angelo with language that echoes the *Sonnets*, this time those poems that would rescue the friend from "Devouring Time" (19):

> O, your desert speaks loud, and I should wrong it
> To lock it in the wards of covert bosom,

29. Empson sees Angelo as "an extreme, perhaps not very credible, example of the cold person and the lily," the unmoved mover, subject to corruption, of Sonnet 94 (*Some Versions of Pastoral* [1935; reprint ed. New York: New Directions, 1960], pp. 105–6). Seen from this perspective, Angelo would seem to draw upon a very different dimension of the *Sonnets* from that suggested by Bertram.

> When it deserves with characters of brass
> A forted residence 'gainst the tooth of time
> And razure of oblivion.   (v.i.9–13) [30]

But by this time all traces of Vincentio's personal investment in Angelo have been erased. The rich web of mutually contradictory connections that complicate Vincentio's early efforts to articulate his relation to Angelo has given way to a simple moral polarization. The impulse to idealize the friend of the *Sonnets* is turned back in *Measure for Measure* into idealization of the Duke. The self-depreciation that often accompanies the poet's effort to exalt the friend is projected into the experience of Angelo's self-degradation. Instead of providing a "figure" for the Duke who "can my part in him advertize" (I.i.41), Angelo, with his fall into sensuality, is separated to the opposite extreme from Vincentio as the ideal of wise rule. With the completion of the comic design, Vincentio's "part" in Angelo is no longer part of himself, no longer corresponds to anything in Shakespeare's characterization of the Duke.

Shakespeare, in short, uses Angelo as a scapegoat who suffers in his person the consequences of a conflict Vincentio is thereby spared.[31] This scapegoat strategy culminates in the final scene; its

30. Empson argues that "the obvious uses of the language of the Sonnets about Angelo all come in the first definition of his character by the Duke; once started like this he goes off on his own" (*Pastoral*, p. 107). But the key words in the passage quoted—*desert, bosom* (as container), *characters of brass, tooth of time, razure,* and *oblivion*—strongly recall the language of those sonnets to the friend that address the threat of time. See especially Sonnets 19, 25, 55, 63, 64, 65, 122. It seems a peculiarly Empsonian irony that Angelo should be mockingly offered the eternity of brass, which is itself scoffed at in the *Sonnets*, as in 64:

> When I have seen by Time's fell hand defaced
> The rich proud cost of outworn buried age,
> When sometime lofty towers I see down-rased
> And brass eternal slave to mortal rage; . . .

31. Hans Sachs posed the question: "Did Shakespeare really want to exempt his hero, the Duke, from all contamination of the wickedness around him?"—and came up with a way of seeing Vincentio directly opposite to the view I have developed in this chapter. Sachs regarded Vincentio's proposal to Isabella as the ironic equivalent of Angelo's sexual coercion: "so commits the Duke, in a legitimate and honorable way, the crime which Angelo attempted in vain." Sachs believed that the Duke put Isabella—who would "prefer to go back to the convent from which she was drawn, much against her will, by her brother's peril"—in a position that makes it impossible for her to decline his offer. ("The Measure in *Measure for Measure*," in *The*

essential emblem is the broken Angelo humiliated before the exalted presence of the Duke. But this arrangement simply extends as a moralized resolution a conflict between idealization and degradation that has troubled the entire play. The whole play is in this sense like Angelo, who cannot integrate an obsessive concern with sexuality into an ideal of moral order. The discrepancy between the Duke's wise authority and Lucio's slanderous accusations mirrors the division in Angelo's person between an idealized moral self and the return of repressed desire in the form of debased sexuality. In a still larger sense, Vincentio's relation to Viennese corruption mirrors the conflict that breaks Angelo; what is *in* Angelo *surrounds* the Duke. The use of Angelo as a scapegoat leaves the conflict itself untouched. Vincentio, who represents the ideal paternal self Angelo aspired to become, is the symbolic center of a moral design he imposes on the play; but Shakespeare's idealization of Vincentio's manhood is the most significant indication of the intensity of conflict that qualifies the comic action. As the play turns away from the rich potential for human encounter suggested in the early characterization of Vincentio, the architect of the comic design becomes its unacknowledged victim as well. Shakespeare strands Vincentio in a kind of allegorical no-man's-land, a shadowy figure of justice tempered with mercy, but a lover without plausible desire, a father with no children, a renouncer with nothing in him to renounce, an empty center precariously holding at a distance, rather than holding together, the teeming life that threatens to overwhelm it.

Ghostly Fathers and Spectral Women

ANGELO   *Be that you are,*
That is, a woman; if you be more, you're none.
(ii.iv.134–35)

The tragedies, like *Measure for Measure*, typically center on the experience of a male protagonist. But the tragic protagonist's effort to control his life invariably leads to his own destruction. Vincentio seems to represent Shakespeare's attempt to achieve comic control over conflicts resembling those that overwhelm figures of masculine

Design Within, ed. M. D. Faber [New York: Science House, 1970], pp. 495–96.)

authority in the tragedies. Among Shakespeare's other comedies, there are only two plays comparably dominated by the controlling efforts of a male character—*The Taming of the Shrew,* written very early in his career, and *The Tempest,* written at the very end of it. Although I am not certain that even *The Tempest* includes drama as powerful or as ambitious as that of *Measure for Measure,* both *Shrew* and *The Tempest* deftly integrate psychological conflict into comic action. The relation of action to conflict in these two plays at either end of Shakespeare's career, and in plays from the tragic period, can help clarify the tension between comic design and disruptive psychological developments in *Measure for Measure.*

However subtle and mutually rewarding the final relation of Petruchio and Kate may be in *Shrew,* it is made possible by Petruchio's powerful masculine presence. What is presented as the rich womanhood of Kate in the final scene cannot come into being in the world of her bumbling father and the timid courtiers of Padua. Petruchio's male power and cunning rescue Kate's own considerable strength from the perverse refuge she takes in shrewishness. The action of the play obligingly accommodates Petruchio's social and sexual ambitions. He triumphs not only over Kate but among his friends, who look on with awe at the end of the play when Kate publicly verifies his manly dominance. The play projects a youthful wish for social and sexual triumph free from anxiety, for a mastery unqualified by fears and doubts and illusions, not only through the prospect of bedding Kate, but through the pleasure of being recognized as victor, of having boldly conquered in an endeavor others are too fearful even to attempt. It is the stuff daydreams are made on.[32]

Petruchio's success is minimally disguised oedipal triumph divorced from the anxieties of oedipal conflict. He acknowledges the liberating effect of his father's death:

32. In *Shrew,* Coppélia Kahn persuasively argues, "Shakespeare allows the male to indulge his dream of total mastery over the female without the real-life penalties of her resentment and guilt" ("*The Taming of the Shrew*: Shakespeare's Mirror of Marriage," *Modern Language Studies,* 5 [Spring 1975]: 88). In Kahn's reading, the "greatest irony" in *Shrew* is that it "satirizes not woman herself in the person of the shrew, but male attitudes toward women" (p. 89). I am not sure, however, that either of these possibilities accounts for the main force of Petruchio's wit, which seems to invite an audience to participate in the release of strong feeling it makes possible—in Kate as well as in himself—more than to see him as the object of satiric irony.

> Antonio my father is deceased,
> And I have thrust myself into this maze,
> Haply to wife and thrive as best I may.   (I.ii.52–54)

Baptista, rather than oppose Petruchio's quest for his daughter, urges the bold suitor to speedy action. All the resistance to the marriage is concentrated into Kate's shrewishness, which Petruchio brashly subordinates to his overriding desire to "wive it wealthily in Padua" (I.ii.73). The triumph of the play lies in Petruchio's power to exploit his sexual aggressiveness to evade fears and confusions that will greatly complicate the lives of later comic heroes. Petruchio's long-range significance, however, is that the model of love by male conquest he embodies very soon drops out of the maturing world of Shakespeare's comedy, to be replaced by such forceful, loving heroines as Portia and Rosalind.[33]

With the partial and difficult exception of *Cymbeline*, the late romances are characterized by a shift of emphasis away from the experience of young love dramatized in the earlier comedies through *All's Well*. In these late plays, often centering on an older generation with children of their own, a special place is occupied by fathers. Prospero's role is unique, however, even in the changed world of the late romances, because of the extraordinary control he exerts over the action of *The Tempest*.[34] Ousted from his dukedom while too busy to attend to politics, Prospero turns into an awesome source of power the very art that has made him vulnerable to the ambitions of his trusted and *de facto* deputized brother. He controls the minute-by-minute action of *The Tempest* with a domination unprecedented in Shakespearean drama except, to a degree, for Iago,

---

33. I discuss this transformation of Shakespearean comedy in the second part of ch. 4.

34. By contrast, Pericles' efforts to act significantly and forcefully quickly give way to flight, and flight to loss and suffering passively endured. He plays no active role in recovering his lost daughter, his lost wife, or his lost place in the world, which are all restored to him by forces beyond any power that resides in him. Cymbeline is helpless in relation to his cruel and deceitful wife, and when near tragic consequences follow from his indecisive presence, Shakespeare must call in Jupiter to reorder the bizarre developments of this play. Leontes' violent jealousy costs him his wife, his son, his newly born daughter, his beloved friend, and his most trusted counselor. Only sixteen years of grief, carefully overseen by Paulina, can win him new access to those lost who remain alive.

Prospero's sinister counterpart as on-stage director of the action.[35]

But the drama over which Prospero presides springs directly from his place in the play. The movement through revenge motives to rather testy forgiveness, the intensity of feeling in the difficult relation to Caliban, the surrender of the beloved daughter to Ferdinand, the ultimate subordination of Prospero's awesome powers to the larger and still more potent rhythms of life—in all these contexts the center of experience is in Prospero, who struggles with himself as much as with his surroundings. In Prospero, as Norman Holland has written,

> we find Shakespeare dealing with the impulses of childhood in their latest development, the father's love for a daughter and his resentment of a son-in-law, one recapitulating the child's love for his mother, the other the last version of a child's aggression toward his father or older brother.[36]

One may go on to observe, as Holland does, that these impulses are projected into other characters whom Prospero, like a "writer-director," moves "through a plot toward catharsis" (p. 337). But in *The Tempest*, projection clarifies, rather than denies; it binds Prospero to other characters instead of putting him on a different, more protected, plane of experience. Where Vincentio denies all connections that would link him to Angelo or Lucio or Pompey, Prospero turns to Caliban in the last act and declares: "this thing of darkness I / Acknowledge mine" (V.i.275–76). Lines of tension radiating through the entire body of experience presented in *The Tempest* originate and reconverge in Prospero's experience.

The Taming of the Shrew is about filial assertion and triumph. *The Tempest* is about paternal renunciation, the renunciation that Lear refused, and that Prospero turns into intensely powerful drama. *The Tempest*, for all the charm of its excursions into elegant fantasy, dramatizes a tough and rigorous awareness of familial and social conflict. *Shrew* elaborates a rather easy fantasy of oedipal conquest. But both *Shrew* and *The Tempest* proceed from bases of feeling fully realized in the actions of these plays. In *Measure for Measure*,

35. Stanley Edgar Hyman discusses Iago and Prospero together as evil and benign "metaphor[s] for the artist" in *Iago: Some Approaches to the Illusion of His Motivation* (New York: Atheneum, 1970), pp. 61–100.

36. *Psychoanalysis and Shakespeare* (New York: McGraw-Hill, 1966), p. 337.

deep conflict does not respond fully to the center of comic control. Vincentio's role is comparable to Prospero's only in regard to the control each exerts. Vincentio is himself less realized as a center of feeling than as an escape from feeling more powerfully expressed in the experience of others. His experience, rather than unifying the play, becomes the hidden locus for its deepest inner division. Shakespeare's attempt to control comic action in *Measure for Measure* with a male character and some factors that qualify the success of this effort become clearer when set against roughly contemporaneous developments in the tragedies.

In tragedies written in the period that also produced *Measure for Measure*, the quest for ideal masculine autonomy in a context of paternal heritage produces profound conflict, localized in the action of the tragic protagonist and leading to his destruction. In *Hamlet*, the need to retrieve paternal authority by identification with it creates dramatic tension at the center of the action. Hamlet attempts to take into his own person—to the exclusion of all else—an image of the self derived from the injunctions of his dead father's ghost. But this compulsive and ambivalently regarded effort becomes a deeply self-destructive part of Hamlet's tragic struggle. In *Measure for Measure*, the "ghostly father" Vincentio who "returns" to Vienna is offered as the comic resolution of tensions developed in the play. The idealization of the Duke represents an attempt to reconstruct outside the sphere of conflict an image of the father as wise, good, powerful, and forgiving, an anchor of purity and strength in a world that has otherwise tumbled headlong into corruption. Hamlet is divided within *himself* in a personal struggle that includes protecting and identifying with the ideal image of his father while responding also to pressures of his own flesh and spirit. *Measure for Measure* is divided within *itself* by Shakespeare's attempt to protect and identify with an ideal of paternal authority while responding also to the flesh and spirit of a very worldly Vienna.

A condition, however, of embodying a benign paternal image in the watchful Vincentio is to disembody Vincentio himself. His fatherhood, in order not to be pawn to profound conflict in this drama of sexual corruptibility, must be "ghostly." To keep the Duke aloof from conflict that originates in the antagonistic overlapping of sexuality and family ties, he must be stripped of family ties and sexuality. The effort to elevate the strong and merciful father empties him of his substance, displacing his potential life into his surroundings. *Measure for Measure* ends with an ideal masculine authority about to marry a chaste wife, a bond that in *Hamlet* is relegated to Hamlet's idealized memory of an irretrievable past. The tension between the closing marriage proposal of Vincentio to Isabella and the effort throughout *Measure for Measure* to insulate the Duke from family ties and from conflicted relations to women may be clarified when set against the tragic design of *Macbeth*.

The crimes Macbeth commits disrupt the transmission of family heritage: the murder of the paternal king Duncan, who has just named his own son successor; the murder of Banquo, intended to include Banquo's son as well, in an effort to thwart the line of royal succession prophesied by the witches; the murder of Macduff's "wife, his babes, and all unfortunate souls / That trace him in his line" (IV.i.152–53). These murders proceed from stresses on Macbeth's sense of his own manhood generated in encounters with potent female presences. The idea of the first crime is crystalized by the three witches; it can be committed because of the strength Macbeth finds by provoking and then attaching himself to the fierce determination of his wife, as if he is nurtured by the gall she summons to her woman's breasts.[37] As Macbeth withdraws from that merger (and simultaneously expels his wife from it) he becomes increasingly dependent upon reassurances he constructs out of his next exchange with the witches, who produce apparitions—"an Armed Head," "a Bloody Child," "a Child Crowned," and the "show of eight Kings and Banquo" (IV.i.)—that concentrate images of savage masculinity, familial violence, infantile fantasies of omnipotence, and royal succession dispersed throughout the entire play.

Macbeth belongs at the play's beginning to an ordered hierarchy of all-male relations and masculine values. In that order, subjects are ideally obedient sons who fulfill themselves in service to a paternal king:

> The service and the loyalty I owe,
> In doing pays itself. Your Highness' part

37. Simon O. Lesser observes that Macbeth "skillfully enlists and uses his wife's help" in order to sidestep a severe superego, but gives little attention to the nature of the help Lady Macbeth provides, in "*Macbeth*: Drama and Dream," in *The Whispered Meanings*, ed. Robert Sprich and Richard W. Noland (Amherst: University of Massachusetts Press, 1977), p. 220.

> Is to receive our duties, and our duties
> Are to your throne and state children and servants,
> Which do but what they should by doing everything
> Safe toward your love and honor.   (I.iv.22–27)

Within this masculine order—the vulnerability of which is made clear at the outset by the rebellion of the original Thane of Cawdor —a son's desire to destroy and replace the father is displaced away from the king and into the violence of battle undertaken to serve him. The "single state of man" (I.iii.140) Macbeth has achieved through service to that order is shattered by a new image of manhood catalyzed by the witches and nurtured into action by Lady Macbeth. The witches and Lady Macbeth, who exist outside this order though they are shaped by it, blur its boundaries, distort its rules, and attack its center. Before Macbeth can act on the patricidal desire suppressed by the male order but animated at the very center of his being by the witches' "supernatural soliciting" (I.iii.130), an alternative image of manhood must be sanctioned by Lady Macbeth. Macbeth will "dare do all that may become a man," but Lady Macbeth must extend the idea of manhood so that his new ambition can be assimilated to it:

> What beast was't then
> That made you break this enterprise to me?
> When you durst do it, then you were a man;
> And to be more than what you were, you would
> Be so much more the man.   (I.vii.46–51)

As Macbeth becomes enslaved to aspirations of this form of self-completion, he is desperately alienated both from his wife and from values generated by ideals of male society, "as honor, love, obedience, troops of friends" (V.iii.25), until he is left ultimately with nothing but a private fantasy of his own indestructibility. When Macbeth murders Duncan he destroys, both in himself and in Scotland, a world based on trust in male bonds. Duncan's dead body becomes a grotesque emblem of the world Macbeth brings into being; those who view his corpse see the sight-destroying spectacle of a "new Gorgon" (II.iii.68)—a body simultaneously monstrous and female, castrated and castrating, murdered and raped. The violence and sexual ambiguity suggested by the Gorgon-like corpse reflect deep sexual tension precariously held in check by the ideal male order. In the world of masculine loyalty and service over which Duncan has presided, individual achievement nourishes the whole system: "And in his commendations I am fed," Duncan says of Macbeth, "It is a banquet to me" (I.iv.55–56). Duncan's murder transforms that ideal into an unnatural world in which horses "eat each other" (II.iv.18) and in which Macbeth's actual banquet feeds no one. The imagery of mutual nourishment set, on the one hand, against mutual devouring, and, on the other, against the violent interruption of nurture, recreates infantile experience in which benign relations of infant to nurturing mother yield to fears of maternal violence and deprivation. Macbeth creates a Scotland that "cannot / Be called our mother but our grave" (IV.iii.165–66). But taking up maternal nurture into the ideal of patriarchal bonds itself rests on and conceals a deep fear of actual maternal power that spreads in *Macbeth* into a generalized fear of women.

The figures who will be chiefly responsible for reestablishing the legitimacy of royal, patriarchal heritage are thoroughly and brutally insulated from the potential contamination that has made a monster of Macbeth. Not only are Macduff's wife and children murdered, but he is that mysterious man not "of woman born," from his "mother's womb / Untimely ripped" (V.viii.13, 15–16), and hence, in the play's symbolic logic, motherless. He comes to have, in short, no place in the line of generations whatever—no mother, no father, no wife, no children. Macduff is thus qualified to kill Macbeth, who will be succeeded by someone else, by Malcolm, the son of a royal father violently murdered. Significantly, Malcolm is initially suspected of murdering his father in order that, when this suspicion is proved unfounded, the paricidal impulse may be symbolically purged through his eventual, legitimate assumption of the crown. Malcolm is, furthermore, the son of a mother, also dead, who "Oft'ner upon her knees than on her feet, / Died every day she lived" (IV.iii.110–11). The son of this "most sainted king" (IV.iii.109) and this most saintly mother—symbolically the child of something approximating virgin birth—is himself "yet / Unknown to woman" (IV.iii.125–26), and his virginity is offered as one of his qualifications to rule. Malcolm apparently will father no son to succeed him as king; the kingship will pass to the male descendants of Banquo, another father murdered by Macbeth, whose ghost returns to unman the murderer.

The kingship is thus purged of the evil Macbeth has brought to it by its radical isolation from all possible strife that can arise in familial relationships, which the play associates with the destructiveness of women. The only protection against violence that originates in family ties is produced by the violent destruction of family ties from without. But that destructiveness derives from stresses within family bonds; the separation asserted by the play marks a dramatic, not a psychological, distinction. Macbeth murders a father, another father whose son gets away, a mother and her children; in battle he slays the son of Siward in the play's final sacrifice to the patriarchal ideal of heroic manhood: "Had I as many sons as I have hairs, / I would not wish them to a fairer death" (V.viii.48–49). Symbolically all the victims belong to the same family; dramatically they belong to families whose survivors can avenge their deaths by destroying Macbeth. Each murder Macbeth commits sharpens the stark symbolic design that will make his own defeat possible.

The burden of instigating internal strife, of turning violence inward upon the family and its political extension in the royal, patriarchal state, is placed upon women. The play expresses a deep fear of women as transgressors of masculine autonomy and power grounded in the patriarchal order. The object of this fearfulness is given its emblem in Lady Macbeth's sacrifice of the nurturing maternal bond to a violent masculinity that will be achieved by her and for her through the actions of her husband:

> I have given suck, and know
> How tender 'tis to love the babe that milks me:
> I would, while it was smiling in my face,
> Have plucked my nipple from his boneless gums
> And dashed the brains out, had I so sworn as you
> Have done to this.   (I.vii.54–59)

Fear of the destructiveness potentially present in family bonds is here localized in a powerful woman's violent fantasy of destroying the most basic family bond, an infant's relation to a mother. But Lady Macbeth's repudiation of her maternal self is also an assertion of the demonic maternal role she assumes toward Macbeth, just as the destructive force she directs toward Duncan represents an attempt simultaneously to destroy and participate in the patriarchal order. "Had he not resembled / My father as he slept, I had done't" (II.ii.12–13), Lady Macbeth observes, but she longs to do it precisely because Duncan represents the father's exclusionary power in the patriarchal family.

Macbeth must become her child in order to destroy the father who represents the patriarchal order and to be the husband through whose experience she desires to fulfill herself in a brutal new version of that order. As she empties herself into the fierce masculine ambition of her husband, she completes Macbeth's directive to her:

> Bring forth men-children only;
> For thy undaunted mettle should compose
> Nothing but males. (i.vii.72–74)

Lady Macbeth's infanticidal fantasy and her active identification with her husband's patricide are generated by tension between the exclusion of women from idealized patriarchal bonds and the actual place of women as mothers at the center of family-based feeling. The relations of Macbeth to his wife and the witches concentrate the fears, hatreds, and aspirations engendered in the bond of mother and son in patriarchal society. Through Lady Macbeth and the witches, Macbeth is endowed with a desperate manhood that serves a fantasy of omnipotent power: "Laugh to scorn / The pow'r of man, for none of woman born / Shall harm Macbeth" (IV.i.79–81). But this fantasy, engendered by the witches, remains dependent throughout on the infantile base of Macbeth's bond to those female presences, who share in the demonic, seductive motherhood of Lady Macbeth. In a violent circularity characteristic of this play, the destructiveness they nurture in Macbeth in turn confirms the fear of women's power that the ideal of patriarchy defends against.

I think these developments in *Macbeth* can help explain why the most powerful drama in *Measure for Measure* springs from disturbed relations across sexual boundaries; why *Measure for Measure*, unlike any comedy between *The Taming of the Shrew* and *The Tempest*, is so thoroughly grounded in a comic movement engineered by a male character; and why that comic design strikes so many as unsatisfactory. In *Macbeth* there is little concern with sexuality as an activity uniting man and woman, though the porter jokes about lechery and impotence, and though Malcolm must ritualistically take on the attribute of bottomless "voluptousness" (IV.iii.61) in testing Macduff, before feigned lust gives way to the revelation of true virginity. But Macbeth does dwell centrally on sexual roles; its violence springs from their transgression, the disruption of idealized masculine order by women. *Measure for Measure*, because it is a comedy, brings the social dimension of sexual release into the foreground of its action. But the instinctual conflict that dominates that play proceeds from a psychological core it shares with *Macbeth*. *Macbeth* dramatizes conflict between patriarchal authority and individual aspiration as it generates violence; *Measure for Measure* dramatizes conflict between patriarchal authority and individual desire as it generates sexual degradation. In both cases, the fear of chaos erupting within an ideal masculine order of society and the self points toward a fearful attitude toward women and the responses they engender in men. Macbeth and Angelo are jolted into awareness of alien but essential inner dimensions of the self by confrontations with women; each betrays a vulnerable ideal of manly selfhood to pursue impulses that cannot be denied and cannot be integrated into that self. Malcolm and Vincentio are protected from such psychic disintegration by being isolated from ties of family and sexuality that disrupt the inner order of the self in relations to women; each is thus enabled to reestablish the shattered ideal of social and moral authority.

In *Macbeth*, the tragic outcome proceeds from the cunning "equivocations" of the weird sisters and the seductive power of Lady Macbeth. The disintegration of Macbeth absorbs the force of the play's powerful conflicts, which are played out tragically through the release of his violence and mastered by an action that culminates in his death. Malcolm, who belongs to an ideal order that frames the play, not to its destructive center, is symbolically essential but dramatically secondary. Vincentio, by contrast, increasingly comes to dominate *Measure for Measure* just when the drama has become most intense, thinning out its density with his pervasive, idealized presence. *Measure for Measure* is guided to its comic conclusion by a character whose essence is the denial of family ties and sexuality, the denial, that is to say, of the essence of comedy.

Angelo, when he decides to enforce the law that punishes fornication with death, literalizes one version of an otherwise unstated but undeniable imperative that sets the rules for tragic action in Shakespeare. Relations to women—overpowering women like Lady Macbeth and Volumnia, but also women like Desdemona and Cordelia—are invariably sources of destruction, usually of mutual destruction, in the tragedies. Shakespeare checks the movement of *Measure for Measure* toward a tragic outcome, but can find no way effectively to purge the play of the destructive imperative lodged in its deep base of conflict. Instead the fearful attitude toward women is stabilized as the degradation of sexuality, generalized and displaced into the life of corrupt Vienna. It becomes the very space the play inhabits, and from which it is never released. The evil the witches boil and bubble in *Macbeth* comes to be concentrated in Macbeth's experience. The corruption Vincentio observes boils and bubbles in a cauldron that is Vienna itself; it is distributed throughout a dramatic space essentially unchanged by the action. This can be seen as a special aesthetic strength of *Measure for Measure* and has been an important source of the play's appeal to twentieth-century directors, who have often emphasized just this quality. But it is a strength that cannot easily be reconciled with the illusion of change and providential guidance superimposed upon the play by the Duke's connivances.

All these plays are haunted by an image of woman that no particular female character can embody. Some of her traits are approximated in different ways in Regan and Goneril, in Lady Macbeth, in Cressida, and in others. But the idea of woman that paralyzes Hamlet's will is never identical with Gertrude, certainly not with Ophelia, just as the woman whose sulphurous pit Lear rages against at Dover is not identical with, and does not come into existence with, Regan and Goneril—though they, like Cordelia, are deeply implicated in his fierce revulsion. The experience of the tragic protagonist is shaped by an imaginary specter of woman, outside the masculine order of law, who seduces, betrays, usurps, castrates, who melts Hamlet's virtue (*virtu*), who releases the tears that scald Lear "upon a wheel of fire" (IV.vii.47), who puts Othello's manhood at the mercy of "every puny whispster" (V.ii.245). She is an imaginary woman who ultimately demands death, and from whom life can be freed only by tragic action that sacrifices the most manly of men—and often the best of women—to her. She is the woman for whom Othello mistakes Desdemona, and whom he thinks he can kill by murdering his wife. In *Othello*, as in *King Lear*, the value of the woman who is a source of life and trust can only be fully realized after she is confused with, and sacrificed to, this spectral woman. In *Macbeth*, there is no room at the center of the action for the woman who gives life and love, and the dread female presence can be controlled only by re-establishment of an idealized masculine order. But throughout the period of the great tragedies, from *Hamlet* to *Coriolanus*, she is the specter that must be confronted; she represents a fear that can only be purged through violence; her presence calls for a world established only in the closure of tragic action. From the triumphant entry of Fortinbras to the last entrance of Octavius Caesar, no tragedy closes upon a stage that supports a living woman. The survival of Volumnia in Rome leads to the death of the "boy" Coriolanus in Corioli.

The effort to achieve comic closure in *Measure for Measure* becomes Shakespeare's attempt to circumvent rather than confront fully the specter that shapes symbolic action throughout the drama of the tragic period. In Claudio's bewildered mixture of truepenny loyalty to Juliet and his sense of guilty contamination, in moralist Angelo's desperate struggle with unacceptable and undeniable sexual drives, in Isabella's horror-stricken response to Angelo's assault on her virginity, in Lucio's strident espousal of a sexuality he makes disgusting, in Vincentio's deep longing for release from the urgencies of life expressed in his "be absolute for death" speech, and in Claudio's terror of death, Shakespeare appropriates for comedy ranges of experience commensurate with and often wider than the reach of the great tragedies. The power of *Measure for Measure* is in the dramatization of the felt experience of characters helplessly caught up in potentially tragic situations. But the attempt to resolve such situations through Vincentio fails to make meaningful as comedy the intensely rich drama it brings to a close.

When Lucio visits Isabella in the convent to report her brother's plight, he explains Claudio's crime this way:

> Fewness and truth, 'tis thus:
> Your brother and his lover have embraced;
> As those that feed grow full, as blossoming time
> That from the seedness the bare fallow brings
> To teeming foison, even so her plenteous womb
> Expresseth his full tilth and husbandry.
>
> (i.iv.39–44)

This striking evocation of the procreative process, almost untouched by the ironies with which Lucio elsewhere debases everything concerned with sexuality, points back both to the early stages of Shakespeare's response to the friend as potential creator of new life in the *Sonnets*[38] and to the imperative of earlier comedies to make the marriages that "people every town" (AYL V.iv.137).[39] In *Othello*, the connection Lucio makes through husbandry between human sexuality and nature is sacrificed to Iago's vicious imaging of a "black ram / . . . tupping your white ewe" (I.i.88–89) and to Othello's desperate attempt to give new birth to himself through his marriage to Desdemona. The movement into pastoral Bohemia in *The Winter's Tale* will redeem that play from the crude fantasies of Leontes' cuckolded imagination when the union of Perdita and Florizel is defined against a festive backdrop of "great creating nature" (IV.iv. 88). Comic drama before and after *Measure for Measure* celebrates the movement through the family from one generation to another. The tragedies violently interrupt that movement with disruptive gestures that originate in the family, but often, as in *King Lear*, the centrality of family bonds is confirmed by their destruction:

> Thou hast one daughter
> Who redeems Nature from the general curse
> Which twain have brought her to.   (IV.vi.201–3)

Even *Macbeth*, perhaps the most extreme dramatization of ambitions and fears generated in a family context, uses violence to clear a space for "Banquo's issue," to make "the seeds of Banquo kings" (III.i.65, 70).

In *Measure for Measure*, Lucio's description of procreation stands out in contrast not only to his habitual mode of thought but to the whole movement of the play. Juliet, the bearer of a child by Claudio, regards the "most offenseful act," the "sin that hath brought you to this shame" (II.iii.26, 31), with more dignity and balance than the disguised Duke who questions her about it: "I do repent me as it is an evil, / And take the shame with joy" (II.iii.35–36). But except for an appearance in the last scene, in which she neither speaks nor

---

38. Compare especially the imagery in lines 5–6 of Sonnet 3: "For where is she so fair whose uneared womb / Disdains the tillage of thy husbandry?"

39. Rosalind begins to think of Orlando as "my child's father" (AYL I.iii.11) almost as soon as they meet. Helena "feels her young one kick" (AWW V.iii.299) in the culmination of an action almost entirely concentrated on completing the relationship of a single young couple; in this respect, as in others, *All's Well* stands in a relation to the earlier comedies very different from that of *Measure for Measure*.

is spoken to, Juliet vanishes from the play after the second act. The only child important to the last act is Kate Keepdown's, who will be legitimized when Lucio is forced to marry "the rotten medlar" (IV. iii.169). This marriage, which on the Duke's instructions will be conducted in prison, is an appropriately debased culmination of the play's unpurged tension between sexuality and the moral order. The proposed marriage of Vincentio to Isabella, the ghostly father and the aspiring nun, is the appropriately barren culmination of the play's moralized comic design.

IV

"Since first we were dissevered":
Trust and Autonomy
in Shakespeare's Development

PRESSURES that tend to overburden comic form in the problem
comedies call attention to complex interrelations of genre, character, and psychological conflict throughout Shakespeare's development. In previous chapters I have often turned outward to other
plays to sharpen my focus on *All's Well That Ends Well* and *Measure for Measure*. Now I would like, in effect, to reverse that procedure, and sketch directly some perspectives on the larger world
of Shakespeare implicit in my attempt to clarify the special place
the problem comedies occupy.

In the earlier phases of his career, Shakespeare writes interchange-
ably, perhaps often simultaneously, comedies, history plays, three
widely divergent tragedies, and narrative and lyric poetry. But in the
later phases, the last two of Dowden's four periods, Shakespeare tends
to write within the inclusive framework of a single, exceptionally
flexible genre, tragedy from *Hamlet* to *Coriolanus*, and then, with
some overlap, the late romances.[1] I will try to identify important

1. See Edward Dowden, *Shakspere: A Critical Study of His Mind and
Art*, 3rd ed. (New York: Harper and Brothers, 1881). His division of the
works into periods is entangled with speculations regarding "spiritual tendencies" in Shakespeare's "personality" that occasionally make Dowden's Shakespeare almost unrecognizable to modern readers. But the groups themselves
provide a useful way of identifying important shifts in Shakespeare's development of dramatic form, and I think his insistence that the critic must in some

154

trends in Shakespeare's development that are separated by genre distinctions in the earlier work but which confront each other in the tragedies and the romances. Although I will suggest some of the ways these trends are manifested in various works, my main concern is to state as simply and clearly as I can a complex pattern, itself composed of smaller, interrelated patterns, that emerges from a long view of Shakespeare's development.[2] I hope that the effort to achieve synoptic clarity justifies sacrificing the very detailed reading that would be necessary to situate fully any one play within this developmental outline.

The earlier writings with which I will be most concerned are written in the later years of the first half of Shakespeare's artistic life: the second tetralogy of English history plays; the comedies from *Love's Labors Lost* and *A Midsummer Night's Dream* to *Twelfth Night*; and the *Sonnets*. Characteristics that distinguish these groups from each other demonstrate Shakespeare's development through three distinct genres. Developments within each group suggest sep-

---

way "attempt to pass through the creations of a great dramatic poet to the mind of the creator" (p. xii) is as appropriate to our age, with its speculative tools, as it was to Dowden's (See the third section of ch. 1 above). The chronology Dowden provides has been altered by modern scholarship, which pushes *Julius Caesar* back to 1599 from Dowden's date of 1601–1603. I do not include *Julius Caesar* in my discussion of plays from the tragic "period," although it anticipates them more than it recalls either *Titus Andronicus* or *Romeo and Juliet*. *Twelfth Night*, according to modern dating, may have been written after *Hamlet*, and its comic world reflects some of the concerns of the tragedies, but its deepest affinities, in spirit and form, are to the festive comedies that precede it. Two comedies contemporaneous with the tragedies, *All's Well That Ends Well* and *Measure for Measure*, can be assimilated to the pattern I trace through the tragedies and the romances.

2. The idea of "psychological development," Heinz Lichtenstein has observed, requires the "postulation of an invariant, to which all transformations must be related" ("The Role of Narcissism in the Emergence and Maintenance of a Primary Identity," *The International Journal of Psychoanalysis*, 45 [1964]: 55). In his own work, Lichtenstein postulates "the concept of a primary identity as an invariant the transformations of which we could call development" (p. 55). My purpose is not to disclose a primary identity for Shakespeare, but to establish the presence of polarized modes of self-experience that are repeatedly transformed in the development of Shakespeare's drama without losing their identifying characteristics. Because I see this polarity as both an animating force and a structural principle in Shakespeare's drama, which persists as an "invariant" against which complex variations can be measured, it serves a purpose in my argument analogous to that served by the concept of primary identity in Lichtenstein's work.

arate movements converging toward the central position that tragedy comes to command in Shakespearean drama. Each of these groups, in addressing itself to a different area of experience, engages a relatively discrete range of conflict. Implicit boundaries exclude or greatly qualify psychic hazards potentially disruptive of the purposes of the form. The boundaries of each genre shift and change, expand or contract with each play or poem, but remain in comparatively stable relation to a psychological center they both express and protect. Shakespeare's maturation as an artist is absorbed into the continuous but separate development of each of these groups until the limits of each obstruct further development. Each group moves in a direction that eventually exhausts its possibilities for further development compatible with the overall growth of Shakespeare's powers as a dramatist.

The struggles for power and political identity in the history plays from *Richard II* to *Henry V* tap deep sources of stress in relations of fathers and sons. The psychic consequences of such conflict, however, are confined within a dramatic world that rigorously subordinates that dimension of parental heritage complicated by responses to the feminine. In contrast with the histories, the actions of the festive comedies are often presided over by generous, resourceful women. Despite the familial basis of longing for feminine control and protection that lies at or near the center of these plays, their actions minimize the force of conflict between the generations that could obstruct the movement toward sexual maturity and marriage. Many of the *Sonnets* open much more fully and hazardously onto a range of feeling grounded in infantile and childhood experiences of the maternal. The irresolution of the sequence as a whole reflects its deeper, more conflict-bound psychological base, but individual sonnets handle this source of feeling with great mastery. Possibilities for conflict latent in earlier writings are released in the violent action of tragedy, where boundaries previously provided by separation of genre are broken through, and the drama takes into itself the entire range of family-based conflict in Shakespeare.

Caught up in conditions of extreme crisis that reflect this more complex base of psychological conflict, the protagonists of the tragedies and the romances struggle toward polarized modes of self-fulfillment. This polarity, which persists through an astonishing range of transformations, is itself hardly unique to Shakespeare;

Margaret S. Mahler generalizes its essential qualities when she speaks of "man's eternal struggle against fusion on the one hand and iso-lation on the other."[3] What is characteristic of Shakespeare is a full imaginative investment in mutually necessary but mutually incom-patible modes of self-definition at either end of this spectrum, and a recurrent pattern of oscillation between them. At one extreme, a deeply feared longing for merger subverts trust; at the other, failed autonomy gives way to helpless isolation.

Earlier works are protected from the destructive consequences that attend either end of this polarity. In the festive comedies, the fear of merger is averted in successful movements toward mutuality. The achievement of autonomy is protected from the threat of isolation in the *Henriad*. The poet of the *Sonnets* attempts to establish a re-lation based on merger that can itself be isolated from a larger world that threatens to intrude upon it. But the problem comedies can neither exclude nor fully embrace the deeper range of conflict that characterizes tragedies contemporaneous with them. In *All's Well*, Bertram struggles to achieve the autonomy he feels is denied him at court and in his marriage to Helena, only to be absorbed back into the world of the king's moral authority and the sexual bond he associates with violation of his manhood. Shakespeare can provide the Duke in *Measure for Measure* with autonomous authority only at the expense of isolating him from the conflicts of others and of emptying his characterization of dramatic life. The comic endings of both plays assume a trust—in the authenticity of Bertram's bond to Helena and in the psychological integrity of Vincentio's authority—that has not been fully earned dramatically.

The tragedies, which take their intensified base of conflict fully into their actions, culminate in dramatic realizations of extreme sit-uations either of destructive merger or desperate isolation. The ro-mances move through and beyond such extreme situations to restored trust and renewed autonomy. In this chapter I will try to show how separate developments in the histories, the festive comedies, and the *Sonnets* converge toward tragedy, how *Hamlet* takes into itself crises averted in these earlier works, and how development through the tragedies and the romances extends polarized modes of self-fulfill-ment that, in *Hamlet*, conflict with each other.

3. "On the First Three Subphases of the Separation-Individuation Process," *Psychoanalysis and Contemporary Science*, 3 (1974): 305.

Toward Tragedy: The Henriad

DUCHESS OF GLOUCESTER   *Thou dost consent*
In some large measure to thy father's death
In that thou seest thy wretched brother die,
Who was the model of thy father's life.
                                        (R2 1.ii.25–28)

The second group of history plays centers on royal inheritance
complicated by patricidal motives in relations to actual and symbolic
fathers. Richard's hand in the death of Woodstock, "one vial full
of Edward's sacred blood" (R2 I.ii.17) and a symbolic extension
of Edward's half-legendary fatherhood, initiates a chain of internal
violence not broken until Henry V makes war on France.[4] In a typical
gesture, compounding failure of nerve with characteristic gluttony
for self-display, Richard prevents the deadly encounter of Mowbray
and Bolingbroke, and with it the possibility of nonreciprocal, purga-
tive violence ritualistically isolated from the cycle of revenge initiated by Woodstock's death. After his banishment of Bolingbroke
sets up that ambitious man as a figure around whom the hopes of
discontented Englishmen may gather, Richard again travesties the
father and son bond, this time in its deep relation to English law and
tradition, when he confiscates the property of Bolingbroke's father
Gaunt, whom he has wished dead. Richard's actions could hardly be
better calculated to bring on his overthrow.

Richard proclaims magical omnipotence in the face of external
danger:

> This earth shall have a feeling, and these stones
> Prove armèd soldiers ere her native king
> Shall falter under foul rebellion's arms.   (III.ii.24–26)

4. A. P. Rossiter stresses the importance of Woodstock's death for R2,
and argues that Richard's guilt initiates the chain of violence dramatized in
both tetralogies: "The logic of the eight-play series *and* the exact apprehen-
sion of the 'tragedy' demand that we should know if it was *guilt* (and guilt
of royal blood) which started this momentous sequence" (*Angel with Horns*
[New York: Theatre Arts Books, 1961], p. 35). Rossiter thinks the play fails
to make the matter of Richard's guilt sufficiently clear (clear in the manner
of the anonymous *Woodstock*, a play to which he thinks R2 indebted) because Shakespeare assumed "that everybody must know what, as it happens,
many do *not*" (p. 36).

But as he invokes a maternal earth to destroy his enemies for him, Richard collaborates in his own destruction. His movement through the course of the play is controlled by simultaneous efforts to ward off recognition of his own guilt by emphasizing the guilt of his usurper and to bring punishment upon himself for his guilty actions. Richard proceeds from being a patricidal aggressor to an identification of himself through martyrdom with the victim of such aggression: ". . . you Pilates / Have here delivered me to my sour cross, / And water cannot wash away your sin" (IV.i.240–42). He proclaims through his actions even more clearly, and more futilely, than with his words: I am not the guilty party, but the broken, crucified, innocent victim of the guilty acts of others.

The deposition and murder of Richard eliminate a guilty king but perpetuate his crime, escalating it to open regicide. The self-assured and instinctively powerful Bolingbroke survives as King Henry IV in a state of anxious suspension, continually affirming a role he can neither fill nor abandon. As his inner guilt and his political insecurity mirror each other, and together mirror Richard's situation earlier, power flows away from its official but contaminated center into dangerous pockets of real or apparent subversion. Ernst Kris has carefully shown how in 1 *Henry IV* the lines of conflict are drawn around symbolic displacements of father and son relations: Henry IV and Falstaff as fathers to Hal; Hal and Hotspur as sons to Henry IV; Northumberland and Worcester as weak and deceitful fathers to Hotspur.[5] In 2 *Henry IV*, conflict closes in on the tension between Hal's inner efforts to justify himself—both to himself and to his father—and patricidal motives culminated both in the death of the king and in the repudiation of Falstaff. As Hal confronts treacherous political realities created by his enemies, he must juggle his own ambivalent relation to a real but guilty father; manipulate his bond to the necessary but ultimately unacceptable father substitute provided by Falstaff; act out a controlled, public identification of himself with the irresponsible Richard ("As thou art to this hour was Richard then" [1H4 III.ii.94]); and make the larger effort to align himself with a purified paternal superego, dramatically approximated in the Lord Chief Justice, whom Henry makes "a father to my youth" (2H4 V.ii.118).

5. "Prince Hal's Conflict," *Psychoanalytic Quarterly*, 17 (1948): 493.

Kris notes, as does Robert Ornstein in his study of the histories,[6] that Hal's efforts at self-justification extend into *Henry V*. But the powerful exploratory perspective through which Shakespeare regards these efforts in the two parts of *Henry IV* is blurred in the last play of the tetralogy. In *Henry V*, Shakespeare seems to be drawn toward both patriotic celebration and continued psychological exploration, opting for the former without quite giving up the latter. Henry V's eloquent meditation on the "idol Ceremony" (IV.i.226) before the battle of Agincourt seems designed more to show that the hero is also a man than to reveal the man he is. The immediately following lines regarding his father's "fault" and his own "contrite tears" (IV.i. 279, 282) for Richard's corpse are potentially more revealing, but apart from the main force of Henry's characterization. These lines serve more as a reminder of what is largely missing from this play than as a full effort to understand the inner dimensions of warlike Harry. Henry V attempts to externalize his guilt and seek expiation at a distance: he hires the prayers of "five hundred poor" and enlists "sad and solemn priests" to "sing still / For Richard's soul" (IV.i. 284, 288–89). This gesture parallels his larger goal of redeeming guilt-ridden England and uniting her feuding factions by waging war in France, and recalls his earlier strategies for keeping himself remote from his father's guilt while waiting to inherit his father's crown. But this perspective functions as a sort of half-articulated qualification, a potentially enriching, possibly dissenting vantage point from which to view Henry, that emerges suggestively from time to time, but is never fully integrated into the prevailing effort to applaud his heroic status.

As Rossiter has observed, "the heart of Shakespeare's insight into English history . . . is in the middle of the sequence" (*Angel with Horns*, p. 58), in the intricate study of historical process intersecting psychological reality presented in the two parts of *Henry IV*. C. L. Barber has fully caught the "astonishing development of drama in the

6. See ch. 8 of *A Kingdom for a Stage* (Cambridge, Mass.: Harvard University Press, 1972), pp. 175–202. Norman Rabkin sees Henry V as "the only successful and fully heroic monarch in all of Shakespeare's ten chronicle plays," but also as a character presented "more as a wish than as a paradigm of political reality" (*Shakespeare and the Common Understanding* [New York: Free Press, 1967], p. 98).

direction of inclusiveness" achieved in these two plays.[7] The audacious energies of powerful, independent men that crowd the beleagured king in *Part 1* and the apprehensions, betrayals, and misplaced hopes that qualify the experience of *Part 2* take in so large a range of life that it seems almost ungrateful to dwell on limitations in these plays. But in dramatizing Hal's exuberant triumph in the first part and his somber assumption of regal glory in the second, Shakespeare immerses his prince in a range of conflict less deep and more narrowly circumscribed than that of the later tragedies.

Kris compares the situation Hal faces with conditions in which Hamlet struggles toward tragic heroism. Each inhabits a world defined by the regicidal guilt of a father or father substitute, "while both heroes are battling against the murderous impulses in their own hearts." But in *Hamlet*, the Oedipus situation is "fully developed, centering on the queen" ("Prince Hal's Conflict," p. 502). Hamlet's sense of moral corruption saturating all experience turns on Gertrude's collaboration in the "incestuous" union he abhors:

> Rebellious hell,
> If thou canst mutine in a matron's bones,
> To flaming youth let virtue be as wax
> And melt in her own fire.   (iii.iv.83–86)

As Hamlet struggles toward an identity responsive to impossibly contradictory demands, he is engaged at the deepest level with a crisis of trust that works to devastate his active response to them. Hamlet's suffering and the inhibitions that deflect him away from direct action are compounded by the invasion of his dramatized experience by powerful preoedipal ambivalence. Hamlet's agonized disillusionment with Gertrude paralyzes the core of the self that originates in the first and most decisive accommodation to an external world that a child accomplishes in early infancy. With the severe erosion of trust in himself and in a world that seems to have forsaken him, Hamlet is overwhelmed by matricidal rage, incestuous longings, and the impotent need to find self-trust through the achievement of trust in an all-important other.

In the second group of histories, as Kris notes, "women are absent

7. *Shakespeare's Festive Comedy* (Princeton: Princeton University Press, 1959), p. 192.

or insignificant. Prince Hal's struggle against his father appears therefore in isolation, enacted in male society" ("Prince Hal's Conflict," p. 502). Shakespeare exploits a tendency encouraged by his sources to exclude from Hal's direct experience the dimension of conflict and need that builds on potentialities established in a child's relation to a mother. Although female characters assume notable secondary roles in these plays, their influence does not extend to Hal until his soldierly courtship of Katherine at the ceremonial end of *Henry V*, after the great struggles are over. In the main power struggles of these plays, the heritage of conflict centered in oedipal and preoedipal relations to a mother tends to be absorbed into symbolic objects of political loyalties and anxieties and only indirectly into relations among characters. England herself, richly endowed with maternal attributes, becomes the "teeming womb of royal kings" (R2 II.i.51) whose quarrelsome sons fight for the right to be her favorite and wear her crown. The bloody civil wars are described by Henry IV as an attack on England's maternal body, an "intestine shock" which compels the soil to "daub her lips with her own children's blood" (1H4 I.i.12, 6).

The earlier history plays are replete with female characters who exert great, often destructive, power. Joan de Pucelle, Queen Margaret, and the chorus of grieving mothers in *Richard III* occupy places at the center of conflict throughout the first tetralogy. Henry VI is consistently overpowered by the superior strength of his wife, and eventually becomes pawn to her fierce maternal investment in their son Prince Edward.[8] The misogyny of Richard III seems to lie at the very core of a character most fully expressed in his animosity toward his mother and in the sinister courtships of Anne and of Queen Elizabeth for her daughter.[9] In *King John* the prospect of masculine action would lie suspended between the fierce opposition of two mothers, Constance and Queen Elinor, were it not taken up by Faulconbridge, bastard heir to the manly force of Richard Cordelion.[10] But in the second tetralogy, the heritage of maternal con-

8. Leslie Fiedler emphasizes the importance of powerful women "all bent on betraying the male champion of the English" in the first tetralogy (*The Stranger in Shakespeare* [New York: Stein and Day, 1972], p. 47).

9. See my "History, Character and Conscience in *Richard III*," *Comparative Drama*, 5 (Winter 1971–1972): 301–21.

10. C. L. Barber, in an unpublished book-length manuscript that I am currently editing, explores the strategic importance of Faulconbridge's renun-

flict is kept free of interpersonal drama involving mothers. The deep ambivalence toward maternal power, which for a child provides both a source of wishful omnipotence and the threat of catastrophic terror, is localized in the crown itself, the " 'most fine, most honored, most renowned' " trophy that, as Hal understands his father's experience, has " 'fed upon the body of my father, . . . Hast eat thy bearer up' " (2H4 IV.v.159, 163–64).

But an England infused with symbolic attributes of a mother offers, in the midst of factionalized encounters, not a further source of conflict, but an absolutely undivided loyalty for Hal, which he serves even when he seems to flaunt his father. Amid the struggles to win and hold the crown, transacted in a virtually all-male context of power politics, Hal keeps himself clear not only of rebellion against his father but of crimes against the bodily integrity of maternal England shared by Henry IV and the rebels who would divide the kingdom. Throughout these plays, Henry IV's guilt for deposing Richard is underscored by the deeper guilt for violating England herself. As "the body of our kingdom" grows "foul" with "rank diseases" (2H4 III.i.38–39), the usurping king futilely dreams of atoning for his guilt with a holy crusade to Jerusalem. But he is helpless to eradicate the personal consequences of this symbolic crime. His very successes in politics and war are accompanied by increased sickness and ultimately by his death when the rebels are defeated. Appropriately he likens himself to a man finally presented with the coveted "feast" just as Fortune "takes away the stomach" (2H4 IV.iv.106–7). Psychologically it is the fate of Henry IV to be eaten rather than to eat. But, as he explains to his son, "all the soil of the achievement goes / With me into the earth" (2H4 IV.v.189–90).

Henry IV's deterioration and death purge in a context of public destiny the most primitive layer of guilt in the individual psyche, which is rooted in an infant's murderous, devouring rage against a mother and the fantasies of retaliation in kind that such rage engenders. Henry IV projects such retaliation into the historical future; he fears that in his son's reign England will become "a wilderness again, / Peopled with wolves," a realm in which "the fifth Harry from curbed license plucks / The muzzle of restraint, and the wild

---

ciation of his mother in the design of *King John* and in relation to the role of women in early phases of Shakespeare's drama.

dog / Shall flesh his tooth on every innocent" (2H4 IV.v.136–37, 130–32). But in the symbolic exchange completed with Hal's inheritance, the devouring force of royal cares attached to the crown is displaced onto the grave that opens for Henry IV, leaving his son to identify fully with the power the crown confers upon its wearer. Prince Hal may successfully inherit the crown, not only because of his efforts to separate himself from his father's regicidal guilt, but also because Shakespeare imagines him as essentially motherless, yet absolutely faithful to maternal England. The deepest psychological context of Henry IV's guilt may be skirted by a son who seems, unlike Hamlet, to have come into the world without the aid of a mother. Hal's successful assumption of the crown is a triumph of heroic masculine autonomy made dramatically possible by insulating the prince from psychic hazards that will qualify the autonomy of Shakespeare's tragic heroes. Motives that originate in infantile relations to a mother and threaten to subvert the quest for autonomy from within are deflected into other characters: Glendower's aspiration to magical omnipotence, Hotspur's narcissistic pursuit of self-idealization through honor, Falstaff's gluttony for a world of timeless sensual satiation. At the oedipal level, tensions within the relation of Hal to his father are resolved independently of the sexual dimension of filial rivalry. Henry V takes a wife only after his father is dead and his own kingly autonomy has been thoroughly proved; and he marries a Frenchwoman at that, a princess as independent of his mother country as she is innocent of his mother tongue.

The drama that draws most fully on the deepest strata of infantile experience, however, both gives these plays their largest and most compelling presentation of life and creates for them their most difficult artistic problem. When Hal refuses a necessarily self-defeating identification of himself with his guilty father, he turns to a world of unqualified appetites embodied in Falstaff. Falstaff, who "lards the lean earth as he walks along" (1H4 II.ii.100–101), provides not only indispensible refuge for Hal, but a kind of nurturing, sensual matrix he is, in Henry IV's angry pronouncement, "grafted to" (1H4 III. ii.15). Although at one level Hal finds in Falstaff a temporary father who can absorb tensions generated in the troubled relation of the prince to his royal father, at another level of his relationship with Falstaff Hal can remain in touch with dimensions of himself that have no place in his father's political world. Franz Alexander saw in

Falstaff the "narcissistic nucleus of the human personality,"[11] the core of an engagement with life formed in the earliest relations to a mother, before firm boundaries of self are formed and the quest for autonomous self-definition becomes urgent. As if suspended from the battle for self-control and the control of others, the world of play centered in Falstaff extends the sensual, spontaneous rhythms of infantile narcissism.

In the tense dramatic reality of the *Henry IV* plays, one character after another—Henry IV, Hotspur, Northumberland, Worcester, Douglas, Glendower—is trapped within a limited, inflexible identity that becomes a source of vulnerability as well as strength. But in the fluid world of the tavern, where provisional, playful identities are put on and taken off at whim, Falstaff provides Hal with a space to play in and a relation to time that, like the temporal world of an infant, is not imposed by the constraints of the external world, but is measured by the sensual rhythms of stimulation and gratification. Through his relation to Falstaff, Hal is able to isolate from the anxious, troubled world of his father the growing inner structure of a self able to confront external conflict decisively. By dwelling in the alternative world of Falstaff, Hal protects the essential inner autonomy based on self-trust that for Hamlet is fragmented and debased by the presence of Gertrude in the inescapable world of conflict he inhabits.

Richard II, in his glory, sees himself reflected in a mirror of royal omnipotence, sanctioned theologically by Carlisle and sustained more immediately by the flattery of court favorites. When the mirror is shattered, Richard is shattered with it; he becomes "in one person many people," but his multiple selves add up to "nothing" (*R2* V.v.31, 38). Henry IV, by contrast, can recognize only guilt in his reflection; he sees his precarious hold on the crown mirrored in Hal's dissolute activity. Hal becomes for him both an image of the "skipping king" he has deposed and murdered ("And in that very line, Harry, standest thou" [*1H4* III.ii.60, 85]) and an image of his own guilt for these crimes:

> But thou dost in thy passages of life
> Make me believe that thou art only marked
> For the hot vengeance and the rod of heaven
> To punish my mistreadings.   (*1H4* III.ii.8–11)

11. "A Note on Falstaff," *Psychoanalytic Quarterly*, 2 (1933): 603.

But Hal is able to exploit Falstaff's presence as an extravagant mirror of dimensions in his own life that he can neither surrender nor bring into direct relation with his position as prince. Falstaff's refusal to acknowledge the demands of a world lying just beyond the compass of his great belly—"Banish plump Jack, and banish all the world!" (*1HV* II.iv.55–56)—rests psychologically on an infant's identification of himself with the whole world through all-encompassing symbiotic relations to a mother.[12] Falstaff makes participation in infantile reserves of fantasy and gratification available to Hal in a playful context independent both of Richard's delusion of omnipotence and of the external world Hal is not yet ready to confront. Hal regards his adventures in the tavern world as a surface affair, "base contagious clouds" that hide the "sun" (*1H4* I.ii.185–86). But his relation to Falstaff keeps alive in him aspects of his own status as a son who in his manhood will become king—a playfully, sometimes cruelly aggressive, flexibility in adapting to experience that does not overwhelm him with inner anxiety or force upon him an identity rigidly molded by a time that, like Hamlet's, is drastically out of joint, and that, like Hamlet, he must eventually set right. Falstaff sustains Hal at a deep level comparable to the power of dreaming to keep intact the essential heritage of the infantile past. Upon "being awaked," he may "despise my dream" (*2H4* V.v.52), but the dream has been necessary at a depth that he cannot acknowledge.

The dream is also potentially hazardous. Just as Hal survives difficult times by living through his relation to Sir John Paunch, he must ultimately free himself from the "feeder of my riots" (*2H4* V.v.63), lest Falstaff, who likens himself to the "sow that hath overwhelmed all her litter but one" (*2H4* I.ii.11–12), make a feast of the royal remainder.[13] Barber has shown, however, without recourse to the sentimentality that has flawed many attempts to assess this

12. "Once upon a time we were all Falstaffs," W. H. Auden wrote: "then we became social beings with super-egos" (*The Dyer's Hand* [New York: Random House, 1962], p. 195). Auden likened Falstaff's body to "a cross between a very young child and a pregnant mother," and saw his fatness as "combining mother and child" to become a source of narcissistic self-sufficiency: ". . . for however ashamed he may be of displaying it in public, in private a man with a belly loves it dearly; it may be an unprepossessing child to look at, but he has borne it all by himself" (p. 196).

13. Hal's exploitation, for psychological and ritual effect, of his entrance into Falstaff's tavern world parallels a primitive "initiatory pattern" in which

repudiation, that necessary as Falstaff's banishment is, morally, politically, and psychologically, it is accompanied by a "drastic narrowing of awareness" in the drama. With the rejection of Falstaff goes an "inhibition of irony" that constricts the ritualistic ending of 2 *Henry IV* and diminishes the dramatic reach of *Henry V* (*Shakespeare's Festive Comedy*, pp. 219, 220). Renouncing Falstaff frees Hal from the fate Henry IV meets when he is devoured by cares that attend the crown, but it removes his characterization almost entirely from a psychological dimension that will come to be increasingly important in the tragedies. The imagination of Henry V as a figure of pure masculine autonomy ceremoniously resolves the political troubles of the second tetralogy at the expense of flattening their human content. As Shakespeare extends the drama of political struggle in the tragedies, anxieties and hazards that derive from the bond to the mother, carefully displaced onto other characters in the *Henry IV* plays, and projected into the attack on France in *Henry V*, will occupy a position at the very center of psychological conflict.

Toward Tragedy: The Comedies

ROSALIND *Believe then, if you please, that I can do strange things. . . . Therefore put you in your best array, bid your friends; for if you will be married to-morrow, you shall; and to Rosalind, if you will.*

(AYL v.ii.56–57; 68–70)

After Bassanio wins the right to marry the heiress of Belmont, "the gentle spirit" of his delighted Portia

> Commits itself to yours to be directed,
> As from her lord, her governor, her king.

"the Hero enters the Great Mother's womb without returning to the embyronic state" (Mircea Eliade, *Rites and Symbols of Initiation: The Mysteries of Birth and Rebirth*, trans. Willard R. Trask [New York: Harper and Row, 1958], p. 61). In such instances of "initiatory mythology," Eliade writes, the Hero "runs the risk of being devoured by a female monster" (p. 62). This danger is analogous to the threats Hal averts when he avoids being devoured, not only by Falstaff, but also by the worms that will feed on Percy beneath the field of battle and by the royal cares that devour his father in the moral and political arenas.

> Myself and what is mine to you and yours
> Is now converted. But now I was the lord
> Of this fair mansion, master of my servants,
> Queen o'er myself; and even now, but now,
> This house, these servants, and this same myself
> Are yours, my lord's.   (*MV* iii.ii.163–71)

Portia's words, spoken without guile or deliberate irony on her part, recall Kate's closing speech in *The Taming of the Shrew*, and seem to define for *The Merchant of Venice* a world of patriarchal priorities akin to that of the *Henriad*. But as prophecy, Portia's dedication of herself to such compliant womanhood is far off the mark. After committing herself to a subordinate wifely role, Portia goes on to assert, disguised as a man in the court of Venice, a strength and cunning far beyond the reach of Antonio, Bassanio, their friends, or the Duke of Venice, all of whom are helpless before the wrath of vengeful Shylock. She then teasingly readmits Bassanio into a household clearly hers. Once the ring she gives Bassanio replaces the caskets left behind by her father as the symbolic object that mediates her relations to others, Portia's self-appropriated power orders the movement of the play.

Portia establishes feminine control over the action that more than rivals Petruchio's manly dominance of *Shrew*, and she does so in a dramatic world that opens much more fully and subtly onto conflicts that attend sexual maturation and the movement toward marriage. The reorientation of comedy that goes with Portia's role makes possible the still more sophisticated comedy of *As You Like It*, *Much Ado About Nothing*, and *Twelfth Night*. The movement toward intimacy basic to these plays brings into the center of comic action a psychological dimension pushed to the periphery by the quest for masculine autonomy in the contemporary history plays. The witty, resourceful women of these plays—Portia, Rosalind, Beatrice, Viola—represent a significant departure from earlier comedies, often dominated by men like Petruchio and Theseus. In *A Midsummer Night's Dream* and *Love's Labors Lost*, comedies written in the three or four years that separate *Shrew* and *Merchant*, there is a telling tension between a masculine base for love relations and anticipations of the shift of comic control into the hands of energetic, loving women.

The prior conquest of Hippolyta by Theseus and Oberon's renewal of his power over Titania make possible triumphant ordering of love through marriage in A *Midsummer Night's Dream*. Each presents as an image of successful love a strong male subduing his woman. The four young lovers who pursue one another to exhaustion in the forest are brought to harmony by Oberon's magical intervention and ultimately take their places in the patriarchal Athens of Theseus. But Theseus himself is never tested within the play by direct involvement in the strife of love, and Oberon's triumph relies on magical appropriation of external power. Both Theseus's military prowess and Oberon's magic are unchallengeable givens; they allow the play to happen, rather than undergoing the test of its comic action. Developments centering around Titania, however, anticipate the movement of Shakespearean comedy away from masculine dominance represented by the Duke of Athens and the King of Fairies.

The cause of strife in the fairy world of *Dream* is a young Indian boy, who, as the object of Titania's maternal devotion, undermines Oberon's demand on her sexual love. By bringing the boy into his male order as his "henchman," jealous Oberon is able to rescue his sexual bond from Titania's tender, sensual cherishing of the boy. The threat to Oberon, like that which may confront a new father who finds himself excluded from an all-absorbing intimacy of mother and infant, is mastered by magically redirecting Titania's sensual love, still saturated with maternal solicitousness, toward an object she will come to find hateful. But this turn of events, from the perspective of the plot merely a device for reuniting the fairy king and queen, becomes through Bottom an important emotional center of the play. Endowed with the head of an ass by Puck, and abandoned in the forest by his fellow players, Bottom is found and loved by the enchanted Titania, who is enamored of his gruff voice, enthralled by his ludicrous appearance. After caressing him and feeding him, she winds him in her arms as "the female ivy so / Enrings the barky fingers of the elm" (IV.i.42–43). As Titania lovingly dotes over Bottom, each falls into luxurious sleep. The sight of the sleeping pair appears pitiful and hateful to Oberon, and comic to the play's audience, but Bottom awakes to recall his experience as "a most rare vision," a "dream past the wit of man to say what dream it was," indeed, a dream that "shall be called 'Bottom's dream,' because it hath no bottom" (IV.i.203–4, 212–13). In the arms of Titania, Bottom recovers for a night a place in the lush and protected environment of early childhood, a refusion of self and magically responsive world, of sensual and tender longings, fissured by later developments.[14] Beneath the comic machinery of ass's head and love potion, Shakespeare touches upon a base of love relations that will become more central to the main love plots of ensuing comedies.

Berowne's role in *Love's Labors Lost* anticipates Rosalind's in *As You Like It* more than it resembles those of Oberon and Theseus. Like Rosalind, he is at once participant and ironic commentator in relation to the main love plot, succumbing to romantic love's poeticized illusions at one moment, puncturing them the next. Unlike Rosalind, however, Berowne is unable to guide the four pairs of lovers in his play to marriage. Barber has stressed that the marriages are not completed because the participants mistake a "game of witty wooing" for love (*Shakespeare's Festive Comedy*, p. 112). This wooing game, like the game of academy before it, is a boys' game, which binds its players in a kind of team more than it extends across sexual lines to take in the women by forming new, heterosexual bonds. The lovers, inspired by the eloquent sophistry of Berowne's pep talk, take to the field of love like enthusiastic soldiers to battle or football players to the game of the year:

> KING   Saint Cupid then! And, soldiers, to the field!
> BEROWNE   Advance your standards, and upon them lords!
>   Pell-mell, down with them! But be first advised,
>   In conflict that you get the sun of them.
>   (IV.iii.361–64)

The men are unable, however, to negotiate the transition from strong bonds linking them with each other to bonds of men and women united in marriage. When Berowne, searching frantically for an adequate rhetoric of love, swears that his love is "sound, sans

14. Robert Fliess asks of the exchange in which Titania feeds Bottom, and embraces him in sleep (IV.i.30–44): "Is this not a most poetic description of how a doting mother in fairyland holds, feeds and fondles her baby?" (*Ego and Body Ego* [New York: International Universities Press, 1961], p. 271n). Fliess sees Bottom's confusion, upon awakening, of the functions of the eye, hand, tongue, and heart as a reflection of the "*modality of primal perception*" in which the various senses are not yet fully distinguished in the immature (in Bottom's case, regressed) ego; "it expresses the unity of their function by ascribing the percepts attained through each of these spheres to another (displacement)" (p. 272n).

crack or flaw" (V.ii.416), Rosaline picks on "sans" for its artificiality, and the ladies continue to refuse to take the professing lovers seriously. Finally, with news that the princess's father is dead, the ladies' playful objections take a new turn, and they demand that the gentlemen spend a year purging themselves of sins and jests and of each other. The love plot ends with four young women bound together by mutual grief and with four young men united in mutual frustration but about to be separated by projects of individual reformation. The prospect of marriage is a full year off, "too long," perhaps, as Berowne observes, "for a play" (V.ii.868).

Whether or not Berowne is correct, what is important in the light of later comedies is that the task of establishing the conditions for marriage has been taken from the men and given to the women. The witty appropriation of control over love relations by Rosaline and her three companions stops the movement toward marriage in *Love's Labors Lost*, but holds out the promise of future marriages purged of male folly. The tender, solicitous love Titania lavishes upon Bottom becomes a means to restore her love for virile Oberon, but provides for Bottom an exquisite experience of nurturing love. Rosaline, as she schools Berowne on the nature of love, and Titania, as she falls helplessly in love with Bottom, embody separately qualities that will converge in heroines who, "many fathom deep . . . in love" (AYL IV.i.190) themselves, will provide conditions that make marriages possible in the main love plots of ensuing comedies.

In *Merchant*, tensions like those that lead to elaborate splitting in *Dream* and to the aborted material resolution of *Love's Labors Lost* are taken into an action that, after first establishing the centrality of male friendship and the patriarchal base of marriage, moves beyond them to a new mode of loving. Portia's marriage to Bassanio initially confirms the propriety of her submission to the power and wisdom of her dead father, whose authority Bassanio will apparently inherit. At Antonio's trial, however, the emotional force of Bassanio's new marriage yields to the older and as yet deeper bond of friendship:

> Antonio, I am married to a wife
> Which is as dear to me as life itself;
> But life itself, my wife, and all the world
> Are not with me esteemed above thy life.
> I would lose all, ay sacrifice them all
> Here to this devil, to deliver you.   (iv.i.280–85)

But after Portia, disguised as a lawyer, frees Antonio from Shylock's wrath, she uses the force of Antonio's friendship to secure from Bassanio the ring he has promised to keep forever. The wedding ring, now an unstable symbol for the primacy of friendship over marriage, gives Portia comic leverage for her chastising reacceptance of Bassanio as husband. The marriage itself, first subsidized by Antonio, then violated to honor Antonio's friendship, will not be consummated until Bassanio, under Portia's witty guidance, subordinates all other bonds to his role as husband. Portia underscores this transition by returning Bassanio's ring via Antonio, "th' unhappy subject of these quarrels," who "shall be his surety" (V.i.238, 254).

At the heart of this transformation of relations is Portia's victory over Shylock in a struggle that not only turns this play around but alters the whole development of Shakespearean comedy. Underlying the troubled ironies of this contest of Jew and Christian is a simpler conflict at once more primitive and more immediate. As Norman Holland points out, summarizing and extending several psychoanalytic studies of *Merchant*, Shylock dominates the masculine world of Venice as a vengeful, jealous father, while Belmont presents a "woman's world . . . full of riches and bounty and giving." Psychologically, *Merchant* is largely inhabited by helpless, dependent children, whose fates turn on the contest "between a loving mother, Portia, and a castrating father, Shylock."[15] From this perspective, the defeat of Shylock, though it appears to bring Bassanio and Antonio closer together, eliminates an important element of their bond—the common object of fear and antagonism that can unite brothers against the powerful father. Portia's victory, begun in the court of Venice, is completed in the return to Belmont, where she bestows lost riches on Antonio, provides new wealth for Lorenzo and Jessica, and teasingly reaccepts Bassanio as her husband.

The triumph over Shylock protects *Merchant* from the threat of the vengeful, possessive father. As the action is taken over by Portia and returned to her enchanted Belmont, Shakespeare establishes for comedy a psychological base liberated not only from the direct threat

15. *Psychoanalysis and Shakespeare* (New York: McGraw-Hill, 1966), pp. 235–36. "At the deepest level," Holland argues, "*The Merchant of Venice* works with the feeling of trust a child needs to have toward his mother: I can depend on her, I can take her displeasure without disastrous results" (p. 330).

of paternal power, but from a general orientation toward masculine values based, like those of the history plays, on competition and conquest, and originating in tensions between fathers and sons.[16] The figure of potentially dangerous patriarchal power does not re-appear fully in Shakespeare's comic art until the vindicated descendants of Shylock's fatherhood inhabit the late romances. Attitudes mocked in Shylock, particularly his conception of his daughter as a possession to dispose of as he sees fit, will be restored and reconfirmed in the world of Prospero. But in *Merchant* the powerful father is villainized and humiliated. Shylock is frustrated in his vengeful desire for Antonio's flesh, made to give over many of his possessions to "the gentleman / That hath lately stole his daughter" (IV.i.382–83), and forced to abandon the patriarchal identity grounded in his Jewish heritage. Shylock must "become a Christian" (IV.i.385); the father must become a child again before the altar of an alien god. "In christ'ning shalt thou have two godfathers" (IV. i.396), Gratiano tauntingly observes, bringing home the point of Shylock's reduction from an almost mythic fatherhood: "Verily I say unto you, Whosoever shall not receive the kingdom of God as a little child, he shall not enter therein" (Mark 10.15).

No other festive comedy is dominated so extensively as *Merchant* is by a single, resourceful woman. Even Rosalind, wiser and wittier yet than Portia, has her direct power restricted to the action of love in *As You Like It*, where a generalized, magical sense of comic destiny displaces much of the individual control exercised in *Merchant*. A heightened self-consciousness of comedy as play space, symbolized within the play by the forest of Arden, provides much of the protectiveness Portia must secure with action when she retrieves Bassanio from a world of masculine aggression. The political crisis identified with masculine control in *As You Like It* is relegated to a fairy tale realm kept separate from the forest world of the lovers. This crisis does not impede directly the central experience of love in the forest, and it finally resolves itself, as if in magical response to the culmi-

16. Note that in *Romeo and Juliet*, a play closely contemporaneous with *Merchant*, a tradition of violence is structured along the lines of patriarchal families, and is brought to tragic intensity when Mercutio asserts the primacy of both friendship and feuding over Romeo's claim for love (III.i.). Much later, in *WT*, the renewal of Leontes' friendship with Polixenes will catalyze his fierce reaction against Hermione.

nation of the love plot by Rosalind, when the usurping duke enters "the skirts of this wild wood" (V.iv.153), a green world that shares in the feminine bounty accorded Rosalind.

Viola clearly extends the line of Portia and Rosalind into *Twelfth Night*. Her boy disguise is perhaps even more central than theirs, since it is as Orsino's page that she exerts her charm over him, preparing him with the intimacy of shared pathos for the sexual love that will ensue when she is revealed to be a woman. Viola's keen understanding of love, like Portia's and Rosalind's, is the most sensitive and comprehensive awareness the play offers. But in *Twelfth Night* understanding is divorced almost entirely from an action over which no character exerts decisive control. Viola states her own helplessness: "O Time, thou must untangle this, not I; / It is too hard a knot for me t' untie" (II.ii.39–40). Time and a bounteous ocean respond to furnish the passive and bewildered resolving agent in Sebastian, who, with the aid of Antonio's loving midwifery, is reborn through "the breach in the sea" (II.i.19–20). The sense of a maternal presence that sees things through to a happy ending is dissociated from any of the romantic lovers—who all often seem much like children—and displaced onto an unusually generous ocean. The plot itself serves as a kind of benevolent destiny, nourishing faith that the impulse to love will work itself out happily, but faith qualified by the delicate fragility of a play that repeatedly calls attention to its precarious independence from less benevolent possibilities that seem to lie just beyond the comic boundaries of Illyria.

But the pattern of fulfillment through union with a spirited, versatile woman, established in *Merchant*, is the paradigm that *As You Like It* and *Twelfth Night* extend and qualify as they move toward the limits of Shakespeare's festive comic form. In the *Henriad*, Hal internalizes the requisite images of royal manhood through a largely individual effort; the ultimate success of his relation to his father demands that Hal maintain considerable distance from him. By contrast, the men of these comedies find their identities in mutuality, in relations with women of exceptional sensitivity who draw them out of themselves, and who are often in active control of the relationship. The emphasis for Hal is on self-created autonomy; for Orlando and Orsino, it is on the trust each comes to invest in a relationship of developing intimacy with a woman whose sexuality is veiled by a male disguise. Violence, essential to Hal's effort to prove himself as a trustworthy prince in 1 *Henry IV*, comes closest to invading the main relations of comedy when that disguised woman is thought to have betrayed the trust invested in her, when Orsino believes Viola/ Cesario has betrayed him by marrying Olivia in *Twelfth Night*. Significantly, Orsino's distress does not spring from losing Olivia, the apparent object of his desire, so much as from the apparent betrayal of Viola/Cesario, to whom he has committed his trust.

These comedies dramatize trust in the expectation that situations of frustration and anxiety do not inevitably lead to utter disaster, but may yield to pleasure and fulfillment through the intervention of trustworthy others and the resources of a compliant world. Simple as this expectation is, it is not part of a person's innate equipment, but must be learned from contact with an environment reliable enough to foster trust in it. More than the release of sexual desire, festive comic action dramatizes a rhythm of frustration and fulfillment grounded in trust, focused specifically through the presence of a trustworthy woman. These plays recreate, within the broader context of crises of intimacy, the infantile achievement of finding a trustworthy maternal environment in responsive relation to the emergence of a trustworthy self. I find myself experiencing *As You Like It*, for instance, not so much through my participation in Rosalind's desire, nor through what there is of Orlando's desire for her, but awestruck and grateful in the presence of the wise magician Rosalind who has worked things out harmoniously, who has provided a secure world that includes the promise of future fulfillment of another order. This situation creates a paradox, however, which suggests the limits of dramatization of love in this play, and of the festive comedies as a group. For while Rosalind exorcises through mockery idealizing conventions of love carved into the forest by Orlando, she simultaneously presides over the play as an ideal image of the beloved, an ideal grounded in relations to the mother, and important in a way that implies her being independent of the child's sexual desire.

In order for this comic pattern to succeed, love relations must be protected from directly experienced passion and from explicit interference from family bonds. As I have tried to show above and in the second section of chapter 2, the comic hero's love for the heroine implicitly includes aspects of the relationship never explicitly dramatized in these plays, a boy's relation to a mother. The actions of these plays move through truncated and disguised oedipal situations in which the heroine provides maternal tenderness and control and in which competition among men for the love of a woman, which could evoke the threat of oedipal rivalry with the father, is minimized, displaced into the subplot, or excluded altogether. When Shakespeare comes to dramatize the plight of a young man whose relationship to his beloved is conditioned by his bond to his actual mother, and whose love meets opposition from the young woman's father, the result is not comedy but *Hamlet*. In order for the central love relations of the festive comedies to be protected from violence, degradation, and latent incestuous associations, they must be stripped of compelling sexual desire; the comic movement toward the moment that will make possible the next generation must be sheltered from direct experience of psychological threats that originate in conflicts between generations. Characters are released from anxieties that accompany sexual maturation, but sexual desire, deflected into the fanciful imaginations of Bassanio, Orlando, and Orsino, is further checked by the interrupted wedding of *Merchant* and by the boy disguises of Portia, Rosalind, and Viola.

In *Much Ado*, however, there is no Portia or Rosalind to oversee the complications of love relations, nor is there a sea symbolically rich with maternal power to unravel the thread of potential disaster as in *Twelfth Night*. Semimagical capabilities bestowed on other heroines—to be like men by changing their clothes, to provide a mother's solicitous care for others, to distinguish insight from fantasy through the distancing power of disguise—Shakespeare presents as frustrated impulses in the character of Beatrice. Disguise is reduced to defense in Beatrice; her wit serves self-deception as well as self-protection and shrewd insight into others. Her attempt to oversee the marriage of Claudio and Hero, when abruptly checked, releases in full earnest a necessarily frustrated wish that has been part of the "curst" exterior of Lady Disdain from the beginning: "O that I were a man!" (IV.i.298–99). But her recognition that "I cannot be a man with wishing . . ." (IV.i.316–17) does not dissolve the forceful, witty, competitive social self that partly originates in such wishing. By minimizing in Beatrice the strong maternal qualities of other heroines, Shakespeare can render her energies more sharply, her movement toward a sexual bond in marriage more convincingly. And he can strengthen her male opposite, Benedick, who could scarcely abide in himself the idolatrous sentimentality of an Orlando or the successive dependencies of a Bassanio. Benedick's witty deflation of love proves less an obstacle to a plausible sexual bond than the idealizing tendencies of Bassanio and Orlando, which the actions of *Merchant* and *As You Like It* mock at one level but amplify at another, deeper level through the bountiful powers invested in Portia and Rosalind.

As in *Merchant, As You Like It,* and *Twelfth Night,* the movement in *Much Ado* is toward relations of trust and mutuality. The action must move beyond Claudio's failure to trust Hero's virtue and Benedick's fearful unwillingness to invest trust in any woman: "I will do myself the right to trust none" (I.i.217–18). But this action, obstructed by fears and conflicts in men, cannot be resolved by the play's women: Hero is largely passive as she is courted and then abandoned by Claudio; Beatrice must discover in herself willingness to place trust in a relation of love. The masculinity of Benedick and Claudio is protected by defenses that themselves become sources of conflict and potential violence; as in the tragedies, the inner logic of this masculinity is destructive when it becomes vulnerable to the threat of female sexuality. Claudio's need for masculine self-esteem subverts his tentative trust in Hero once his romanticized image of her is challenged by Don John's plot. His honor, tested in the context of love, retreats into destructive vanity. Benedick is driven by the same masculine code of honor, held up before him by an outraged Beatrice, to avenge Claudio. The ironic distance provided by Beatrice's keen wit collapses under the pressure of the action, as she urges Benedick to take the vengeful measures she longs to take herself.

The psychological base of comedy altered in *Much Ado* minimizes the controlling presence of resourceful women and intensifies conflict in the search for male identity. This alteration, which both links *Much Ado* more closely than the other comedies I have been discussing to earlier plays like *Two Gentlemen of Verona* and *The Taming of the Shrew* and points forward, with Hero's apparent death, to *All's Well That Ends Well* and the late romances, puts a severe strain on the comic action. In order to subdue the potential for violence engendered in what is ostensibly the main love plot of *Much Ado,* Shakespeare must trim the parts of Claudio and Hero to shallow conventionality. These thinly portrayed lovers seem hardly adequate dramatically to the most severe crisis in a love relation presented in any of the festive comedies. To secure an ultimately comic outcome, Shakespeare must turn to forces altogether independent of the dynamics of love. Dogberry's happy, unlikely discovery that proves Hero's innocence must be introduced to break the circle of vengeful, masculine violence from the outside.

"I can live no longer by thinking" (V.ii.48), Orlando laments to Rosalind (as Ganymede), but in *As You Like It* Shakespeare protects his lovers, his audience, and his comic art from difficulties that go with expanding the relation of "thinking"—of loving as idealized expectation—to sexual intimacy in the sustained bond of marriage. The basis of festive comic rhythm in experiences of the maternal can lead comic characters to marriage, but not beyond it. Bassanio wins Portia's hand in the third act of *Merchant*, but developments in Venice both defer the completion of this union until the last scene and radically redefine the conditions that make its completion possible. The movement toward marriage deflects more than it embodies passionate longing, taking a course through male friendship to Bassanio's reverence for his "thrice-fair lady" (III.ii.146), then back to male friendship and the triangular, sado-masochistic intricacies binding Bassanio, Antonio, and Shylock, before culminating in the magical dispensations (and the slightly uneasy sexual jesting) of Portia's Belmont. The relation of Rosalind and Orlando in *As You Like It* is mediated by disguise and double-disguise until the very end. Although Rosalind feels the sexual dimension of her attraction to Orlando fully and directly, the passion she provokes in the play is either highly sentimentalized, in Orlando's doggerel verse, or comically perverse, in Phebe's passion for Ganymede. Rosalind is never regarded as the object of directly experienced sexual desire by her suitor, a condition she recognizes fully and addresses in Ganymede's manipulation of Orlando, but does not change.

When the prospect of sexual consummation becomes more immediate, or when the comic hero makes a larger claim for his own manhood, the comic resolution of marriage becomes more precarious. *The Merry Wives of Windsor*, a play that protects already established marriages by mocking the licentious intentions of Falstaff and the easily aroused jealousy of Master Ford, takes a form that isolates it from the main line of development of Shakespeare's comic art. In *Twelfth Night*, when the comic hero is presented as a man of power and substance, as the Duke of Illyria rather than as the son of a worthy father or the boyish friend of a Venetian merchant, the central love relation takes tragic potentiality into itself: Orsino, in a sacrificial gesture anticipating Othello's, threatens to "kill what I love" (V.i.113) when he thinks his trust has been betrayed. Comedy veers toward violence when Claudio and Hero are scheduled to be married in the fourth act of *Much Ado*. When marriage is moved into the second act of *All's Well*, Bertram flees with disgust and fear a sexual bond to a woman who exaggerates qualities of Portia and Rosalind, and whom other characters idealize. When marriage is moved into the first act of *Othello*, sexual tensions yield to the nightmarish destruction of both trust and autonomy; the action culminates in a consummation of death for husband and wife. As Shakespeare moves comedy away from a psychological base of trust in feminine control, sheltered from the full range of conflicted male sexuality by the exclusion or minimization of generational conflict, he moves it toward the world of tragic action that will succeed it.

Toward Tragedy: The *Sonnets*

Thou art the grave where buried love doth live,
Hung with the trophies of my lovers gone,
Who all their parts of me to thee did give;
That due of many now is thine alone.
 Their images I loved in view of thee,
 And thou, all they, hast all the all of me.

(SON. 31)

The early sonnets state a goal identical with that of the festive comedies: a young man is urged to marry and procreate. As they move through their various phases, however, the *Sonnets* dwell on kinds of relationships subordinated to or deflected from the claims of matrimony in the comedies: the binding power of friendship and the contamination of sexual relations by promiscuity or degradation. In the *Sonnets*, Shakespeare seems to be caught up in a situation over which he often has as little control, beyond poetic utterance, as a character in a play. But in them there is no consistent dramatic perspective larger than that presented by the declarations of love. When in *As You Like It* Orlando persuades himself that he will die if his love is not returned, Rosalind, disguised as Ganymede,

stands outside this illusion and uses her wit to put it into larger
perspective: "Men have died from time to time, and worms have
eaten them, but not for love" (IV.i.96–98). Many of the *Sonnets*
are written from inside an awareness that can declare, without reservation, that "life no longer than thy love will stay, / For it depends
upon that love of thine" (92). In *The Merchant of Venice*, Antonio's effort to live and die through his love for Bassanio is contained by the ironies of a comic action that culminates when male
friendship yields to marriage as the center of the social order; in
the *Sonnets*, Shakespeare's effort to live and die through his friend,
whom he would withdraw from the larger world of an intruding society, is expressed in nearly endless ironic variations that never yield
to comprehensive understanding.[17] The festive comedies mock illu-

17. Within the comic frame of *MV*, the parallels between Antonio's love
for Bassanio and Shakespeare's love for the friend are striking. Antonio, like
the poet of the *Sonnets*, uses the prospect of his own death to dramatize his
willingness to die as a validation of the primacy of his love for Bassanio over
that of all others:

> Commend me to your honorable wife.
> Tell her the process of Antonio's end,
> Say how I loved you, speak me fair in death;
> And when the tale is told, bid her be judge
> Whether Bassanio had not once a love.
> (IV.i.271–75)

As with the *Sonnets* poet, self-effacement for Antonio links the purity of his
love with a sense of personal shame or unworthiness:

> I am a tainted wether of the flock,
> Meetest for death. The weakest kind of fuit
> Drops earliest to the ground, and so let me.
> (*MV* IV.i.114–16)
>
> O, lest the world should task you to recite
> What merit lived in me that you should love
> After my death, dear love, forget me quite,
> For you to me can nothing worthy prove. . . .
> (*Son.* 72)

And like the poet of the *Sonnets*, Antonio can indulge in a kind of disingenu-
ously covert extortion aimed at provoking love laced with pity: " '. . . all debts
are cleared between you and I,' " he writes in the letter summoning Bassanio
back to Venice, " 'if I might but see you at my death. Notwithstanding, use
your pleasure. If your love do not persuade you to come, let not my letter' "
(*MV* III.ii.318–21).

> Nay, if you read this line, remember not
> The hand that writ it, for I love you so
> That I in your sweet thoughts would be forgot
> If thinking on me then should make you woe.
> (*Son.* 71)

sions that attend and obstruct romantic love; love in the *Sonnets* discovers itself in necessary illusion, subordinating all other claims of living to itself.

Rosalind, I have tried to show, provides for the lovers of *As You Like It* shrewd guidance and a protected environment that reflect the experience of childhood relations to a maternal presence. In early sonnets Shakespeare playfully evokes the friend's mother as an incentive to marriage and procreation. But as the relationship intensifies, the friend is absolved of this imperative, and the poetry becomes the means of perpetuating the friend's presence. Shakespeare, who in his cherishing love identifies himself with nurturing, protective aspects of a maternal presence, will rescue the friend from "Devouring Time": "My love shall in my verse ever live young" (19). Where Rosalind provides an objectified presence that enhances the movement toward self-discovery and stable object relations in others, Shakespeare, in the *Sonnets*, seeks through a maternal identification a further identification of himself with the figure of the beloved.[18] "Many of the sonnets can be seen," as C. L. Barber observes in his review of Stephen Booth's extraordinary edition of the *Sonnets*, "as play aimed at evoking, by way of the young man, a sense of the original maternal presence—and reckoning with its vulnerability to 'never resting time' [5] and other betrayals."[19] Both when that play strains the limits of playfulness and when it is an exercise of joy, self-effacement can become a means to achieve self-fulfillment: ". . . I in thy abundance am sufficed / And by a part of all thy glory live" (37).

18. Otto Fenichel, in an account of psychic developments that can lead to a narcissistic object choice, describes a key purpose served by such an identification: "Having identified himself with his mother, he behaves as he previously had wished his mother to behave toward him. He chooses as love objects young men or boys who, for him, are similar to himself, and he loves them and treats them with the tenderness he had desired from his mother. While he acts as if he were his mother, emotionally he is centered in his love object, and thus enjoys being loved by himself" (*The Psychoanalytic Theory of Neurosis* [New York: Norton, 1945], p. 332).

19. *New York Review of Books*, 25 (April 6, 1978): 36. My own reading of the *Sonnets* owes much to Professor Barber's understanding of them, as conveyed in this review, in an article cited below (note 24), in a chapter of his unpublished book-length manuscript, and in many conversations. The following remarks reflect my attempt to follow Barber's directive "to read them with awareness of what they themselves convey about the use Shakespeare is making of them, enigmatic as this use often is" (p. 32).

Shakespeare does not so much bring into these poems the young man they address as create an idealized image of the beloved that answers to deep needs in himself.[20] Through the poet's identification of himself with this image, the friend becomes "all the better part of me" (39). The attempt to consolidate in the friend the "trophies" and "images" of all past loving gestures, and to venerate them at the "grave where buried love doth live" (31), in itself points toward ritualistic repetition marked by the kind of intimate reverence caught wonderfully in 108:

> What's new to speak, what now to register,
> That may express my love or thy dear merit?
> Nothing, sweet boy; but yet, like prayers divine,
> I must each day say o'er the very same;
> Counting no old thing old, thou mine, I thine,
> Even as when first I hallowed thy fair name.

Efforts to contain the beloved in a "hallowed" image of him, however, clearly meet with difficulty. A tension underlies many of the sonnets, and is unresolved by the whole group of them, which springs from the pain of recognizing that the friend the poet creates out of inner needs and images is not identical with the friend who exists independently of his love.[21]

Shakespeare seeks to make of his love a total bond that demands all and promises all, to live through his love for the friend by making him into an absolute presence. The *Sonnets* aspire to a love resembling Montaigne's friendship with the poet La Boetie, a love that

> hath no other *Idea* than of it selfe, and can have no reference but to it selfe. It is not one especiall consideration, nor two, nor three, nor foure, nor a thousand: It is I wot not what kinde of quintessence, of all this commixture, which having seized all my will, induced the same to plunge and lose it self in his, which likewise having seized all his will, brought it to lose and plunge it selfe in mine, with a mutuall greediness, and with a semblable concurrence. I may truly say, lose, reserving nothing unto us, that might properly be called our owne, nor that was either his, or mine.[22]

20. I discuss the function of idealization in the *Sonnets* in more detail in "Poetry and Fantasy in Shakespeare's Sonnets 88–96," *Literature and Psychology,* 17 (November 1972): 151–62.

21. In the third section of chapter 2 above I discuss this tension in exploring the relation between Shakespeare's love for the friend and Bertram's place in AWW.

22. "Of Friendship," in *The Essayes of Montaigne,* tr. John Florio, introd.

The experiences recounted by Montaigne and Shakespeare participate in a process which M. Masud R. Khan calls the "secularization
of self-experience"; each is an effort to fill a "gap left by the absence
of God's presence" with a secular bond cherished as sacred and to
which all is surrendered with complete devotion.[23] In both Montaigne and Shakespeare the love is everything, compared to which
"all the world besides methinks are dead" (*Son.* 112), all else is
"nought but a vapour" (*Essayes*, p. 153). Both are loves by identification. La Boetie is "no other but my selfe," writes Montaigne;
their minds are joined in "so universall a commixture, that they weare
out, and can no more finde the seame that hath conjoyned them
together" (*Essayes*, pp. 152, 149). Shakespeare's friend is enclosed
in a beauty that "Is but the seemly raiment of my heart, / Which in
thy breast doth live, as thine in me" (22).

Khan offers his remarks on Montaigne in a short, speculative paper
in which he stresses the importance of "crucial friendships" (p. 99)
in the lives of Montaigne, Rousseau, and Freud. Each of these figures puts intimate friendship to very different uses: Montaigne internalizes the image of La Boetie, after the poet's death, as the core
of his own life; Rousseau "needed to have friends in order to hate
them and in order to love himself better" (p. 105); Freud's friendship
with Wilhelm Fliess, severed abruptly and with mutual bitterness
after twelve years, "supplied the supportive presence in the background to Freud's most audacious and unique undertaking: his self-
analysis" (p. 107). Each of these friendships, however, was marked
by a pronounced trend toward projection and idealization that localized inner strengths (in Rousseau's case, inner weaknesses) in
the image of the friend. In all these instances, Khan argues, crucial
friendship "was of formative importance toward the crystallization
of their particular vision or theory" (p. 99). Like Montaigne and
Freud, Shakespeare seems to have entered into the deep bond of

J. I. M. Stewart (New York: Modern Library, n.d.), Bk. 1, p. 149. Rodney
Poisson compares the love for the friend with classical and Renaissance declarations of the ideal of friendship, including Montaigne's, in "Unequal Friendship: Shakespeare's Sonnets 18–122," in *New Essays on Shakespeare's Sonnets*, ed. Hilton Landry (New York: AMS Press, 1976), pp. 1–19.

23. "Montaigne, Rousseau and Freud," in *The Privacy of the Self* (New
York: International Universities Press, 1974), pp. 103, 100. See J. B. Leishman, *Themes and Variations in Shakespeare's Sonnets*, 2nd ed. (London:
Hutchinson University Library, 1963), for a moving and perceptive account
of the "religious" dimension of Shakespeare's love.

friendship recounted in the *Sonnets* at a time when he was already a man of considerable accomplishments, but had yet to open his exploration of human experience to the depths it would ultimately reach. The strategic place of the *Sonnets* in Shakespeare's artistic development suggests that the love for the friend they express played a role in the development of his art analogous in importance to the place Khan assigns to intimate friendship in Montaigne and Freud.

The complete mutuality achieved in the friendship of Montaigne and La Boetie, however, contrasts sharply with the unstable mix of deferential submission to and one-sided appropriation of the beloved in Shakespeare's love, where even the "mutual render" of 125 suggests a one-way movement, "only me for thee." Montaigne, according to Khan, "internalized this relationship and idealized it into a private presence that was to guide him for the rest of his life" (p. 101). But this idealization seems to have been remarkably consistent with the actuality of their comparatively brief but fully reciprocated love for each other. For Shakespeare, lack of reciprocity necessitates extraordinary efforts to stay in vital contact with the presence he would make the center of his experience. Unable to abide the gap that repeatedly threatens to open up before him with the prospect of losing the friend, Shakespeare denies that potential absence with the illusion of merger with the ideal beloved. Illusory oneness supersedes and disavows betrayed trust: "For do thy worst to steal thyself away, / For term of life thou art assurèd mine" (92). Masochistic passivity is the price the poet is not only willing but relieved to pay for a wishful sense of participation in the friend's magical abundance: "Such is my love, to thee I so belong, / That for thy right myself will bear all wrong" (88). But just beyond the illusion of merger is an isolation stripped of autonomy, an abandoned self that has forfeited its own claims to selfhood. Barber aptly summarizes the poet's situation: "The poet's sense of himself hinges on the identification: elation in realizing himself in the friend's self is matched by desolation when he is left in the lurch of selflessness." [24]

The terrible simplicity of self-denial transcended by merger with an idealized other cannot easily sustain itself in the context of this troubled friendship. The effort to live through the presence of an

24. "An Essay on the Sonnets," in *Elizabethan Poetry: Modern Essays in Criticism*, ed. Paul J. Alpers (New York: Oxford University Press, 1967), p. 314.

illusory ideal, in the image of which Shakespeare creates his beloved friend, is qualified by a counter effort, more difficult to describe because it is never completed and fully articulated in the poems. This counter trend includes, but is not identical with, confronting disillusionment and recognizing the ambivalence engendered within the poet by strains on the friendship. Such poems as 33 ("Full many a glorious morning have I seen") and 95 ("How sweet and lovely dost thou make the shame") make gestures toward disillusionment, and express, if only fleetingly, the hostility that builds up toward the friend, and is more often aligned in the *Sonnets* with the project of self-accusation. But beyond such transitory efforts to cut the figure of the friend down to human size, the *Sonnets* as a cumulative expression seem to allow Shakespeare to approach an awareness of dimensions of his love for the friend that cannot be fully articulated in them, because to do so would (and presumably, in the experience behind the *Sonnets*, did) break the bondage for which the poetry exists and out of which it grows.

Perhaps the larger significance of the *Sonnets*, in all the inconclusiveness they together present, is that they do not need to go on, not that the relationship from which they spring is brought to some kind of resolution in them (which it is not), but that it is made no longer necessary. Shakespeare does not so much comprehend the experience as exhaust it; in doing so, he enables himself to go beyond it, to master in drama situations that often center on conditions like those that elude mastery in the love for the friend. In the relatively isolated experience recounted in the *Sonnets*, Shakespeare brings into the concretizing processes of poetry, not the secure and dignified idealization Montaigne finds in the relation to La Boetie, but awesome and often disturbing dimensions of ambivalent inner experience that will be taken into the core of the great dramatic art that follows.[25] What the consequences of all this were in Shakespeare's

25. Although linked closely to Montaigne's friendship by historical situation and by the quality of sacred devotion in each, Shakespeare's love for the friend resembles in complexity Freud's bond to Fliess. Freud's "transference" relation with Fliess, Khan observes, was characterized by "his lurid over-idealization of Fliess, his over-estimation of Fliess's intellect, his impassioned dependence on Fliess's judgement and approval, and its transience." But Khan also observes:

I do not think it is too much to claim for this friendship that it alone made Freud's self-analysis possible and helped him to discover his analytic method,

personal life there is no way of knowing. But the consequences for
that part of his life he draws on for the drama we can see in the
drama itself, in those dramatic actions where Shakespeare presents
the protagonist's total, ambivalent investment of self in the object
of his love.

In the *Sonnets*, the idealization that takes the place of trust in
the bond to the friend blocks gestures toward disillusionment and a
fully clarified recognition of the ambivalence the friendship engenders. Unresolved tensions, denied, averted, or given covert expression
in the private relationship to the friend, give way to the dramatic mastery of ambivalence in the public realm of tragic art. Through a shift
in relations to inner needs and hazards that beset the self in an all-
or-nothing love, "or gluttoning on all, or all away" (75), discoveries
that intrude upon the experience recounted in the *Sonnets* become
resources for the intensified exploration of human vulnerability undertaken in the tragedies. Tragic protagonists like Othello, Lear, and
Antony, who are given the exalted status Shakespeare associates
with the friend, are also, like the poet of the *Sonnets*, made the sub-
jective centers of love relations that threaten catastrophic loss. In
tragic form, the experience of devastating loss, repeatedly denied in
the *Sonnets*, can be embraced and fully objectified. Magnificent
heroes, for whom the investment of trust in self and other is brought
into irreconcilable conflict with the need to assert or maintain au-

---

the essence of which is that a person can observe himself as–if the other through
the presence and instrumentality of an actual other. (p. 108)

The tension Khan sees between Fliess as an "actual other" and as the carrier
of Freud's projected ideal self is analogous to the tension in Shakespeare's
regard for the friend of the *Sonnets*. The assurance provided by idealization
of the friend makes possible the liberation and ultimate mastery both of
potential strengths and of potential hazards: in Freud through self-analysis
facilitated by a relation with Fliess sustained mostly by letter; in Shakespeare
through poems written to celebrate in the friend "all the better part of me"
(*Son.* 39). Illusory assurance engenders actual vulnerability; the failure of
idealization provokes hatred of the actual other; but both facilitate heightened,
objectified awareness of inner motives that have formed the hidden core of
the relationship. Tensions in the friendship with Fliess, Khan argues, lead
Freud to an understanding of ambivalence, of the inseparability of "love and
hate in his self-experience" (p. 110). Love carries the burden of suppressing
hostility engendered in the poet's bond with the friend of the *Sonnets*. The
ambivalence Freud reluctantly and painfully discovers in his self-analysis becomes the cornerstone of the analytic situation; the ambivalence Shakespeare
labors not to discover in the *Sonnets* is taken up at the center of his tragic art.

tonomous selfhood, can be created and then destroyed in actions
that disclose the protagonists' vulnerable humanity. The destruction
of these characters is an integral part of their creation, a process
through which they are not lost—as the Sonnets poet fears the loss
of the friend—but fully possessed and integrated into enduring dramatic reality. A comprehensive tragic perspective that includes disillusionment can reveal the limits of protagonists, themselves caught
up in violent swings from idealization to degradation, both of self
and others, without diminishing their greatness. The plays themselves achieve the wholeness that the tragic protagonists—like the
poet of the Sonnets—are unable to achieve in their own experience.

This relation between the Sonnets and the directions in which
Shakespeare's later art moves can be further clarified by one more
contrast with Montaigne's Essayes. In the essay celebrating the
friendship with La Boetie, Montaigne makes it clear that "affection
toward women" cannot be put "in this ranke":

> Her fire, I confesse it . . . to be more active, more fervent, and more
> sharpe. But it is a rash and wavering fire, waving and divers: the fire
> of an ague subject to fits and stints, and that hath but a slender
> hold-fast of us. (Essayes, p. 146)

Though this description would understate significantly both the
compulsiveness and the sense of contamination in many of the
poems to the dark lady, Montaigne here expresses an attitude toward
women comparable to the sometimes feverish, sometimes whimsical
attitude Shakespeare brings to Sonnets 127–52. The affair presented
in these poems, like the relations to women Montaigne describes,
does not call out the all-encompassing response elicited by the love
for the friend. They present a love that holds the poet strongly, but
against simultaneous repulsion, and with "but a slender hold-fast":
"If thy unworthiness raised love in me, / More worthy I to be beloved
of thee" (150).

For Montaigne, his life stabilized around the internalized ideal
of his friend, there is no subsequent swerve in later essays toward relations to women. Although other essays contain generous comments
about particular women (often in connection with sacrificial gestures within subordinate relations with men),[26] and although a num-

26. In "Of Three Good Women," for instance, two of the women are
notable for exemplary suicides that inspired their wavering husbands—one

ber of impressively talented and powerful women were important to
Montaigne in his life, the passage on "affection toward women"
quoted from "Of Friendship" hits a note repeatedly sounded
throughout the *Essayes*. What is perhaps most striking, in connection with Shakespeare, is not the cynicism that often attends such
comments, but the limits of Montaigne's imagination in response to
experience that turns on relations of men to women. Womanly
powers could, for Montaigne, come into prominence only as a result of masculine folly, a part of the human comedy he surveys with
exquisite detachment:

> me thinkes, we seldome see that woman borne, to whom the superi-
> oritie or majestie over men is due, except the motherly and naturall;
> unless it be for the chastisement of such, as by some fond-febricitant
> humor have voluntarily submitted themselves unto them. . . .
>   ("Of the Affection of Fathers to
>   Their Children." *Essayes*, II, viii, p. 352)

One need only set this passage beside the tragic action of *King Lear*,
which it describes in a crabbed sort of way, or beside the ending of
The Winter's Tale, to glimpse an essential difference between Montaigne's imagination and Shakespeare's development beyond the
Sonnets.

The bond to La Boetie, free of ambivalence and enshrined at the
very center of experience, fulfilled for Montaigne an impulse that
comes to exercise a potently central force in Shakespearean tragedy
and romance. "Replete" with the presence of his friend in a stable
way never achieved in the *Sonnets*, Montaigne's imagination provides no impetus toward the tragic reach that in Shakespeare is
grounded in familial patterns of experience and is often embodied
in relations to women. The need in Montaigne that fulfills itself in
idealized friendship recenters itself in Shakespeare's tragic drama in
relations of men to women that hold out the promise of ideal, absolute fulfillment and that culminate in mutual destruction. The
nourishing, maternal presence Shakespeare becomes in his relation

---

condemned to live in incurable pain, the other under the sentence of death—
to do likewise; the third, Seneca's young wife Paulina, attempts to join her
husband in his self-inflicted death. Montaigne finds the three examples "as
pleasant and as tragicall, as any we devise at our pleasures, to please the vul-
gar sort withall . . ." (II, xxxv, p. 672); but the vision into which he incorporates them in the *Essayes* is not a tragic one.

to the friend is sought out, tragically, by King Lear, who "mad'st thy daughters thy mothers" (I.iv.163–64), by Othello, who makes of Desdemona "the fountain from the which my current runs / Or else dries up" (IV.ii.59–60). The self-effacing, submissive posture the *Sonnets* poet often embraces in his relation to the beloved is experienced in the tragedies as excruciating shame, helplessness, and rage. The suppressed ambivalence that just edges into the sonnets to the friend emerges directly, and in countless forms, tragically interweaving love with hate, fear, and violence. Both feared loss of autonomy through submission and the torment of intolerable ambivalence are focused chiefly through conflicting needs tragic protagonists bring to other characters indispensable to their own identities.

The feverous love for the dark lady in the *Sonnets* exists in tension in one direction with the chaste, idealized, all-consuming love for the friend and, in another direction, with the love relations—protected from sexual degradation, but also much less intense in themselves than the poet's love for the friend—orchestrated by chaste, trustworthy young women in the festive comedies. These three modes of loving maintain their separate characteristic qualities throughout the phase of Shakespeare's development to which they belong, even when the poet's "man right fair" and "woman colored ill" (144) pair off with each other in the *Sonnets*. But the essential qualities of all three modes converge in the later drama in all-consuming relations of men to women often perceived in the images of both the treacherous dark lady of the *Sonnets* and the trustworthy heroines of the festive comedies. The image of the dark lady, which exists at the compulsive, degraded periphery of the *Sonnets*, is often reinscribed in the tragedies and the late romances, as when Othello addresses Desdemona: "Was this fair paper, this most goodly book, / Made to write 'whore' upon?" (IV.ii.71–72). But when Othello writes whore upon Desdemona, he does not write in the margins of experience, but upon the idealized presence he has made the center of his life. Nor does he write the truth.

An essential form of tragic intensity in Shakespeare, as well as an essential route toward the recovery of lost relations in the late romances, resides in the protagonist's need to find an image of his own completion reflected in the most goodly books held up to him by Desdemona and Cordelia, by Cleopatra, Marina, and Hermione.

When in such quests, the heritage of the dark lady—a fearful distrust of female power and sexuality—returns again and again, it does not provoke bawdy accommodation to "seeming trust" (138) and "th' uncertain sickly appetite" (147), but failed trust and violence. The *Sonnets* poet labors to separate "better angel" from "worser spirit" (144), and to isolate both from the great world of "Fortune and men's eyes" (29). Adoration and degradation, intimacy and awe, private anguish and catastrophe that shakes a whole society, converge at the centers of the later plays, most typically in relations of men to women:

> OTHELLO Excellent wretch! Perdition catch my soul
> But I do love thee! and when I love thee not,
> Chaos is come again. (III.iii.90–92)

Trust and Autonomy: *Hamlet*

> HAMLET   *Once more good night,*
> *And when you are desirous to be blest,*
> *I'll blessing beg of you.* (III.iv.171–73)

Richard II and the *Henry IV* plays dramatize intense struggles for political power and autonomous manhood centered in the identity of the king. But the idealized autonomy that Henry brings into *Henry V* is so secure, and therein so untested, that Shakespeare's prior exploration of Hal's inner conflict gives way almost entirely to public celebration of royal heroism and wisdom. Among the festive comedies, ranges of drama not explored earlier are fully realized in *Much Ado* and *Twelfth Night*. But as the comedies move away from the center of trust in feminine control most securely embodied in *Merchant* and *As You Like It*, they move closer to the potential for violent action released in the tragedies. In the *Sonnets*, idealization is unable ultimately to replace the secure trust for which it substitutes. But gestures toward the reestablishment of the autonomy the poet forfeits can only erode a relationship grounded in self-denial and identification with the other. Developments in each group edge Shakespeare's art toward the necessity for a new kind of drama, which can comprehensively dramatize converging ranges of experience earlier explored separately in distinct genres.

The experience isolated in the *Sonnets* from the political realities and social rhythms rendered so fully in the histories and comedies perhaps has special importance in expanding the psychological base of Shakespearean drama. The mastery the *Sonnets* poet seeks by merging with a projected ideal, and which he quietly subverts by making himself (like his readers) aware of the futility of this effort, releases depths of feeling Shakespeare will master in tragedies that open outward to the larger public world. In a discussion of "fusion states," Gilbert J. Rose describes the shift in relation to potentialities within oneself that can be made possible by abandoning oneself fully to another:

> Mastering something by "fusing" with it, temporarily obscuring the boundaries between the self and object representations, recalls the primary narcissism of the infant and the psychotic. But to merge in order to re-emerge, may be part of the fundamental process of psychological growth on all developmental levels. Although fusion may dominate the most primitive levels, it contributes a richness of texture and quality to the others. Such operations may result in nothing more remarkable than normally creative adaptation to circumstance. . . . [But they] may result in transcending the limitations of earlier stages of narcissism to simplify, unify anew, and recreate an expanded reality.[27]

Shakespeare creates such an expanded reality for his art in the tragedies.

The impact of opening up the drama to a greatly expanded range of conflict is reflected in the action and the imagery of *Hamlet*. Horatio and the sentinels, in the first scene, struggle to take in the "dreaded sight" (I.i.25) of old Hamlet's ghost without being overwhelmed by it. They exploit the resources of political knowledge, myth, superstition, and finally the reassuring natural order embodied in the sunrise to cope with an overpowering presence at once familiar ("Look's a not like the king? Mark it Horatio"); alien and mysterious ("What art thou that usurp'st this time of night? . . ."); and undeniably real ("How now, Horatio? You tremble and look pale. / Is this not something more than fantasy?" [I.i.43, 46, 53–54]). The efforts of these men not only anticipate Hamlet's larger effort to accommodate experience that threatens to nullify his whole prior relation to himself and to the world, but mirror Shakespeare's effort

27. "Fusion States," in *Tactics and Techniques of Psychoanalytic Therapy*, ed. Peter L. Giovacchini (London: Hogarth Press, 1972), p. 185.

to take into the order of his art dimensions of experience never approached in the previous drama.

"It harrows me with fear and wonder" (I.i.44), Horatio observes, initiating an image pattern especially important to the early parts of the play. This pattern suggests a self that has its integrity as a whole, unified being threatened with violent destruction by an intrusion of alien, overpowering force. Horatio describes to Hamlet the ghost's appearance before the sentinels:

> Thrice he walked
> By their oppressed and fear-surprisèd eyes
> Within his truncheon's length, whilst they, distilled
> Almost to jelly with the act of fear,
> Stand dumb and speak not to him.   (I.ii.202–6)

When Hamlet first sees the ghost, he faces the same threat, magnified by his special situation, but expressed in a rhetoric of terror and imminent disintegration that recalls the language of Horatio. "Let me not burst in ignorance," Hamlet cries, as if about to explode from the force of the ghost's unassimilable presence, which he both recognizes as his father and regards as utterly mysterious:

> What may this mean
> That thou, dead corse, again in complete steel,
> Revisits thus the glimpses of the moon,
> Making night hideous, and we fools of nature
> So horridly to shake our disposition
> With thoughts beyond the reaches of our souls?
>   (I.iv.46, 51–56)

After confronting the ghost directly, Hamlet first turns outward— "O all you host of heaven! O earth! What else? / And shall I couple hell?" (I.v.92–93)—then inward in the attempt to compose himself in relation to an experience that can neither be absorbed into the self nor refused admittance to it. The turn inward recalls the earlier imagery of a body harrowed by an alien intrusion:

> O fie! Hold, hold, my heart,
> And you, my sinews, grow not instant old,
> But bear me stiffly up.   (I.v.93–95)

The solution Hamlet automatically attempts is to take in entirely the "commandment" of the ghost, which "all alone shall live / Within the book and volume of my brain, / Unmixed with baser matter" (I.v.102–4). The "baser matter" Hamlet would exclude from the purified role of avenger he longs to adopt comprises "all trivial fond records, / All saws of books, all forms, all pressures past / That youth and observation copied there" (I.v.99–101), and perhaps also the "sullied flesh" (I.ii.129) that is a source of anguish prior to the ghost's appearance. His fear of collapse from the force of the ghost's violent intrusion, however, proves to be more prophetic than his resolution to follow the ghost's command through a complete surrender of himself to it. The self he longs to remake in the image of the ghost's command has a resilience of its own.

Prior to the ghost's appearance to him, Hamlet is locked into a withdrawn state of mourning by conditions that have so radically altered the world he has known before his father's death he has no way and apparently little desire to reenter it. His retreat into mourning includes a wish for self-destruction, but its main purpose seems to be to protect the battered integrity of a self whose only accessible authentic feeling toward the world outside him—outrage with his mother's remarriage—would be violated by any conciliatory step toward that world. The confrontation with the ghost validates that outrage, and seems at first to promise a source of unified, fateful power:

> My fate cries out
> And makes each petty artere in this body
> As hardy as the Nemean lion's nerve.   (1.iv.81–83)

But the commandment of his dead father ultimately threatens to usurp Hamlet's inner world as completely as Claudius has usurped the outer world of family and politics. This problem is extravagantly compounded by Hamlet's necessary attempt to collaborate in this usurpation. Hamlet is placed in a position in which the affirmation of self through his commitment to action enjoined by his father's ghost is identical with absolute surrender of individual autonomy.

Hamlet's delaying tactics express his resistance to the self-surrender he wills upon himself. In Ernest Jones's argument, Hamlet's "uncle incorporates the deepest and most buried part of his own personality, so that he cannot kill him without also killing himself." [28]

28. *Hamlet and Oedipus* (1949; reprint ed. New York: Norton, 1976), p. 88. K. R. Eissler (*Discourse on Hamlet and "Hamlet"* [New York: International Universities Press, 1971], p. 85) and Theodore Lidz (*Hamlet's*

But Hamlet does not fear his own death so much as he recoils from his own willed effort to nullify the ground, already put out of his reach by his response to his mother's remarriage, upon which relations to the self, including self-destructive relations, are ordered. Hamlet struggles against his own declared intention at a level deeper than his will and in a way not entirely explained by fear of repressed motives. He involuntarily seeks to preserve the potential integrity of self violated by his own attempt to take in and identify totally with the image of his father embodied in the ghost's command. This psychological resistance is analogous to the expulsion reaction in the biochemistry of an organism, set into action by the intrusion of alien tissue. Hamlet attempts to perform a kind of self-transplant upon his own person, and the core of his individual self will not accept the foreign intruder.

Hamlet's oscillating commitment to revenge expresses mutually subverting imperatives to be himself and to surrender himself totally to an other in inner and outer environments hostile to both efforts. M. Masud R. Khan has found, for persons driven to subvert their own latent capacity for autonomous, integrated self-experience, that the "typical anxiety affect is threat of annihilation and its pervasive defence mechanism is staying dissociated and hidden, not repressed."[29] Khan's observation helps identify an essential threat Hamlet confronts in the play, the threat of self-annihilation he both wills upon himself and tenaciously resists. It also helps explain Hamlet's remarkable dexterity in hiding himself through the dissociated self of madness, while he brings the repressed content of his situation very close to the surface. In the play Hamlet stages for Claudius, for instance, the player king is murdered, not by a brother, but by a nephew, edging the play within a play that much closer to the oedipal situation of the larger drama.

As a public gesture, the "mouse-trap" amounts to a virtual confession of his secret knowledge of Claudius's guilt; Hamlet confirms what he already knows, while Claudius is presented with the aware-

---

Enemy [New York: Basic Books, 1975], pp. 173–74) believe that Hamlet delays killing Claudius out of fear of foreclosing the possibility of reunion with a mother purged of guilt. Avi Erlich, by contrast, argues that the apparent delay is part of a larger pattern centered in Hamlet's "unfulfilled need for a strong father" (*Hamlet's Absent Father* [Princeton: Princeton University Press, 1977], p. 49).

29. "The Finding and Becoming of Self," *The Privacy of the Self*, p. 294.

ness Hamlet has thus far kept hidden. Hamlet is more concerned to hide what he is than what he knows, but what he is is hidden from himself as well. Even the desire to avenge his father's murder Hamlet confronts by futilely trying to find the essence of himself in a radically simplified role of revenger—as if he learned it from Elizabethan revenge tragedy:

> Now could I drink hot blood
> And do such bitter business as the day
> Would quake to look on. (III.ii.375–77)
> O, from this time forth,
> My thoughts be bloody, or be nothing worth. (IV.iv.65–66)

Hamlet turns to the role of avenger to give structure and meaning and power to a life that has been made chaotic and empty and powerless. But like an individual who develops what D. W. Winnicott calls a "false self" organization to defend against exploitation and possible annihilation of the core of his identity, Hamlet cannot fully exist—cannot "be"—within the revenger's role.[30]

Hamlet is caught between two forms of self-estrangement that exacerbate each other. One, engendered by the loss of his father and greatly intensified by what he perceives as the betrayal of his mother, undermines the base of identity in internalized trust. The other, engendered by the appearance of his father's ghost, imposes an unacceptable identity upon Hamlet that he wills to accept but cannot. But of the polarized forms of identity that Hamlet does find authentically compelling, neither the inviolate selfhood of Horatio, "whose blood and judgment are so well commeddled / That they are not a pipe for Fortune's finger / To play what stop she please" (III. ii.66–68), nor the multiple selfhood of an actor, who can identify himself with any role in the protected play space of drama, is available to him as an ultimate resolution in his search for autonomous selfhood. As Hamlet recognizes from the time of his encounter with the ghost, he is being played by circumstances of Fortune over which he has no control ("The time is out of joint. O cursèd spite / That ever I was born to set it right!" [I.v.188–89]); playing mad, putting on an "antic disposition" (I.v.172), will neither restore the lost inner

30. See "Ego Distortion in Terms of True and False Self," in *The Maturational Processes and the Facilitating Environment* (London: Hogarth Press, 1965), pp. 140–52.

sense of self nor alter the external circumstances that have trauma-tized it.

What such exacerbated experience demands for self-recovery, Khan writes, "is mutuality—that is, shared trust." [31] The unacknowledged quest that dominates Hamlet, engaging him more deeply than his desire for revenge, is the quest for such trust. The ghost of his dead father, rather than resolve this quest, compounds its difficulties; the ghost transgresses mutuality, usurping rather than enlarging and strengthening the self that seeks to recover a base for its own opera-tions. For Hamlet trust has been stripped of its place in relations to self and others and reduced to imprisoned potentiality by the muti-nous frailty of a coveted mother. Horatio provides a kind of holding relation that keeps the potential for mutuality alive, but cannot change the conditions that have created and sustained the failure of trust. The relationship to Ophelia, because it inherits the violent mistrust of women and female sexuality that derives from Gertrude's incestuous union, is put beyond the reach of the trust and absolution Hamlet seems to want to seek in it:

> Soft you now,
> The fair Ophelia!—Nymph, in thy orisons
> Be all my sins remembered.   (iii.i.88–90)

At the center of Hamlet's search for self is his need to repurify and rediscover himself in the trustworthy, internalized maternal pres-ence that Gertrude has contaminated by her "o'erhasty marriage" (II.ii.57), sullying Hamlet's flesh even as she sullies her own.

The ghost's command that his death be avenged includes a stipu-lation that greatly complicates Hamlet's attempt to abide by it:

> But howsomever thou pursues this act,
> Taint not thy mind, nor let thy soul contrive
> Against thy mother aught. Leave her to heaven
> And to those thorns that in her bosom lodge
> To prick and sting her.   (i.v.84–88)

It is, however, his relation to his mother that preys most deeply on Hamlet's mind; the "taint" and the precariously suppressed rage it engenders are precisely what link him most closely both to his dev-astated inner world and to the "solidity and compound mass" of a

31. "The Finding and Becoming of Self," p. 294.

world beyond him that Gertrude's remarriage makes "thought-sick" (III.iv.50, 52). The bond the ghost commands him to ignore, the source of his deepest torment, provides the only potential route to restored trust and autonomy available to Hamlet.

Hamlet is driven by his rage against Gertrude more powerfully than by his desire to kill Claudius. He steels himself not to murder Gertrude, but he must in some way act in the context of this rage to move toward the trust imprisoned by it. Not until the matricidal impulse is released and deflected onto Polonius, hiding behind the arras in Gertrude's closet, can Hamlet envision what he thinks, at least, is a rapprochement with his repentent mother whom he wants "to be blest" so he may "blessing beg" of her (III.iv.172–73). Gertrude dies when she drinks a poisoned cup of wine that, as part of its meaning, represents her contamination of the nurturing bond of trust with her son.[32] As she dies, Gertrude absorbs the destructiveness that has bound Hamlet to her throughout the play. Only after her death is Hamlet finally able to act, in his own person, to destroy the usurping king. In the complexities surrounding Gertrude's death, the killing of Claudius, and his own approaching death, Hamlet seems to be able to control for himself the conditions of the incestuous union that earlier made him powerless ("Is thy union here?" he asks of Claudius, "Follow my mother" [V.ii.315–16]); to separate himself from his mother's contamination ("Wretched queen, adieu!" [V.ii.322]); to stop the chain of mutual poisoning and contamination initiated by the murder of his father ("Give me the cup. Let go. By heaven, I'll ha't!" [V.ii.332]); and to establish, in dying, the sense of manly righteousness denied him throughout the play ("Horatio, I am dead; / Thou livest; report me and my cause aright / To the unsatisfied" [V.ii.327–29]).

In the play's closing, Hamlet apparently approaches an integrated relation to experience that embodies trust as a base for the self, a self-trust he comes to understand in the context of divine providence. It is not clear, however, to what extent this quest is resolved dramatically—whether Hamlet's discovery of an all-encompassing providence, present even in "the fall of a sparrow" (V.ii.209), represents a

32. Compare Leontes as he likens his loss of trust in Hermione to the plight of one who drinks from a cup "steeped" with the venom of a spider: "I have drunk and seen the spider. . . . All's true that is mistrusted" (*WT* II.i.45, 48).

truer relation to the world of the play than he has known before, or whether it is a final attempt to endow that world with attributes that answer to private needs in himself. But it is clear, I think, that one trend in the drama moves to restore for Hamlet the inner strength and integrity of an individual self threatened with annihilation from within as well as from external circumstances, and that the restoration of the capacity for trust is essential to the restoration of self. Perhaps Hamlet's last words suggest a confirmation of the importance of this movement within the troubled ambiguities of the last scene.

Although there are obvious dangers of overloading, or rather of misloading, Hamlet's final cryptic expression, "the rest is silence" (V.ii.347), I would like to view it here through a perspective provided by D. W. Winnicott in an essay on forms of communication. Winnicott finds that the center of health in the personality is a necessarily isolated core of the self that exists beyond communication with external reality, but makes communication with reality possible. He regards the violation of this core as the essential "sin against the self."[33] It is at this core that the individual enters into communication with himself, and the medium of this communication is silence. Winnicott defines this core of the self—his way, I think, of understanding what Erikson calls the establishment of basic trust—as

> the non-communicating central self, for ever immune from the reality principle, and for ever silent. Here communication is not non-verbal; it is, like the music of the spheres, absolutely personal. It belongs to being alive. And in health, it is out of this that communication naturally arises. (p. 192)[34]

"The question is," Winnicott states, "how to be isolated without having to be insulated?" (p. 187). This question seems to go right to the heart of Hamlet's excruciating efforts to establish a self while hiding it from others, and to keep himself at a distance from external realities that threaten to violate his inner self while remaining in touch with a world of potential meaning beyond him.

The delight Hamlet takes in madness as camouflage celebrates his success at hiding himself from others and in keeping at least part of

---

33. "Communicating and Not Communicating Leading to a Study of Certain Opposites," *The Maturational Processes*, p. 187.

34. Winnicott here puts the "music of the spheres" to metaphorical use virtually identical with its dramatic function in *Pericles* V.i.

encroaching reality at a distance. But the "words, words, words" (II. ii.191) into which Hamlet channels his antic disposition, his rage at Gertrude and at women generally, his vows of vengeance, his meditations on life's meaning, and his disgust at his own inaction, cannot consolidate an inner sense of identity.[35] The core of the self Hamlet hides from others remains for most of the play out of his own reach as well. His fear is not simply of being found, but, in a phrase of Winnicott's, of "being found before being there to be found" (p. 190). The full burden of Hamlet's crisis as it is compounded by the ghost is first registered in the awesomely sinister silence of the exchange Ophelia reports to her father. There Hamlet's departure from the woman he has loved dramatizes also the intensity of his own self-estrangement:

> He raised a sigh so piteous and profound
> As it did seem to shatter all his bulk
> And end his being. (II.i.94–96)

Perhaps the silence Hamlet refers to in his last utterance issues from a final sense of "being there," of having found himself in relation to that silent core of the self violently usurped by circumstances in which he "must like a whore unpack my heart with words / And fall a-cursing like a very drab, / A stallion!" (II.ii.571–73).

Or, to shift the frame to include Hamlet's creator, perhaps Shakespeare, having confronted, in a play that takes drama to previously unexplored depths, psychic hazards that threaten the self with annihilation, offers *Hamlet* as a "communication [that] arises out of silence" ("Communicating . . ." [p. 191]), the silence at the core of a self that has risked all in order to find and affirm itself through the drama. Hamlet's quest leads to destruction. By comprehending this destruction in drama, Shakespeare finds the strength to confront through tragic action deep sources of destruction and estrangement in human experience.[36]

The crisis of trust as it exacerbates Hamlet's effort to achieve an

35. Janet Adelman has helped me see this, and much else that I address in this chapter, more clearly by her painstaking commentary on it.

36. In a 1922 paper on "The Impatience of Hamlet," Ella Freeman Sharpe made this distinction succinctly and clearly: "The poet is not Hamlet. Hamlet is what he might have been if he had not written the play of *Hamlet*" (*Collected Papers on Psycho-Analysis*, ed. Marjorie Brierley [London: Hogarth Press, 1950], p. 205).

autonomous identity consolidates the psychological base of the
drama that follows, both for the destructive action of tragedy and
for the reconstructive movements of the late romances. *Hamlet*
is unique among Shakespeare's tragedies in that it moves, or seems
to move, through tragic action toward the establishment of an inclusive identity earlier denied to the tragic protagonist. Troilus,
hopelessly divided within himself when he loses the identity he
thinks he has found in his love for Cressida, will attempt desperately
to exorcise that part of himself based on relations to the feminine:

> For th' love of all the gods,
> Let's leave the hermit pity with our mother,
> And when we have our armors buckled on,
> The venomed vengeance ride upon our swords,
> Spur them to ruthful work, rein them from ruth.   (v.iii.44–48)

By contrast, Cleopatra will dream the completion of "an Emperor
Antony" (V.ii.76) who synthesizes elements that tear the actual
Antony apart; the tragic sense of *Antony and Cleopatra* arises out
of the gap separating dream and actuality, which relegates the consummation of Antony's manhood to the realm of dream. But Hamlet's effort to incorporate an image of heroic manhood, stripped of
ties to women, stipulated by his father's ghost, and his conflicting
effort to recover the capacity for trust shattered by Gertrude's incestuous union identify the psychological directions in which the
ensuing drama will move.

Turn and Counter-Turn: The Tragedies and Romances

> LEAR   *Filial ingratitude,*
> *Is it not as this mouth should tear this hand*
> *For lifting food to't?*   (iii.iv.14–16)

Conflicting impulses within the needs for trust and autonomy,
averted in the festive comedies and displaced away from Hal's quest
for power in the *Henriad*, shape the drama in a new way in *Hamlet*.
A polarity based in this conflict, which begins to take form in the
movement from *Hamlet* to *Troilus and Cressida*, recurs regularly
in the drama that follows; it is refined to exceptional purity in *An-*

tony and Cleopatra and *Coriolanus* at the end of the period of the tragedies, and again in *The Winter's Tale* and *The Tempest*. This polarization, which indicates emphasis and subordination, not exclusion, points to shifts in relations among basic needs and psychological hazards present in all the plays. It is expressed in a pattern of contrast that cuts across other lines of development; with varying degrees of clarity and comprehensiveness, it tends to sort the later drama into two groups of plays. The fear of and the longing for merger with another provide the primary driving force in the plays of one of these groups. In the other, a comparably ambivalent relation to the prospect of omnipotent autonomy provides the psychic context in which the protagonists seek self-definition. I will refer to the two groups as the *trust/merger* group and the *autonomy/isolation* group. The terms paired across a slash mark designate the primary positive and negative trends—the need and the characteristic danger that accompanies it—held in tension within the plays of each group.

The tragedies I include in the trust/merger group are *Hamlet*, *Othello*, *King Lear*, and *Antony and Cleopatra*. In these plays, the effort to establish power and autonomy is ultimately subordinated to what proves to be a stronger need for a lost or jeopardized bond to another. The need for mutuality in a relation of trust, however, contains within it a longing for merger with another. This longing provides the primitive prototype for mutuality, but, because its aim is to eradicate the identity of both parties, is antagonistic to it. A characteristic fear underlying the experience of the protagonists of these plays is loss of autonomy in a union that destroys both self and other. But longing for merger shapes the action, and is culminated, tragically, in the endings of these plays. Hamlet's final sense of enclosing himself within the sphere of "a divinity that shapes our ends, / Rough-hew them how we will" (V.ii.10–11), completes in a dramatically ambiguous religious resolution a movement more directly realized in the human context of the other plays of this group. Othello, after he labors desperately to reconstruct an image of his heroic self, joins Desdemona on her death bed, "to die upon a kiss" (V.ii.359). The dying Lear, with dead Cordelia in his arms, tragically consummates the overreaching longing that has driven him throughout the play. Antony dies in the arms of Cleopatra, to be reborn through the fertile womb of her imagination into a transcendent image of manhood he has been unable to achieve in his life. In each instance, an extravagant effort to protect a deeply threatened ideal of manly selfhood gives way to a more powerful longing, completed with tragic irony, for merger with another. In skeletal form, the culminating action of these plays moves through loss of identity in isolation toward tragic realization, in mutual destruction, of the longing for merger.

The tragedies I include in the autonomy/isolation group are *Troilus and Cressida, Macbeth, Timon of Athens,* and *Coriolanus.* In these plays, relations of the self to others that promise fulfillment instead prohibit the achievement of stable autonomy. In contrast to the movement toward union in the trust/merger group, tragic protagonists in the autonomy/isolation group move away from relations of unqualified trust that ultimately prove to be destructive. Each of these relationships is grounded in a perilous overinvestment of self in others—a mistress, a wife, a whole society, a mother—that negates the autonomy these characters will make desperate efforts to retrieve. Troilus's naive faith in Cressida, Macbeth's desperate reliance on the will of his powerful wife, Timon's bizarre attempt to appropriate for himself the role of nurturing mother to all of Athens, and Coriolanus's bond to his mother shape dependent, contingent identities that define both the strength and the vulnerability of these characters. The psychic separateness each initially either denies or surrenders is tragically realized as complete estrangement, isolation, and impotent rage against a world perceived as hostile, intrusive other. The culminating action of these plays moves through destructive merger toward isolation and emptiness. Rather than die, like the protagonists of the trust/merger group, in a union with a beloved other, Troilus is left in impotent, empty rage; Macbeth and Coriolanus, desperately and defiantly alone, are hacked to death by enemies; Timon dies, in a grave of his own making, after petitioning the "common mother," the "common whore of mankind": "Ensear thy fertile and conceptious womb; / Let it no more bring out ingrateful man!" (IV.iii.177; 43; 187–88).

The contrasting movements of the two groups can be summarized by a glance at key developments in the experience of Lear and Macbeth. In the opening scene of *King Lear,* there is a clear incompatibility between Lear's implicit assumption of absolute power and freedom and his actual forfeiture of political power to his daughters. Driving Lear, and underscoring his desire to "shake all cares and business from our age," is his longing for a condition of childlike dependency with his beloved Cordelia: "I loved her most, and thought to set my rest / On her kind nursery . . ." (I.i.39; 123–24). After he banishes Cordelia, and after Regan and Goneril have refused to comply with his demands on them, Lear is unable to articulate the "true need" (II.iv.265) they have failed to accommodate. But after the shattering experience of the storm, in which his effort to assert hallucinatory omnipotence by commanding the heavens to serve his will gives way to his own collapse, Lear can express that need and the joy that attends its apparent fulfillment, when he would transform imprisonment into the earthly paradise of a sacred union with Cordelia:

> Come, let's away to prison.
> We two alone will sing like birds i' th' cage.
> When thou dost ask me blessing, I'll kneel down
> And ask of thee forgiveness.　(v.iii.8–11)

Lear's final experience oscillates between unbearable awareness of Cordelia's death—"Thou'lt come no more, / Never, never, never, never, never . . ."—and undeniable longing to retrieve her, to exist in the presence of the radiant, human, feminine face and voice that alone can confer wholeness and meaning—"Look on her! Look her lips, / Look there, look there— . . ." (V.iii.308–9; 311–12). The sum of Macbeth's experience, by contrast, is realized as absolute aloneness, bereft even of desire for relations with others. The death of Lady Macbeth offstage releases Macbeth's vision of life as a "walking shadow, a poor player," emptied of any context, within the self or external to it, that could provide meaning: "It is a tale / Told by an idiot, full of sound and fury, / Signifying nothing" (V.v.24; 26–28). There is an enormous gulf between Lear's "never" and Macbeth's "nothing." Lear necessarily fails to achieve the conditions he covets for living through Cordelia's presence. Macbeth annihilates in himself the capacity even to imagine a context that would redeem him from absolute, empty isolation.

Whereas *King Lear* begins with the separation of Lear from his daughters, the quest for royal manhood in *Macbeth* (as I suggest in the somewhat fuller discussion of this play in the fourth section of chapter 3) requires that Macbeth's ambition be nurtured into action by others upon whom he becomes dependent. After the first exchange with the witches, Macbeth is driven to achieve a magically compelling ideal of manhood articulated for him by his wife. Macbeth cannot refuse this ideal, but he cannot pursue it except by making himself a child to the demonic motherhood held out to him by Lady Macbeth. This psychological paradox, in which a sense of invulnerable power is grounded in total dependence, repeats the conditions that generate infantile fantasies of omnipotence and makes Macbeth's new manhood desperately unstable from the outset. As the merger of these two characters dissolves, Macbeth's reliance upon the equivocations of the witches only isolates him further within the sterile assumption of absolute power: "Our castle's strength / Will laugh a siege to scorn" (V.v.2–3). After having "supped full with horrors" (V.v.13), Macbeth finds that even the illusion of omnipotence nurtured by the witches collapses before the force of a man "not born of woman" (V.vii.3).

As my emphasis on family bonds and symbolic extensions of them in *King Lear* and *Macbeth* suggests, the psychological patterns I am tracing are grounded in experience in a family, particularly in the crises that accompany the maturational process of forming a separate self out of an originally undifferentiated matrix. Early development comprises, according to Margaret Mahler, "a gradual growing away from the normal state of human symbiosis, of 'oneness' with the mother."[37] As the child discovers that he is not identical with the essential source of nurture provided by the mother and that his world is not magically responsive to urgent demands originating in him, he must struggle to master the first and most profound divisions in the development of the human self. This development proceeds along the lines of what Mahler calls the "gradual process of separation-individuation." The movement through individuation is

37. "On the First Three Subphases of the Separation-Individuation Process," p. 295. Mahler's theory of "the psychological birth of the individual" (p. 296) specifies a series of subphases, each of which contributes differently to the separation-individuation process, and each of which has its specific forms of psychic hazard. But all the subphases are understood within the larger context of opposing gestures toward fusion and separation, a context she sees as active throughout the life span. It is this larger context that I have found most pertinent in formulating an overview of Shakespeare's development in the tragedies and the romances. Mahler's full-length studies of early development, which summarize and extend work reported on in many articles, are: *On Human Symbiosis and the Vicissitudes of Individuation* (London: Hogarth Press, 1969) and *The Psychological Birth of the Human Infant* (New York: Basic Books, 1975).

essential to the establishment of autonomous identity, but is accompanied by unavoidable and repeated traumata of separation. This leads Mahler, with other analysts, to see the "growing away process" as a "lifelong mourning process" (p. 296).

Erik Erikson calls the achievement of the early phases of the separation-individuation process "basic trust," the confidence manifest at the very core of experience that inner urges and external providers are trustworthy enough to allow further development of the self and its relations to others.[38] The establishment of basic trust, and out of it the first gains toward autonomy, underlie all later development, both toward relations with others and toward the consolidation of individual identity. Mahler suggests that "the entire life cycle" pivots on the double "process of distancing from and introjection of the lost symbiotic mother, . . . the 'all-good' mother, who was at one time part of the self in a blissful state of well-being" (Mahler, p. 305).[39] But as the ego develops along boundaries that distinguish the world from the self, crises in the process of separation can engender the wish to reinhabit the symbiotic unity of infant and mother; crises within the environment provided by the mother, including those that provoke fears of "reengulfment," can lead to the defiant repudiation of essential others and to fantasies of a powerful autonomous self that magically incorporates symbiotic omnipotence.

Neither longing for fusion nor longing for omnipotent autonomy can be integrated fully into the contingencies of living, and the separation-individuation process to which they are bound is never complete. Arnold H. Modell emphasizes that in the development of an individual self,

> the acceptance of separateness, as is true for the establishment of one's identity, is never absolute or final. Even if one has established the capacity for mature love, established a sense of identity and accepted the uniqueness of the beloved—there is a wish to merge, to fuse, to lose one's separateness.[40]

38. See especially *Childhood and Society*, 2nd ed. (New York: Norton, 1963), pp. 247–51. I discuss basic trust in relation to the comedies and the late romances in the fourth section of chapter 2 above.

39. The " 'all-good' mother" is not an actual person, but an aspect of the infant's experience of maternal care as a "blissful state of well-being." Mahler links this experience with an "actual or fantasied 'ideal state of self' " (p. 305), a source of longing identical with the longing for fusion.

40. *Object Love and Reality* (New York: International Universities Press, 1968), pp. 61–62.

The wish to merge with another, however, if felt to endanger one's need to be separate, may in turn intensify the effort to establish total separation through withdrawal and isolation. Both the movement toward separation and the longing for fusion may jeopardize the equilibrium of the self that emerges from their interaction: the longing for merger threatens to destroy precariously achieved autonomy; the longing for complete autonomy threatens to isolate the self from its base of trust in actual and internalized relations to others.

Shakespearean tragedy dramatizes conditions of extreme crisis that bring these longings directly into the experience of the protagonist's vulnerable, heroic identity. As C. L. Barber observes, "the roots in infancy from which identity grows outward in healthy situations become, in tragic situations, the source of impossible, destructive and self-destructive demands." [41] *Hamlet*, because it brings into tragic drama the full range of family-based conflict, forecloses solutions available in earlier works that exclude or minimize potentially disruptive conflict. The tragedies that culminate in relations of destructive merger seem to seek to reinhabit the world of love grounded in trust, often presided over by benign female presences, dramatized in the festive comedies. The women of these tragedies— Ophelia, Desdemona, Cordelia, Cleopatra—often recall the women who establish the conditions of loving in the festive comedies, but they cannot accomplish comic goals of stable relations of mutuality. By contrast, the desperate recoil into movements toward travestied autonomy in Troilus, Macbeth, Timon, and Coriolanus recall the simpler world of masculine authority, uncomplicated by the presence of captivating women, that Prince Hal negotiates in the *Henriad*. The split in the *Sonnets* between the chaste, almost sacred idealization of the friend and the degraded sexuality of the dark lady, a split that originates in conflicted responses to a single maternal figure, is taken up and refocused in the tragedies of the trust/merger group, usually in a single relation to a woman, as when Othello inscribes "whore" upon the brow of "divine Desdemona" (IV.ii.72; II.i.73). A sense of desperate isolation, which emerges in those sonnets that suggest failures in Shakespeare's identification with the friend, anticipates the tragic intensity of helpless separation in the plays of

41. I quote from the opening chapter of Barber's unpublished book-length manuscript on the place of the tragedies in the development of Shakespeare's drama and the drama of the Elizabethan stage.

the autonomy/isolation group. In *Timon of Athens*, this helplessness is given dramatic shape by Timon's desperate denial of it when he rails savagely against a society that has failed to reciprocate his nurturing generosity.

In the development of Shakespeare's later drama, the two groups balance and perhaps beget each other in a rhythmic unfolding of plays or, in one instance, pairs of plays, in the same genre. From this vantage point, *Hamlet* in the trust/merger group is closely linked to *Troilus and Cressida* in the autonomy/isolation group, *Othello* and *King Lear* to *Macbeth* and *Timon of Athens*, *Antony and Cleopatra* to *Coriolanus*, as if the movement through isolation to union and the movement through union to isolation recurrently engender each other.[42] This rhythmic, oscillating pattern can be traced into the reconstructive actions of the late romances, blurred a little in the experimental gestures toward new form in *Pericles* and *Cymbeline*, and worked to great clarity in *The Winter's Tale* and *The Tempest*. Like Roethke's woman, "lovely in her bones," Shakespeare's art "moved in circles, and those circles moved."[43] The interinanimations of turn and counter-turn within this psychic dance are virtually infinite, and occur at every level. But it is useful to conceive of four separable contexts in which a movement through an enduring polarity—of trust linked with the threat of destructive merger and of autonomy entangled with the threat of isolation and emptiness—is realized in these plays: in the interaction of conflicting needs for trust and autonomy in the protagonist of a single play; in the oscillating movement from a play in the trust/merger group to a play in the autonomy/isolation group, from *King Lear* to *Macbeth*, for instance, or from *Antony and Cleopatra* to *Coriolanus*; in a spiraling movement toward increased polarization in the de-

42. Although the chronology can never be made totally secure, there is considerable consensus among recent scholars and editors. Harbage provides the following dates for the tragedies, which vary little from those supplied by G. Blakemore Evans in the Riverside ed. (Boston: Houghton Mifflin, 1974) and by Sylvan Barnet in the Signet Classic ed. (New York: Harcourt, Brace, Jovanovich, 1963, 1972): *Hamlet*, 1601; *Troilus and Cressida*, 1602; *Othello*, 1604; *King Lear*, 1605; *Macbeth*, 1605; *Timon of Athens*, 1606; *Antony and Cleopatra*, 1607; *Coriolanus*, 1608. Harbage's dates for the late romances are: *Pericles*, 1607; *Cymbeline*, 1609; *The Winter's Tale*, 1610; *The Tempest*, 1611.

43. Theodore Roethke, "I Knew a Woman," in *Words for the Wind* (Bloomington: Indiana University Press, 1958), p. 151.

velopment first of tragic and then of romance form; and in the polarized relation of the two genres to each other, as the central experience
of loss in the tragedies gives way to the restoration of lost relations
in the late romances.

Lying behind these developments, as a half-mythic paradigm of
stable family harmony, is Hamlet's nostalgic remembrance of his
father's kingly authority complemented by the loving union of royal
husband and wife. But at the outset of *Hamlet*, this private paradise
of familial order has become an "unweeded garden" (I.ii.135). The
tragedies pursue fragmentary, aberrant, self-destructive gestures toward reestablishing either half of the balance of trust and autonomy
Hamlet recalls in his idealization of the past. The late romances
move toward reinstatements of the identity, anchored in images of
manly autonomy and familial unity, Hamlet has lost through his
father's murder and his mother's remarriage. Although in *Hamlet*
the need to be an autonomous, active self and the need to find a relation of trust in which to ground that self are closely balanced, Hamlet must locate himself within a relation to transcendent providence
before completing his personal mission, and both achievements are
dramatically ambiguous. The tragedies that follow intensify and
clarify the polarization between a quest for mutuality subverted by
merger and a quest for autonomy that results in separation. This
polarization reaches extreme form in Antony's death in the arms of
Cleopatra set against Coriolanus's death in an alien city. The late
romances, by extension and by contrast, culminate in the mutuality
reachieved in *The Winter's Tale* and in Prospero's movement toward benevolent autonomy in *The Tempest*.

Antony's bond to Cleopatra expresses a longing denied by the
Roman ideal of manly honor and autonomy. Once he has been en-
snared by Cleopatra's "strong toil of grace" (V.ii.346), Antony can
neither retrieve full rapport with that ideal nor fully articulate an
identity for himself independent of it. When he fails to live up to
a Roman ego-ideal he cannot abandon or qualify, the essential
imagery of self-experience becomes for him as "indistinct / As water
is in water" (IV.xiv.10–11).[44] The deep antagonism between An-

---

44. Janet Adelman perceptively explores the movement in the play by
which Antony's Roman identity is dissolved and transcended through its

tony's Roman self and the mode of relatedness into which he is drawn by Cleopatra is ironically manifest in Antony's death: he declares himself "a Roman, by a Roman / Valiantly vanquished" (IV. xv.57–58) while lying in the arms of the woman who has led him beyond the experiential limits of Roman manhood. Shakespeare makes it clear that Antony's failure to integrate the two poles of his experience is a necessary, tragic failure. To be Cleopatra's "man of men" (I.v.72) is to be enmeshed in the contradictory imperatives realized as paradox in Antony's death. In his life, they are realized by a series of circular movements in which the union of Antony and Cleopatra is severed and then renewed with heightened intensity. The longing for this union is the most powerful need driving Antony: it at once allows him to achieve a richer, more inclusive humanity and estranges him from political resources established by Caesar's deflection of all human impulse into the quest for power.

The longing for identity in mutuality continues to seek elaboration after Antony has been sacrificed to it. It remains for Cleopatra to articulate a dream of an Antony adequate to her own shrewdly exploited dream of herself. From Cleopatra's vantage point, " 'Tis paltry to be Caesar" (V.ii.2). In the dream she describes to Dolabella, an extravagant consummation of human longing for transcendent identity finds in her vigorous, earthy imagination the home it cannot maintain in ongoing human experience: "his delights / Were dolphin-like, they showed his back above / The element they lived in . . ." (V.ii.88–90). This dream of her lover's endless "bounty" ("an autumn 'twas / That grew the more by reaping" [V.ii.86–88]), which embraces Antony in Cleopatra's bountiful imagination of him, is the exalted counterpart of Lady Macbeth's effort to live through her husband in the image of a manhood she covets. Underlying this dream is the longing to reinhabit the serenely mysterious realm of complete unity that Lady Macbeth shatters in her violent repudiation of maternal nurture:

immersion in the fluid, hyperbolical, erotic world of Cleopatra's Egypt in *The Common Liar: An Essay on "Antony and Cleopatra"* (New Haven and London: Yale University Press, 1973): "The Roman horror of that loss [of oneself in the sexual process] and the ecstatic union which the lovers feel as they die are two elements in the same process: for the dissolution of personal boundaries is both our greatest fear and our highest desire" (p. 149).

CLEOPATRA   Peace, peace!
Dost thou not see my baby at my breast,
That sucks the nurse asleep? . . . .
As sweet as balm, as soft as air, as gentle—
O Antony! (v.ii.307–11)

Cleopatra has offered Antony a mode of relating in which his manhood is completed in his response to the feminine in Cleopatra and
which releases the mutual interchange of masculine and feminine
in both lovers.[45] Although this union is tragically incompatible with
the structures of sustained life as they are understood in this play,
its ideal imaginative completion holds the stage even as Cleopatra's
corpse is scrutinized by curious Romans seeking a cause of death in
a world that does not crack, even with "the breaking of so great a
thing" (V.i.14).

The restless expansiveness that often makes Antony and Cleopatra
seem as much like comedy or romance as tragedy, the inclusiveness
of an action that holds contradictory modes of living and understanding in its wide embrace, and the rich lyrical imperialism that can melt
Rome in Tiber to establish new heaven, new earth make this play a
fitting culmination of the tragedies of the trust/merger group. Wide-
ranging dramatic movements that establish a source of irreducible
value characterize these plays: Hamlet's imperiled nobility is set
off by the rotten world of Denmark; the precious womanhood of
Desdemona is dramatized against Othello's "lust-stained" imagination of her; Cordelia's truth survives the sacrifice of Cordelia in Lear's
quest to fulfill "true need." More than in any of these plays, in
Antony and Cleopatra Shakespeare dramatizes value in a dream of

45. Murray M. Schwartz emphasizes the "interpenetration of opposites,
self and other, male and female," in Antony and Cleopatra, as he explores
shifts in Shakespeare's use of the "play space" of drama in the development
from the tragedies to the late romances. Schwartz's paper, "Shakespeare
through Contemporary Psychoanalysis," was delivered at the International
Shakespeare Association Congress, Washington, D.C., April, 1976. In the
same session, Janet Adelman presented a paper, " 'Anger's my meat': Feeding
and Dependency in Coriolanus," which has helped focus for me the discussion
of Coriolanus that follows. Schwartz's paper is in Hebrew Studies in Literature, 5 (1977): 182–198; Adelman's is in Patterns of Excelling Nature, ed.
David Bevington and Jay L. Halio (Newark: University of Delaware Press,
1978); both are included in Representing Shakespeare: New Psychoanalytic
Essays, ed. Murray M. Schwartz and Coppélia Kahn (Baltimore: Johns Hopkins University Press, 1980).

fulfillment plainly incompatible with pragmatic reality. Cleopatra's folly, as Janet Adelman observes, "is the folly of vision; and the whole play moves toward the acknowledgment of its truth" (*Common Liar*, p. 163).

Coriolanus, by contrast, completes a group of tragedies centered from the beginning in movements toward disillusionment and devaluation: Cressida's infidelity and the bankruptcy of heroic ideals define the world of *Troilus and Cressida*; the "imperial theme" is transformed into royal butchery in the action of *Macbeth*; Timon's grand generosity collapses into vindictive misanthropy in *Timon of Athens*. Like *Antony and Cleopatra*, *Coriolanus* exaggerates trends in the group it completes. The strong Egyptian fetters that bind Antony are liberating as well as destructive; Cleopatra's immortal longings are illusions that illuminate a human truth; together the two lovers appropriate the right to define, against Caesar's might, what is noble, what is great. On the other hand, psychological patterns that entrap Coriolanus are explored in ways that severely qualify the glory of Roman manhood to which he aspires; the "lonely dragon" is accorded no visionary power to counterpoise the relentlessly reductive force of the action in the last tragedy of the autonomy/isolation group.

Volumnia creates in Coriolanus a self that expresses "my very wishes / And the buildings of my fancy" (II.i.188–89). As Coriolanus fulfills her wish to be a man, embodying the "valiantness" he has sucked from her (III.ii.129), the relation also takes into itself a deep maternal antagonism toward the son who becomes the man such a mother longs to be herself.[46] Within the context of her exalted identification of herself with her son, the glory Volumnia takes in Coriolanus's wounds expresses a deep resentment toward a manhood she cannot realize in her own person. The inseparability of the nurturing maternal bond and violent attack on the infant become manly warrior is established strikingly in Volumnia's own imagery:

---

46. Cf. Phillip E. Slater's analysis of the "oral-narcissistic dilemma" in Greek family structure and mythology in *The Glory of Hera* (Boston: Beacon Press, 1968). Slater describes "a deeply narcissistic ambivalence in which the mother does not respond to the child as a separate person, but as both an expression of and a cure for her narcissistic wounds. Her need for self-expansion and vindication requires her both to exalt and to belittle her son, to feed on and to destroy him" (p. 33).

> The breasts of Hecuba,
> When she did suckle Hector, looked not lovelier
> Than Hector's forehead when it spit forth blood
> At Grecian sword, contemning.   (I.iii.38–41)

In his brutal successes at war, Coriolanus both localizes his mother's ideal of manhood and absorbs her fierce inner rage. In battle, Coriolanus will display his bloody body to urge on the Roman troops, for the wounds he receives are in balance with the destruction he metes out, in a kind of desperate homeostasis of violence. But in peace, his wounds become a source of vulnerability and shame. Coriolanus's angry refusal to show his wounds to the citizens reflects a fear of exposing himself as incomplete, piecemeal, a collection of fragments held together only by his mother's idea of him.

Coriolanus's fear of gaps in himself—represented by the wounds his mother has enjoined him to suffer, and which she regards as emblems of her own self-fulfillment—betrays his perpetual indebtedness to Volumnia for what provisional psychic wholeness he possesses. Coriolanus is ashamed to show the wounds that reflect his own fear of being female, of being identical with that part of his mother she repudiates by identifying herself with him. This fear of being female, of being possessed by "some harlot's spirit" (III.ii.112), is linked to a hidden hatred of the bond with his mother, which the play expresses by dwelling on Coriolanus's turning against his motherland and on his role as destroyer of family units in battle. But the action bends this resentful impulse back toward its origins, until Coriolanus's imminent assault on Rome is equated with an assault on "thy mother's womb / That brought thee to this world" (V.iii. 124–25). Coriolanus is forced to renounce in direct confrontation a matricidal impulse implicit in his desperate effort to "stand / As if a man were author of himself / And knew no other kin" (V.iii. 35–37).

The impotent rage released in Coriolanus when Aufidius calls him "boy" completes an understanding developed throughout the play—that Coriolanus's savage masculinity remains bound to the overpowering mother who invented it and filled it with her son. Coriolanus would rather die than acknowledge this psychic incompleteness:

> Cut me to pieces, Volsces. Men and lads,
> Stain all your edges on me. Boy? False hound!

> If you have writ your annals true, 'tis there
> That, like an eagle in a dovecoat, I
> Fluttered your Volscians in Corioles.
> Alone I did it. Boy?   (v.vi.110–15)

He is destroyed amid cries that define him as the archenemy of the family, and that reflect his deep hostility toward the familial constraints that underlie his very being:

> ALL PEOPLE   Tear him to pieces!—Do it presently!—He killed my
> son!—My daughter!—He killed my cousin Marcus!—
> He killed my father!   (v.vi.119–21)

Like his own challenge to the Volscians, the cry of the people to tear the hero to pieces clarifies the fragmentation that results from Coriolanus's futile effort to assert a manly autonomy independent of his bond to Volumnia.

The polarity that divides the tragedies into two groups, culminating in *Antony and Cleopatra* and *Coriolanus*, extends into the late romances, which retrieve a place for basic needs sacrificed to destructive impulses within those needs in the tragedies. *Pericles* and *The Winter's Tale* follow in the line of those plays that move toward tragically achieved relations of merger, and I regard them as part of the trust/merger group. *Cymbeline* and *The Tempest* have stronger affinities with the tragedies of the autonomy/isolation group, whose protagonists move toward isolation and emptiness. The resolution of *Pericles* in the reunion of the protagonist with his daughter and wife is facilitated by the intervention of the goddess Diana. Like that of *Pericles*, the ending of *The Winter's Tale* is centered emotionally in the protagonist's recovery of lost relations of mutuality and trust. Hermione's reappearance in *The Winter's Tale* takes into itself the quality of sacredness suggested in *Pericles* by the appearance of the goddess Diana, heralded by the cosmic harmony of the music of the spheres. By contrast, Jupiter, god of masculine power and autonomy, must intervene to allow the resolution of the tangled action of *Cymbeline*. Autonomous patriarchal power is restored to the human sphere in *The Tempest* through the actions of Prospero. In the ending of *The Tempest*, and to a lesser extent in *Cymbeline*, feelings of loss and separation qualify the spirit of restoration and renewal. Cymbeline must be freed from the trust betrayed by a wicked queen ("It had been vicious / To have mistrusted her" [V.v. 65–66]) to be united with his daughter; Belarius, surrogate father to the king's sons, must "lose / Two of the sweet'st companions in the world" (V.v.348–49) so that he can become brother to the king in *Cymbeline. The Tempest* closes on a Prospero who has given up his beloved daughter, his beloved Ariel, and his beloved magic, and for whom henceforth "every third thought shall be my grave" (V.i.311).

Each of the romances culminates in the restoration of characters who survive aggression that has endangered their lives, often expressed in symbolic deaths regarded as real by other characters. A psychological index to the development through the destructive actions of the tragedies to the restorative movements of the romances can be constructed from D. W. Winnicott's understanding of the role of aggression in the formation of the self. Winnicott specifies conditions that enable the self to "use" objects that exist "out in the world."[47] This "capacity to use objects" includes the capability of relating to others in a manner that acknowledges their full, independent existence. In locating others in a world outside the realm of mere projection and exploitation, Winnicott argues, "it is the destructive drive that creates the quality of externality" (p. 93). The object can be "used" in a world recognized as external to the self only if it is first destroyed in a psychic world not yet differentiated from a world beyond it: "it is the destruction of the object that places the object outside the area of the subject's omnipotent control" (p. 90). Winnicott points to the importance of the mother (and the often analogous role of the analyst) as "the first person to take the baby through this first version of the many that will be encountered, of attack that is survived" (p. 92). Acknowledgment of a separate world, not completely independent of projective fantasy, but which does not exist simply as a creation of projection, can only be achieved when a trustworthy world beyond omnipotent control reveals itself as such by surviving its destruction within the sphere of omnipotence. The completion of this process is crucial to the establishment of both trust and autonomy; it makes possible relations to others that can unite persons who acknowledge the separateness of one another.[48]

47. Winnicott, "The Use of an Object and Relating through Identification," in *Playing and Reality* (New York: Basic Books, 1971), p. 91.

48. Winnicott summarizes his argument by providing the following sequence of development:

(1) Subject *relates* to object. (2) Object is in process of being found instead of placed by the subject in the world. (3) Subject *destroys* object. (4) Object survives destruction. (5) Subject can *use* object. (p. 94)

In the crises of Shakespeare's later drama, the boundary that establishes the condition of externality is blurred by protagonists who replace actuality with worlds that reflect inner need and conflict. In movements either toward fusion or radical isolation, encounters with essential others recreate in drama the conditions of infantile destruction Winnicott describes. But in these plays, the implications of this aggression extend far beyond a two-person encounter grounded in one individual's regression to deep conflict; destructiveness based in fantasy leads to actual destruction in the plays' dramatic reality. Often, as in *King Lear*, this destruction becomes the image of permanent, generalized loss:

KENT   Is this the promised end?
EDGAR Or image of that horror?
ALBANY   Fall and cease.
            (v.iii.264–65)

But each of these plays, at its psychological core, participates in part or all of the process Winnicott describes, in which an essential other is denied a place in reality, is destroyed in fantasy, survives that destruction, and thus becomes a part of the actual world, separate from the subject, but united with him in a bond of trust. Within the complexities of their whole dramatic movements, the romances dramatize the renewed completion of this process, but the tragedies return it to and abort it at the destructive phase.

In the tragedies, essential others, replaced by projective fantasies, are denied places in the actual world. Tragic protagonists who lose touch with actuality attempt to recapture it within the sphere of omnipotent control: "Now he'll outstare the lightning" (III.xiii. 195), Enobarbus observes of Antony, who has forfeited his actual resources of power; "I banish you!" (III.iii.124), cries Coriolanus, to the Rome that has banished him. Frustrations that penetrate the assumption of omnipotent control, rather than lead to its dissolution, tend to divert magical, projective thinking toward a negative vision no less grandiosely self-centered. Othello, "the noble Moor whom our full Senate / Call all in all sufficient" (IV.i.257–58), expects the universe to suffer a cosmic repetition of his own unbearable loss after he murders Desdemona:

I have no wife.
O, insupportable! O heavy hour!

> Methinks it should be now a huge eclipse
> Of sun and moon, and that th' affrighted globe
> Should yawn at alteration.   (v.ii.98–102)

Timon would annihilate Athens, indeed humanity ("Destruction fang mankind!" [IV.iii.23]), when Athenian ingratitude annihilates in him the illusion of a world defined by the nurturing generosity through which he has lived. But Timon's raging belongs no less to the projective realm of omnipotent control than his earlier generosity, and it is Timon, not mankind, who cannot survive his destructiveness: " 'Timon is dead, who hath outstretched his span. / Some beast read this; there does not live a man' " (V.iii.3–4).

More than that of any other tragic protagonist, Timon's fate reflects the catastrophe of infantile self-annihilation that Winnicott associates with failure to be able to create the quality of externality. It is a limitation of *Timon of Athens* that Timon's misanthropic reconstruction of the world is inadequately balanced by a dramatic reality independent of it: the Athenian world Timon rejects is never compellingly established in the first place, and it is scarcely affected by Timon's withdrawal of himself from it into impotent rage. More typically in the tragedies, destructiveness that originates in the sphere of omnipotent control does lead to actual destruction in a fully rendered world that sustains life for the protagonist who has belonged to it. When Lear gives up his kingdom he relinquishes such a world, one Cordelia and Kent struggle at the outset to keep intact and struggle throughout to reinstate. In doing so, Lear trades actual power for illusory omnipotence. When he banishes Cordelia, he does not send her out into the world, but expels her from an imaginary world of omnipotent control defined by magical, automatic responsiveness to the demands of his psyche. When Lear is ready to go with her to prison, he continues to deny her a place in a world beyond that created by his own need. In his longing Lear destroys Cordelia by creating her presence in the image of his own need and imprisoning her in that image.[49] But the consequences of Lear's actions extend

49. M. Masud R. Khan provides a clinical instance of this process in a discussion of three patients whose progress in analysis was blocked by their incapacity to relinquish "symbiotic omnipotence": "They needed my *presence*—in the analytic situation so they could disregard and negate me, and in their life so they could be related to themselves" ("On Symbiotic Omnipotence," *The Privacy of the Self*, p. 84).

throughout the world of the play. He has tragically altered the conditions of an actual world in which Cordelia must be destroyed, cannot be retrieved, cannot be used. In the play's symbolic action, the malevolence of that outer world mirrors the inner destructiveness of Lear.

The late romances create a comparable intermingling of symbolic and actual destruction. The resolutions of these plays hinge on the restored presence of those who "survive destruction," but often at considerable cost in the actual world. After Leontes retreats into persecutory fantasy in *The Winter's Tale*, he cannot begin to recover a world apart from his omnipotent recreation of it until his "psychic murder of Hermione." [50] The eventual recovery of Hermione, who survives Leontes' hatred, will reinstate the creative rapport between inner need and external reality that Leontes annihilates in jealous delusion. But this process of recovery is decisively complicated when the attack on Hermione destroys in actuality the one figure who provides for Leontes a link between the world of fantasy and the actual world. That link is Mamillius, whom Leontes both loves as a son in the world and endows with projected attributes that reflect his persecutory fantasies: "Though he does bear some signs of me, yet you / Have too much blood in him" (II.i.57–58).

In the infantile struggle that Winnicott interprets, the external world can only be recognized and lived in after it survives destruction, but in the complex dramatic reality of *The Winter's Tale*, Leontes can recognize a world apart from fantasy only when an essential part of it does not survive. Even the oracle of Apollo is powerless to free Leontes from his delusion until news comes of Mamillius's death. Mamillius is a real victim of the assault on Hermione that takes place within the sphere of Leontes' destructive omnipotence; Mamillius dies when he is deprived of the essential maternal presence Leontes destroys in fantasy. The loss of Mamillius in the actual world confirms its independent existence, but cannot enable Le-

50. Schwartz, "*The Winter's Tale*: Loss and Transformation," *American Imago*, 32 (Summer 1975): 156. This illuminating discussion of "how Shakespeare transforms the fears and realities of loss into the theatrical revelation of fulfillment" (p. 146) completes a thorough psychoanalytic interpretation begun in "Leontes' Jealousy in *The Winter's Tale*," *American Imago*, 30 (Fall 1973): 250–73. I am also indebted to Stephen Greenblatt for emphasizing the importance of Mamillius's death in the whole design of *The Winter's Tale* (personal communication).

ontes fully to assume his own place in it. The completion of Leontes' mourning must reestablish the boundary that both connects and separates the inner and outer world, and must prepare him to acknowledge that outer world as a place to live in. Only then can he and his wife be newly united, in a bond of trust that confirms the autonomy of each, "at the point in time and space of the initiation of their state of separateness."[51]

In *The Winter's Tale* the longing for merger and the violent recoil from it are ultimately subordinated to achieved trust and mutuality. Perdita, Hermione, and Paulina together enable Leontes to recover a place in the world of relations he has himself destroyed in the delusional rages of the first three acts. In the hallowed presence of Hermione, maternal and wifely, sacred and human, Leontes recovers the base for potent, sustained selfhood lost to Hamlet, Lear, Othello, and Antony. In *The Tempest,* the need for autonomy is purged of the drive toward omnipotence and the collapse into failure. Rendered helpless by his misplaced trust in Antonio, Prospero wrests new power away from the savage legacy of the "foul witch Sycorax" (I.ii.258), malevolent symbol of feared maternal power. In Prospero, Troilus's "venomed vengeance" yields to the "rarer action" (V.i.27) of a mercy that seems to contain, rather than transcend, his vindictive impulses; Macbeth's usurpation by a demonic wife and three cunning witches is superseded by the liberation of those powers imprisoned by Sycorax; Timon's fantastic quest for maternal omnipotence and his collapse into misanthropic rage are transformed into artfully exploited magical power and Prospero's final resignation of himself to his own human limitations; the mutual banishment of Coriolanus and Rome gives way to the mutual recovery of Prospero and Italy.

In Leontes, Shakespeare allows the richness of relations grounded in mutual trust to flow back into the life of a character who has fearfully transformed those riches into a nightmare of violent jealousy. *The Winter's Tale* moves beyond the poisoned cup that fragments psychic wholeness to the mutuality Leontes finds through a magic "lawful as eating" (V.iii.111). In Prospero, Shakespeare provides a

---

51. Winnicott, "The Location of Cultural Experience," *Playing and Reality,* p. 97. The quoted words are italicized in the original.

character who subdues the longing for omnipotent control to responsible power, who can release the daughter whose loss leaves an unfillable void in himself and not collapse around his own experience of emptiness. Leontes' recovery of himself in the embrace of Hermione and Prospero's assertion of self-sufficient autonomy through the power of his mind extend and perhaps embody in its purest form the division I have tried to trace through the drama leading up to these plays.

The restoration of Leontes in the facilitating presence of Hermione reverberates back through the plays of the trust/merger group to complete an image of manhood complementary to the feminine powers invested in Portia and Rosalind in the festive comedies. Hermione "hangs about his neck" (V.iii.112), restoring to health not only the mind that has imagined a Polixenes who "wears her like her medal, hanging / About his neck" (I.ii.306–7), but also Hamlet's anguished memory of Gertrude, who would "hang on [King Hamlet] / As if increase of appetite had grown / By what it fed on" (I.ii. 143–45). Essential to the comic achievement that takes *The Winter's Tale* beyond the catastrophic world of tragedy is the movement toward a reciprocal, mutually creative relation between a vigorously rendered manhood and a comparably complete realization of essential womanly power. But the play can only come to this point through Leontes' trusting submission of himself to the active, guiding spirit of Paulina.

The trusting investment of self in others gives way in *The Tempest* to exacting control and shrewd vigilance; the mature womanly powers embodied in Paulina and Hermione drop out altogether. In order to dramatize the controlling presence of Prospero, Shakespeare must split his imagination of the feminine into the compliant, innocent daughterhood of Miranda and the evil maternal power bequeathed to the island by Sycorax. The maternal capacities to give and withhold essential nurture, which inform Timon's initial generosity and his subsequent withdrawal of nurture in the feast of stones and water, are incorporated into Prospero's magic, as in the banquet Ariel first provides and then withdraws from the distraught visitors to the island. Prospero's autonomy, which completes with new intensity an ideal of manhood anticipated in the *Henriad*, is achieved by the rigorous subordination of trust to power. In the world of *The Tem-*

pest, trust exercised within the sphere of human activity "like a good parent" (I.ii.94) begets a contrary falsehood great as itself.

The Winter's Tale and *The Tempest* also look back to the two comedies from the tragic period that have been the main concern of this book, whose problematic actions are subjected to stress by virtually every facet of Shakespeare's development touched on in this chapter. As I tried to show in detail in chapter 2, Helena's efforts to resolve the action of *All's Well* suggest the earlier comic roles of Portia and Rosalind, while her adoration of Bertram recalls the love for the friend expressed in the *Sonnets.* But mistrust of female power and sexuality, which Shakespeare masters dramatically in tragic action, greatly complicates Helena's comic role, and qualifies her success in bringing this play to a comic conclusion. Helena's mysterious cure of the king's fatal disease and her arrangement for her own miraculous recovery after rejection and apparent death anticipate the roles divided up among Paulina, Perdita, and Hermione in *The Winter's Tale,* but confer upon her presence conflicting psychological meanings for other characters that disrupt the mutuality she seeks. The design of *All's Well* places it among the plays of the trust/merger group ("We should submit ourselves to an unknown fear" [II.iii.5–6] says Lafew), in which the need for trust invariably provokes the fear of lost autonomy. But Bertram resists trusting submission until the very end and does not then embrace it very convincingly, or in a manner that suggests his fears have been fully dispelled.

Measure for Measure, by contrast, comes under the control of a man, Vincentio, who, as many have noted, anticipates the role of Prospero in *The Tempest. Measure for Measure* belongs with the autonomy/isolation group. Tragic protagonists in this group of plays are pitched into desperate isolation in the effort to achieve omnipotent autonomy; Vincentio's autonomy is purchased at the expense of isolating him from direct involvement in conflicts that beset lesser mortals in *Measure for Measure.* His proposal to Isabella in the comic resolution suggests more a denial of that isolation than a fully successful triumph over it. As in *All's Well,* a deep mistrust of sexuality obstructs the comic movement toward marriage in *Measure for Measure.* But whereas Helena, in order to complete her marriage, must virtually prostitute herself to sexual drives that seek release from social and familial constraints, Vincentio attempts to preside, lofty and aloof, autonomous but emptied of psychic content, over a city that boils and bubbles with debased sexuality.

All's Well and *Measure for Measure*, like *The Winter's Tale* and *The Tempest*, relate to each other across a division in Shakespeare's imagination that is never closed nor completely bridged. This division separates a potential identity sought in a trusting investment of self in an other and that turns on the mutual dependence of male and female, from a potential identity sought in a counter-turn toward the assertion of self-willed masculine autonomy over destructive female power or over compliant feminine goodness. But *The Winter's Tale* and *The Tempest* look across this division toward needs that form the separate, incompatible centers of the previous drama. Perhaps, like Leontes and Polixenes, these two plays, written at the end of Shakespeare's career, "shook hands, as over a vast; and embraced, as it were, from the ends of opposed winds" (I.i.28–30). From the vantage point of this conceit, it is well to recall what happens when that vast is dissolved by intimate contact in *The Winter's Tale*. But nonetheless, Leontes, restored fully to himself in the arms of Hermione, presides over the ending of *The Winter's Tale* with kingly power and autonomy. And Prospero, having willed his own autonomy in triumph over the threatening power invested in Sycorax's heritage, submits himself, in the epilogue to *The Tempest*, to the playwright's ultimate other for the life-giving applause that only can save him from isolation and despair. Together, these plays culminate a vast dramatic enterprise that encounters with incomparable courage and skill human vulnerabilities that entered into Shakespeare's life, and enter into our own, in that "wide gap of time since first / We were dissevered" (*WT* V.iii.154–55).

Index

223

Compositor: Heritage Printers, Inc.
Printer: Heritage Printers, Inc.
Binder: The Delmar Company
Text: Linotype Electra
Display: Handset Deepdene
Cloth: Holliston Roxite B 53596
Paper: 55 lb. P&S Offset